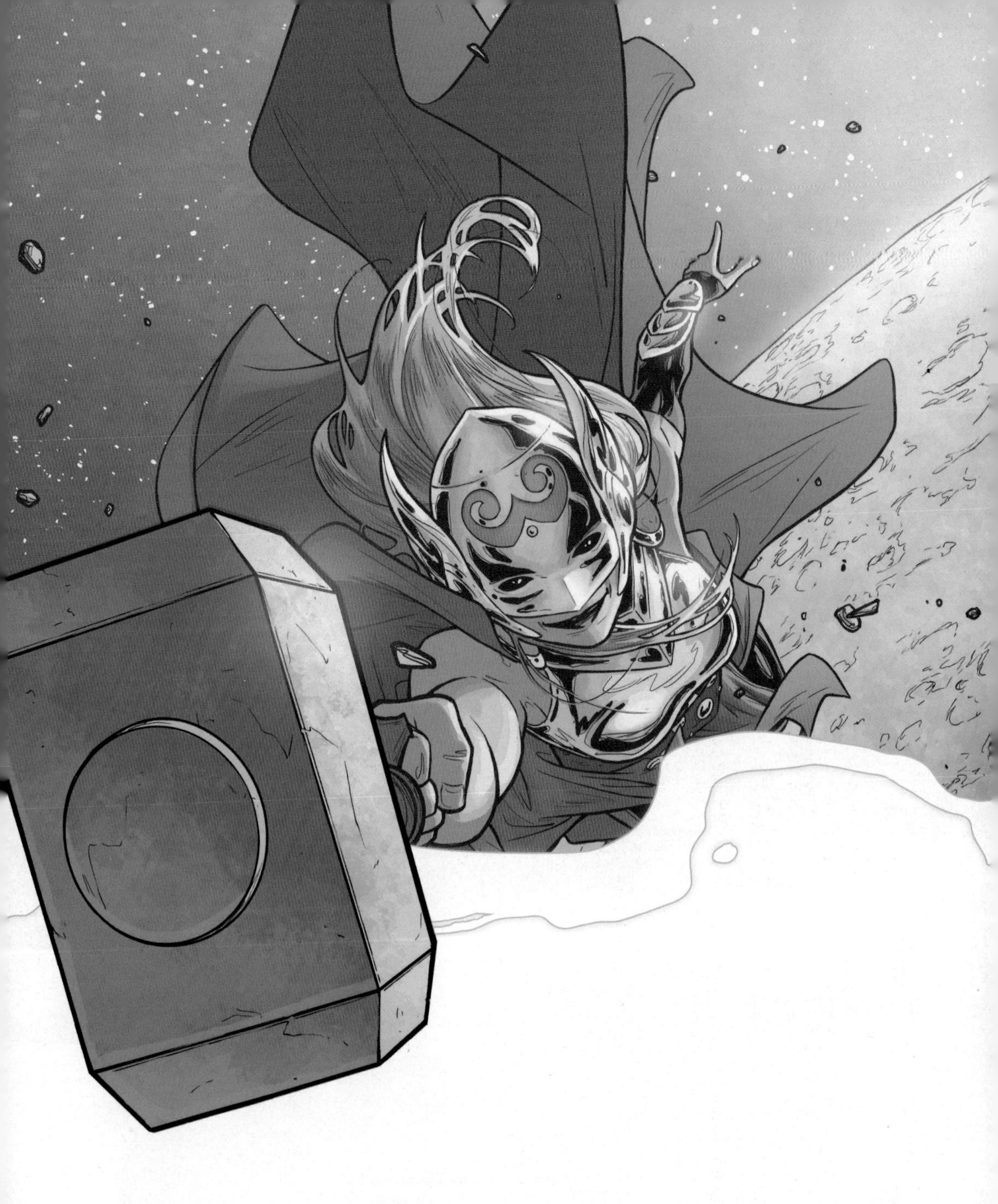

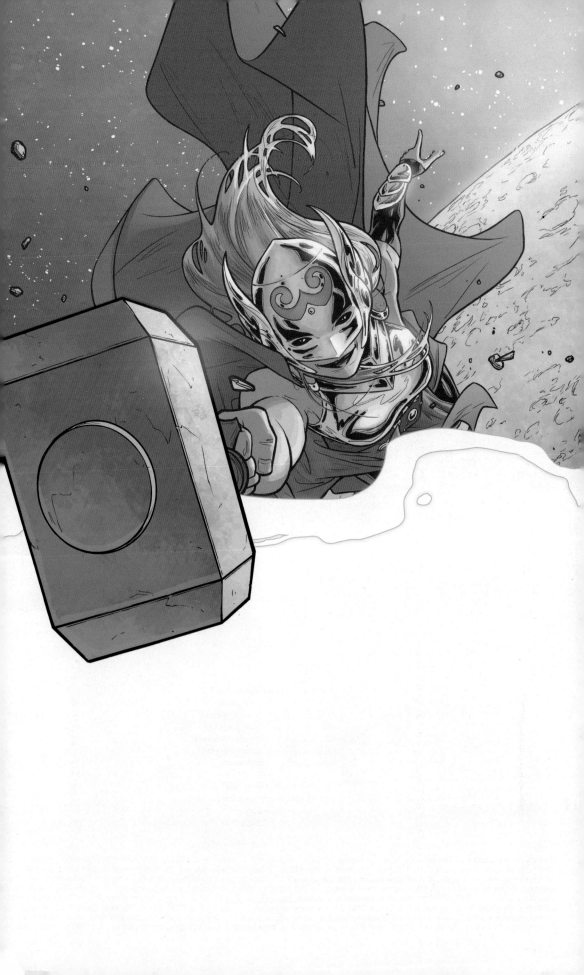

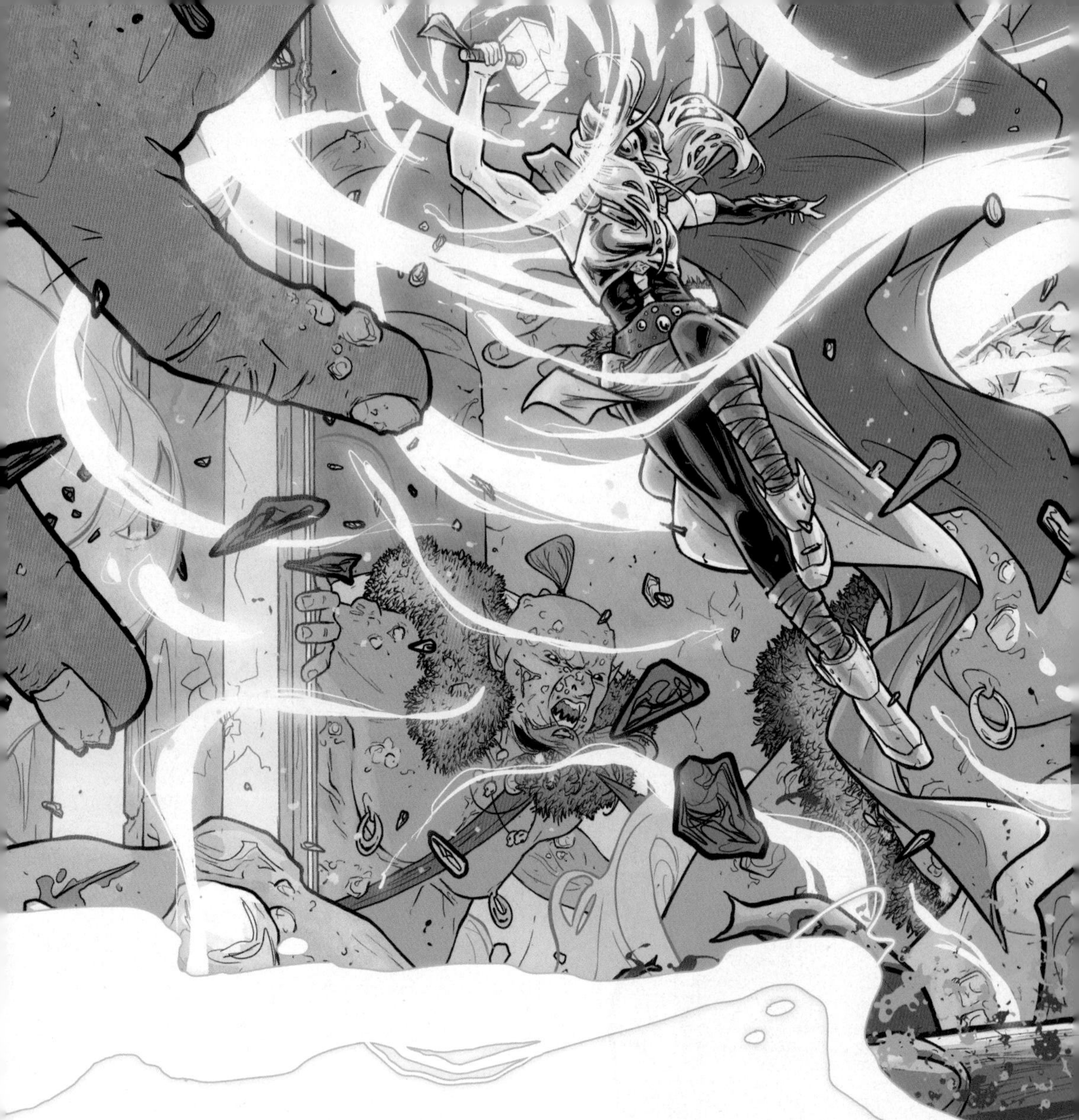

COLLECTION EDITOR: **JENNIFER GRÜNWALD**

ASSISTANT EDITOR: **SARAH BRUNSTAD**

ASSOCIATE MANAGING EDITOR: **ALEX STARBUCK**

EDITOR, SPECIAL PROJECTS: **MARK D. BEAZLEY**

SENIOR EDITOR, SPECIAL PROJECTS: **JEFF YOUNGQUIST**

SVP PRINT, SALES & MARKETING: **DAVID GABRIEL**

BOOK DESIGNER: **JEFF POWELL**

EDITOR IN CHIEF: **AXEL ALONSO**

CHIEF CREATIVE OFFICER: **JOE QUESADA**

PUBLISHER: **DAN BUCKLEY**

EXECUTIVE PRODUCER: **ALAN FINE**

THOR VOL. 1: THE GODDESS OF THUNDER. Contains material originally published in magazine form as THOR #1-5. First printing 2015. ISBN# 978-0-7851-9238-1. Published by MA WORLDWIDE, INC., a subsidiary of MARVEL ENTERTAINMENT, LLC. OFFICE OF PUBLICATION: 135 West 50th Street, New York, NY 10020.

Printed in the U.S.A. ALAN FINE, President, Marvel Entertainment; DAN BUCKLEY, President, TV, Publishing and Brand Management; JOE QUESADA, Chief Creative O TOM BREVOORT, SVP of Publishing; DAVID BOGART, SVP of Operations & Procurement, Publishing; C.B. CEBULSKI, SVP of Creator & Content Development; DAVID GABRIEL, SVP Print, & Marketing; JIM O'KEEFE, VP of Operations & Logistics; DAN CARR, Executive Director of Publishing Technology; SUSAN CRESPI, Editorial Operations Manager; ALEX MORALES, Publi Operations Manager; STAN LEE, Chairman Emeritus. For information regarding advertising in Marvel Comics or on Marvel.com, please contact Jonathan Rheingold, VP of Custom Solutions Sales, at jrheingold@marvel.com. For Marvel subscription inquiries, please call 800-217-9158. **Manufactured between 3/13/2015 and 4/27/2015 by R.R. DONNELLEY, INC., SALEM, VA,**

10 9 8 7 6 5 4 3 2 1

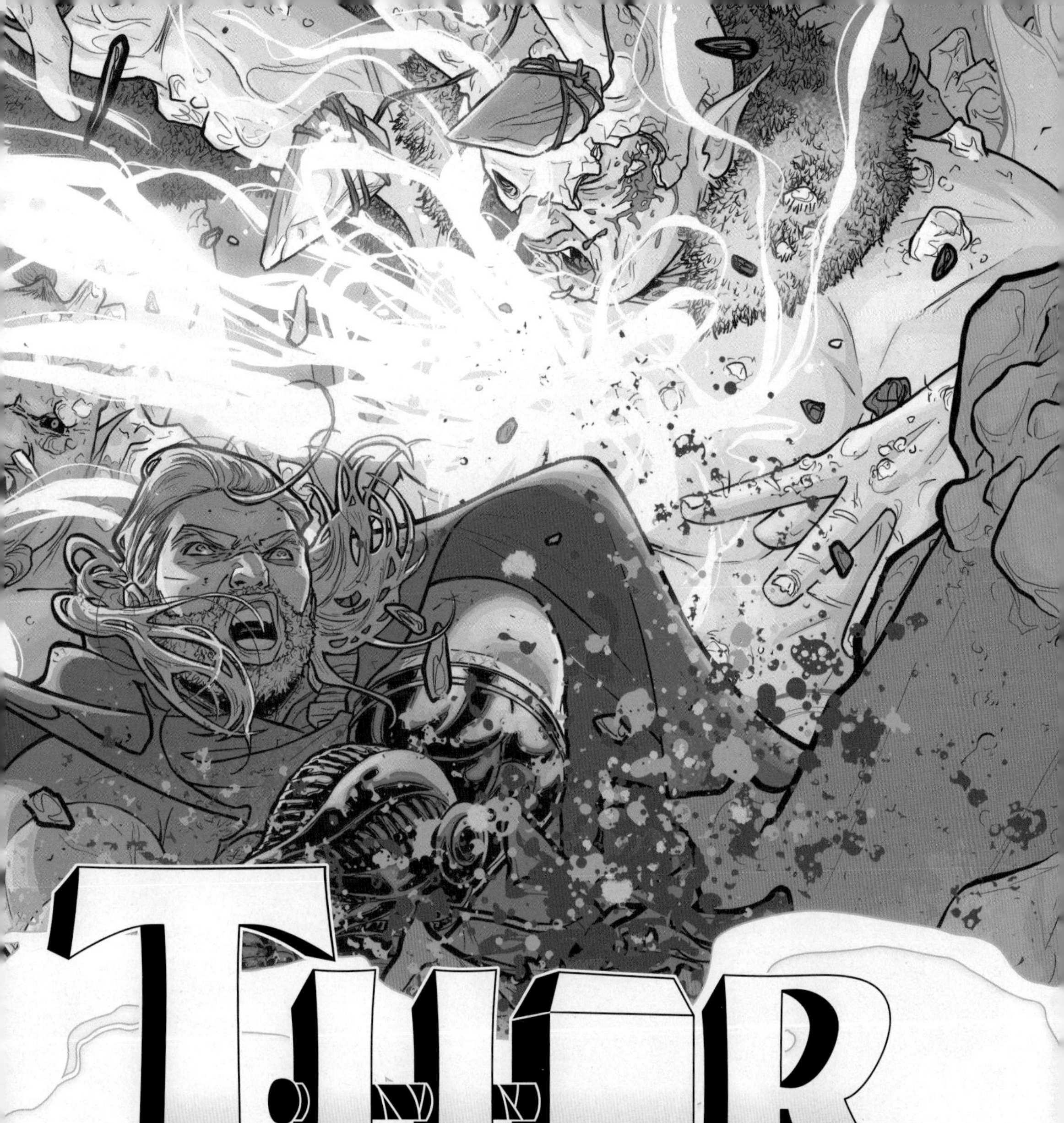

THOR

THE GODDESS OF THUNDER

WRITER
JASON AARON

ARTISTS
RUSSELL DAUTERMAN (#1-4)
& JORGE MOLINA (#5)

COLOR ARTISTS
MATTHEW WILSON (#1-4)
& JORGE MOLINA (#5)

LETTERER
VC'S JOE SABINO

COVER ART
RUSSELL DAUTERMAN
& FRANK MARTIN

ASSISTANT EDITOR
JON MOISAN

EDITOR
WIL MOSS

THOR CREATED BY STAN LEE, LARRY LIEBER & JACK KIRBY

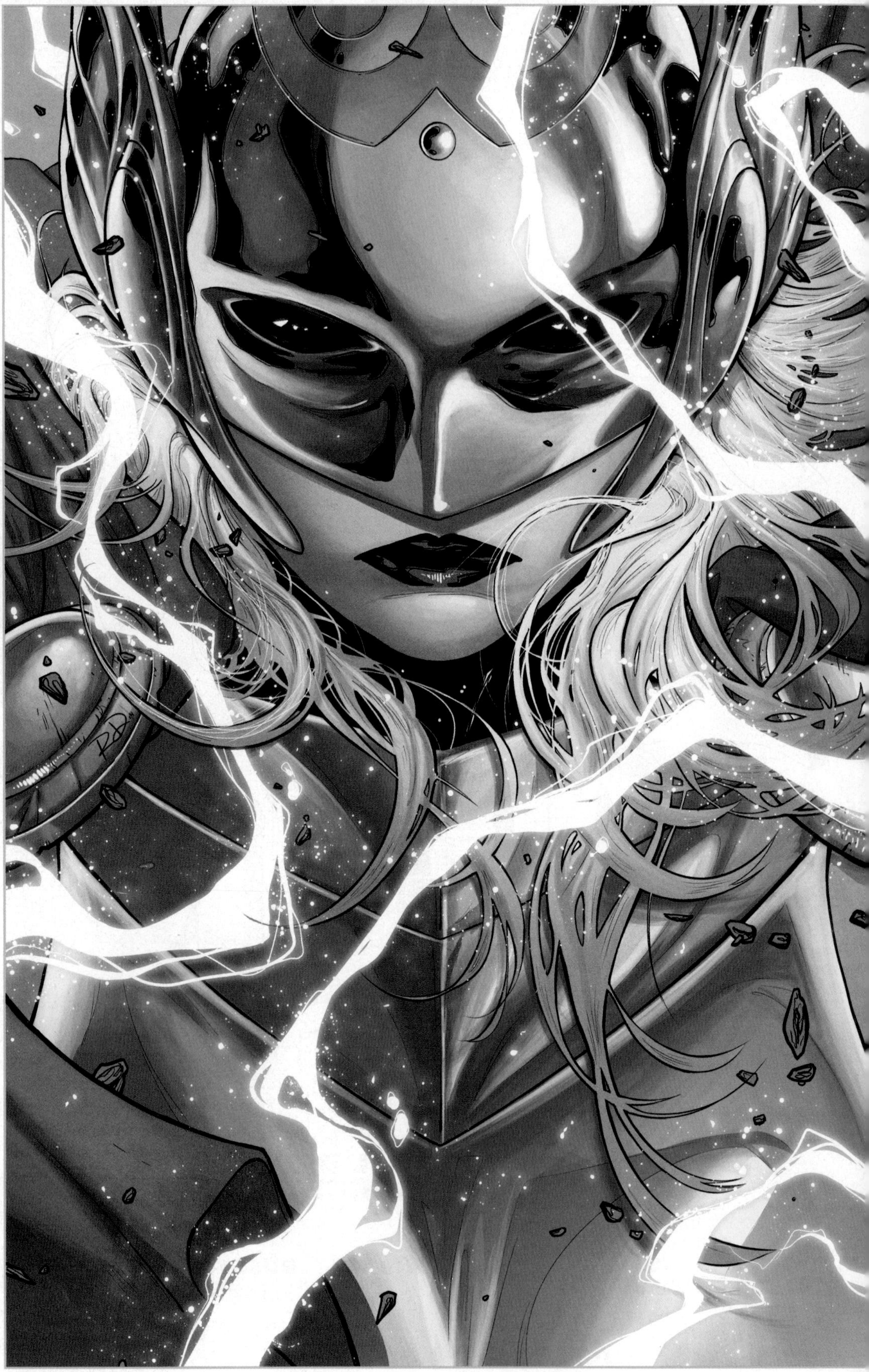

— 1 —

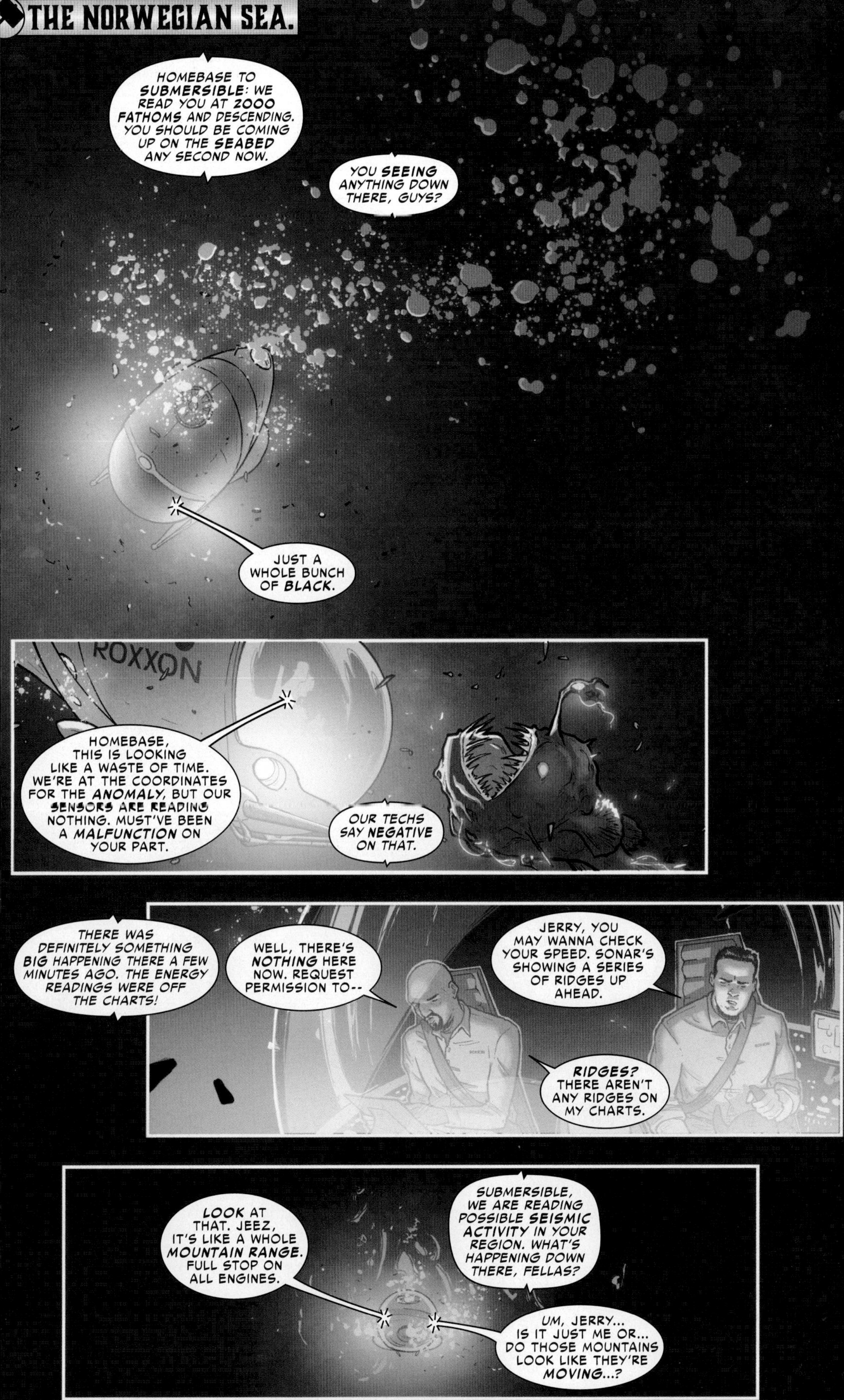
THE NORWEGIAN SEA.
HOMEBASE TO SUBMERSIBLE: WE READ YOU AT 2000 FATHOMS AND DESCENDING. YOU SHOULD BE COMING UP ON THE SEABED ANY SECOND NOW.
YOU SEEING ANYTHING DOWN THERE, GUYS?
JUST A WHOLE BUNCH OF BLACK.
ROXXON
HOMEBASE, THIS IS LOOKING LIKE A WASTE OF TIME. WE'RE AT THE COORDINATES FOR THE ANOMALY, BUT OUR SENSORS ARE READING NOTHING. MUST'VE BEEN A MALFUNCTION ON YOUR PART.
OUR TECHS SAY NEGATIVE ON THAT.
THERE WAS DEFINITELY SOMETHING BIG HAPPENING THERE A FEW MINUTES AGO. THE ENERGY READINGS WERE OFF THE CHARTS!
WELL, THERE'S NOTHING HERE NOW. REQUEST PERMISSION TO--
JERRY, YOU MAY WANNA CHECK YOUR SPEED. SONAR'S SHOWING A SERIES OF RIDGES UP AHEAD.
RIDGES? THERE AREN'T ANY RIDGES ON MY CHARTS.
LOOK AT THAT. JEEZ, IT'S LIKE A WHOLE MOUNTAIN RANGE. FULL STOP ON ALL ENGINES.
SUBMERSIBLE, WE ARE READING POSSIBLE SEISMIC ACTIVITY IN YOUR REGION. WHAT'S HAPPENING DOWN THERE, FELLAS?
UM, JERRY... IS IT JUST ME OR... DO THOSE MOUNTAINS LOOK LIKE THEY'RE MOVING...?

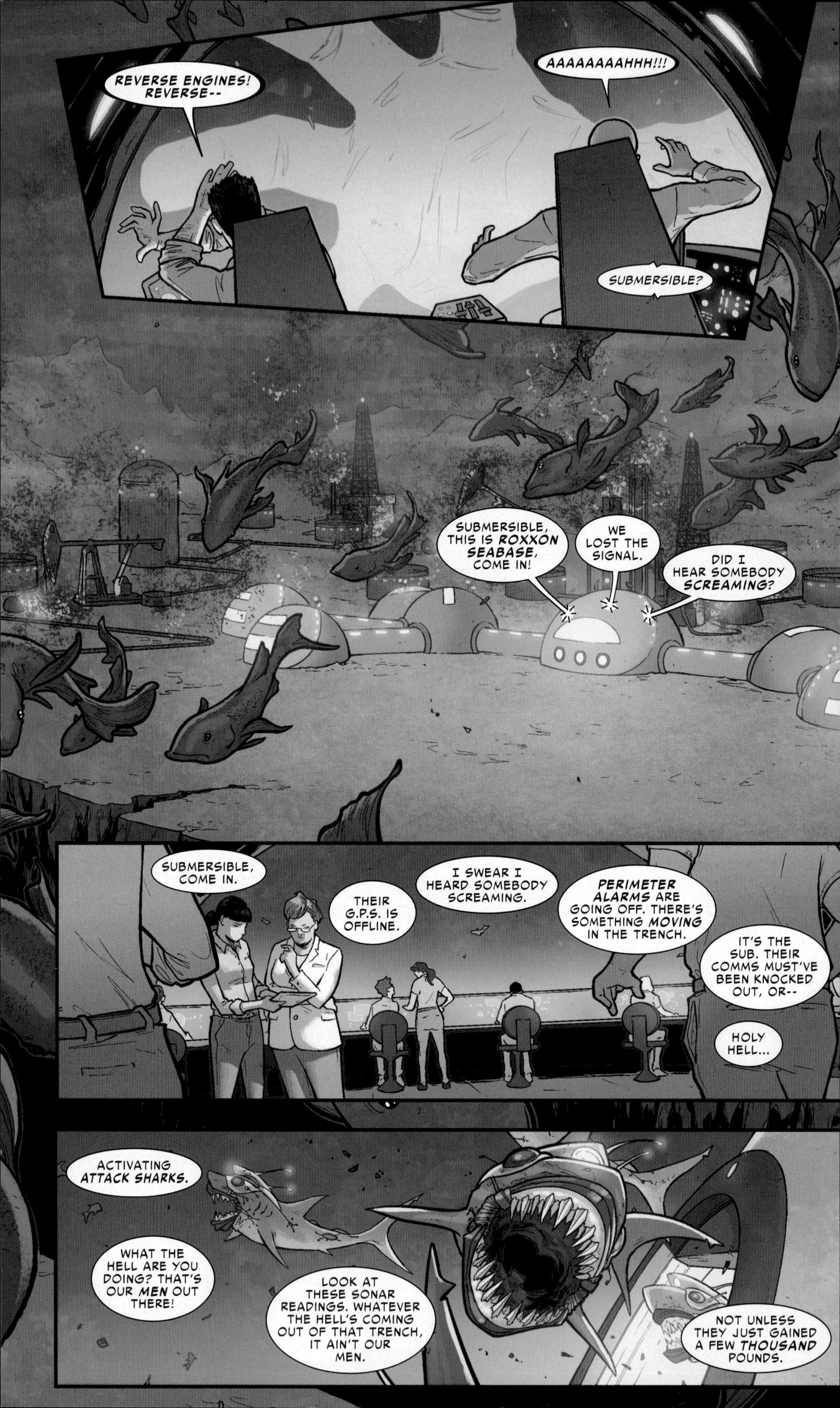

REVERSE ENGINES! REVERSE--
AAAAAAAAHHH!!!
SUBMERSIBLE?
SUBMERSIBLE, THIS IS ROXXON SEABASE, COME IN!
WE LOST THE SIGNAL.
DID I HEAR SOMEBODY SCREAMING?
SUBMERSIBLE, COME IN.
THEIR G.P.S. IS OFFLINE.
I SWEAR I HEARD SOMEBODY SCREAMING.
PERIMETER ALARMS ARE GOING OFF. THERE'S SOMETHING MOVING IN THE TRENCH.
IT'S THE SUB. THEIR COMMS MUST'VE BEEN KNOCKED OUT, OR--
HOLY HELL...
ACTIVATING ATTACK SHARKS.
WHAT THE HELL ARE YOU DOING? THAT'S OUR MEN OUT THERE!
LOOK AT THESE SONAR READINGS. WHATEVER THE HELL'S COMING OUT OF THAT TRENCH, IT AIN'T OUR MEN.
NOT UNLESS THEY JUST GAINED A FEW THOUSAND POUNDS.

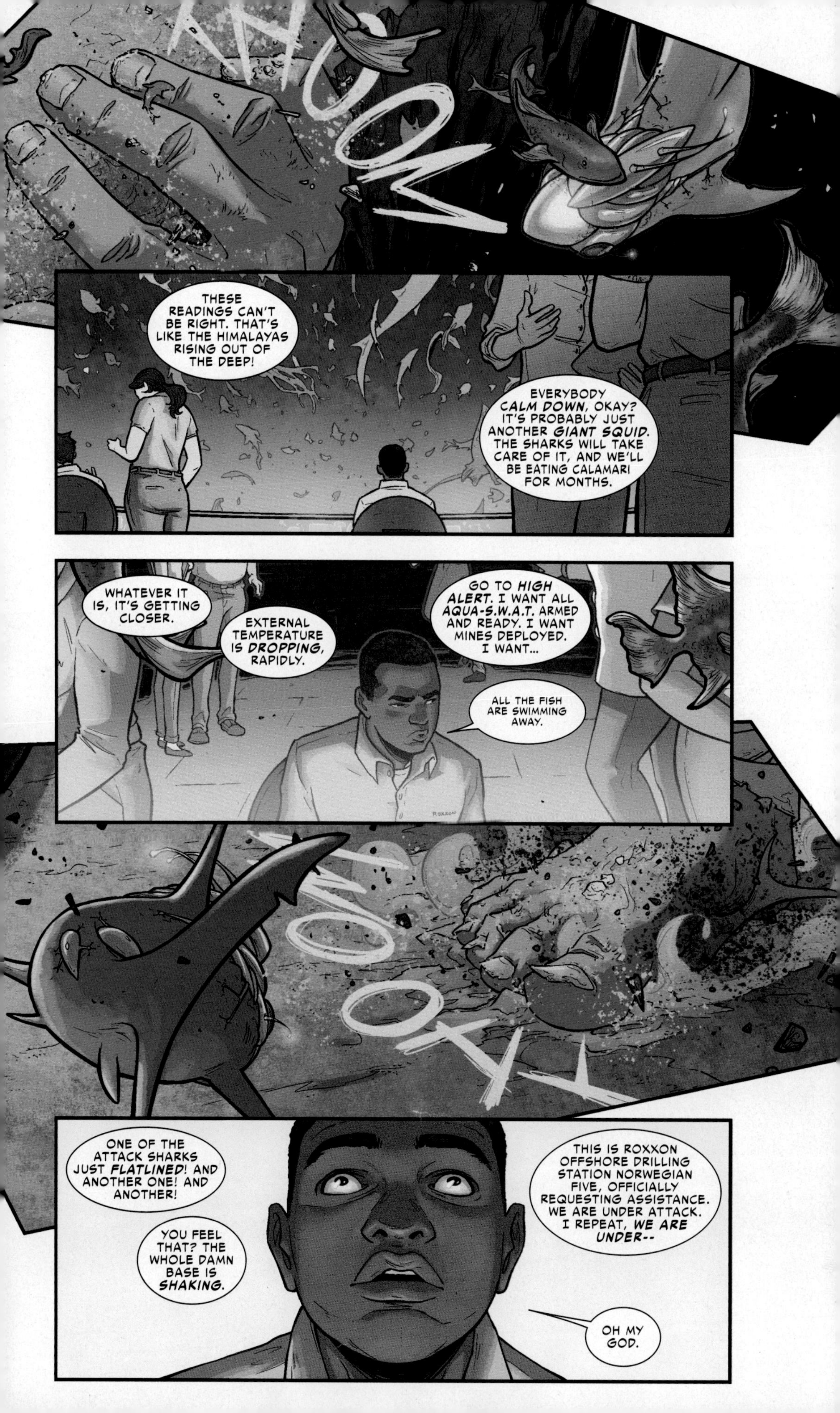

THESE READINGS CAN'T BE RIGHT. THAT'S LIKE THE HIMALAYAS RISING OUT OF THE DEEP!
EVERYBODY CALM DOWN, OKAY? IT'S PROBABLY JUST ANOTHER GIANT SQUID. THE SHARKS WILL TAKE CARE OF IT, AND WE'LL BE EATING CALAMARI FOR MONTHS.
WHATEVER IT IS, IT'S GETTING CLOSER.
EXTERNAL TEMPERATURE IS DROPPING, RAPIDLY.
GO TO HIGH ALERT. I WANT ALL AQUA-S.W.A.T. ARMED AND READY. I WANT MINES DEPLOYED. I WANT...
ALL THE FISH ARE SWIMMING AWAY.
ROXXON
ONE OF THE ATTACK SHARKS JUST FLATLINED! AND ANOTHER ONE! AND ANOTHER!
YOU FEEL THAT? THE WHOLE DAMN BASE IS SHAKING.
THIS IS ROXXON OFFSHORE DRILLING STATION NORWEGIAN FIVE, OFFICIALLY REQUESTING ASSISTANCE. WE ARE UNDER ATTACK. I REPEAT, WE ARE UNDER--
OH MY GOD.

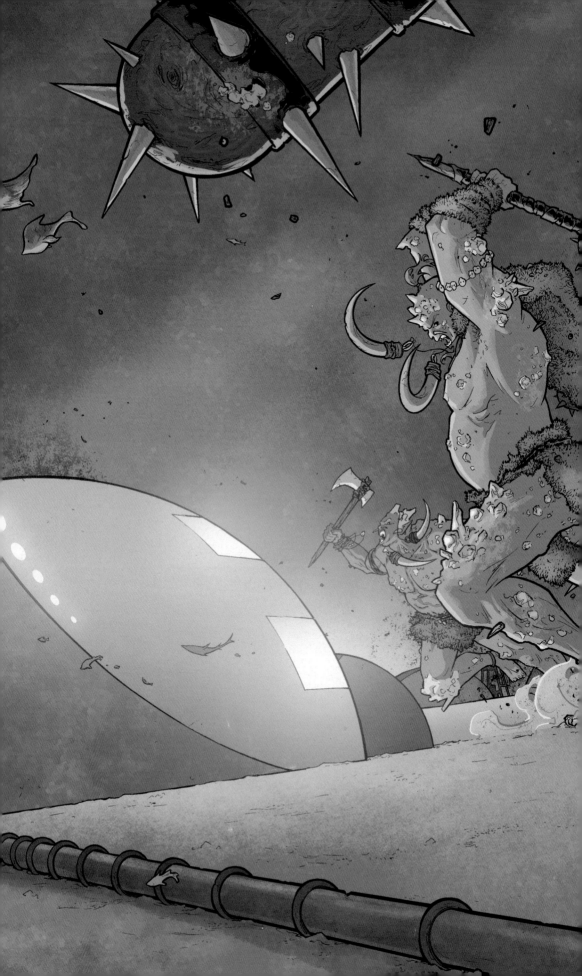

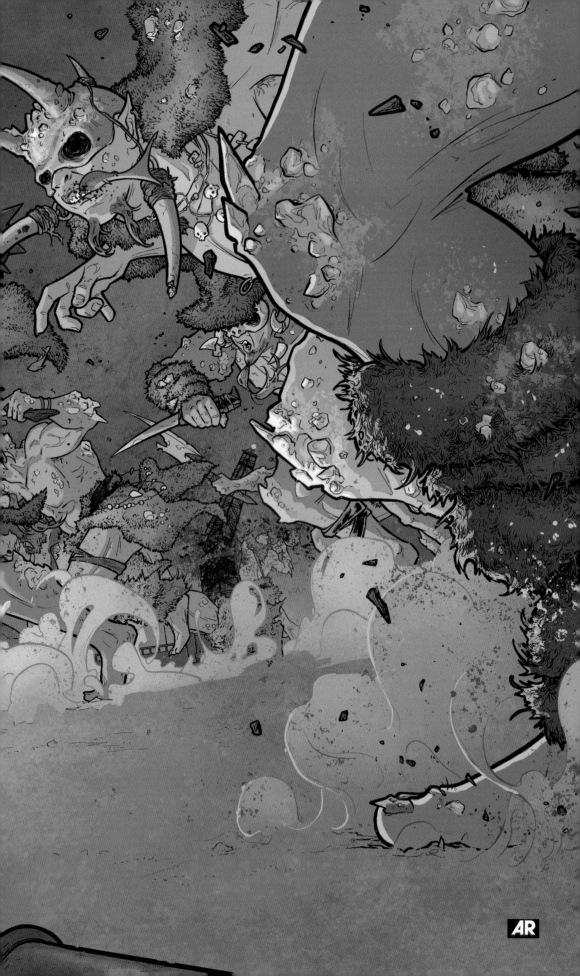

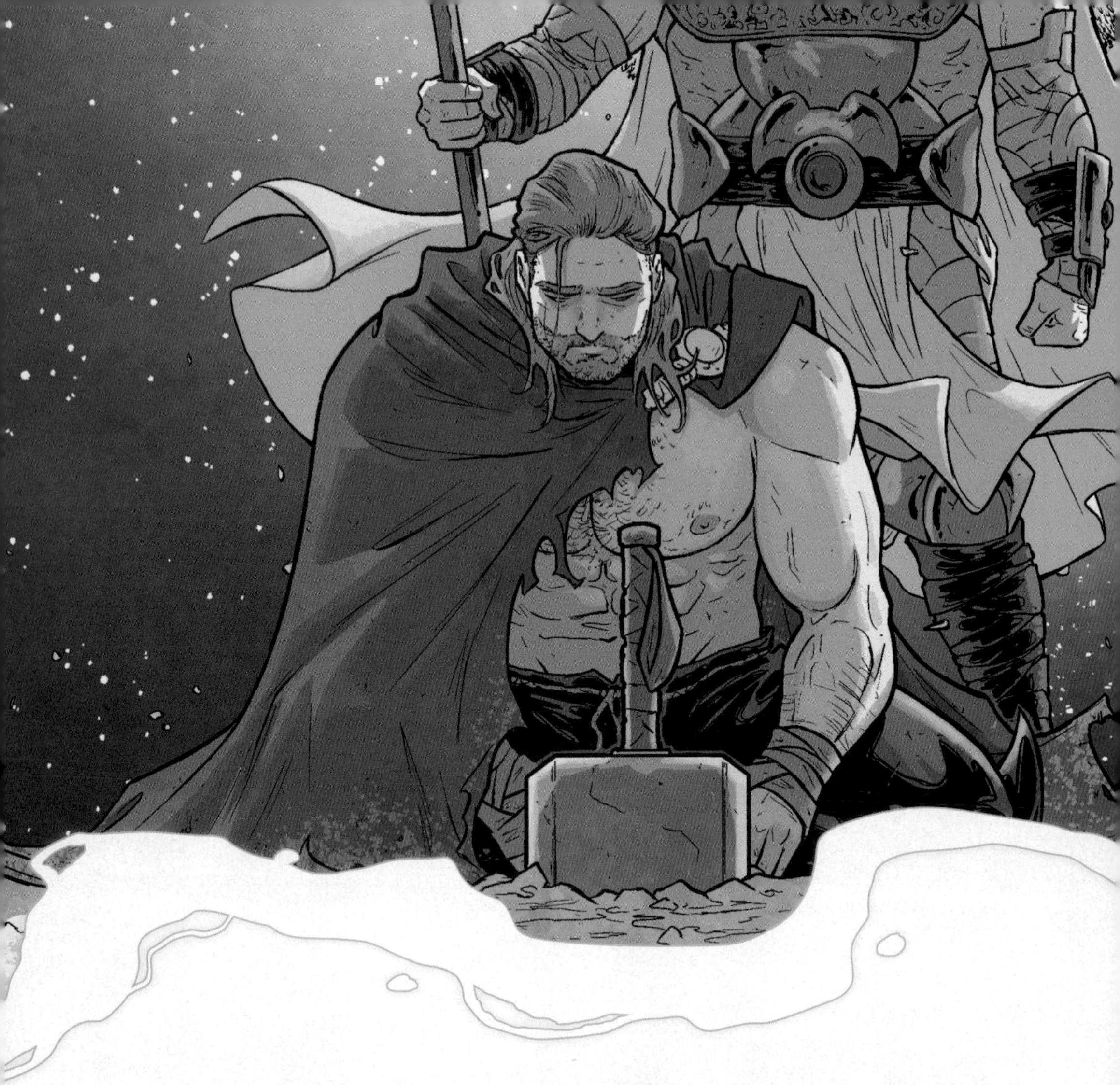

CHANGE HAS COME TO ASGARD.

After a self-imposed exile, Odin the All-Father has returned to his former kingdom (now called Asgardia). But his wife Freyja, who had been ruling Asgardia in his stead as the All-Mother, has no intention of letting things go back to the way the were before Odin left.

The biggest change, though, is that their son, Thor, the God of Thunder, now finds himself no longer worthy of weilding Mjolnir, his enchanted hammer. In a recent battle on the moon, superspy Nick Fury—empowered with secrets he stole from the Watcher—whispered something that caused Thor to drop Mjolnir to the moon's surface, where it has remained ever since. No matter how hard he tries, Thor cannot lift it.

With the leadership of Asgardia uncertain and Thor now in a severly weakened state, it is only a matter of time before enemies of Asgard strike, bringing doom to both the fabled realm and Earth itself.

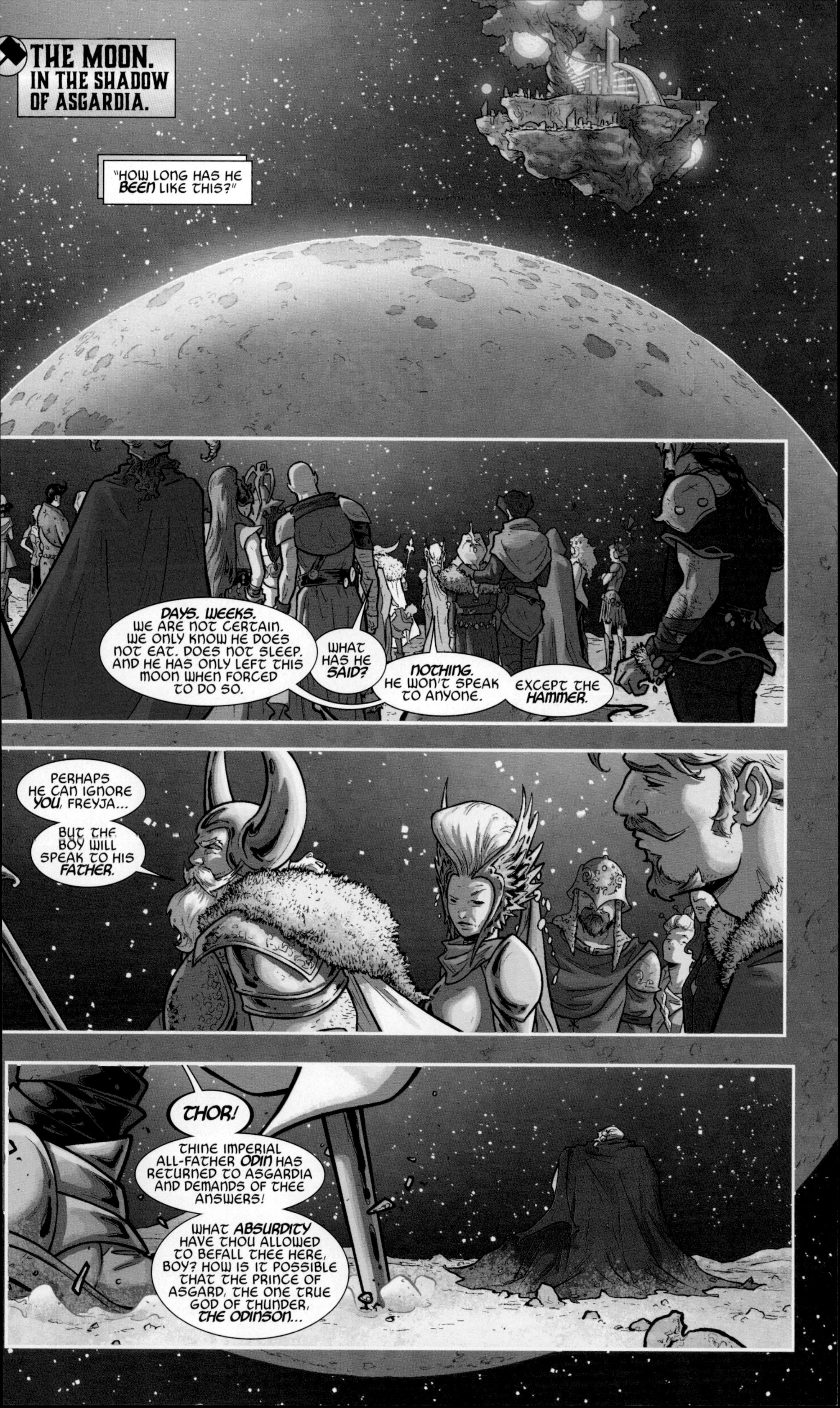
THE MOON. IN THE SHADOW OF ASGARDIA.
"HOW LONG HAS HE BEEN LIKE THIS?"
DAYS. WEEKS. WE ARE NOT CERTAIN. WE ONLY KNOW HE DOES NOT EAT. DOES NOT SLEEP. AND HE HAS ONLY LEFT THIS MOON WHEN FORCED TO DO SO.
WHAT HAS HE SAID?
NOTHING. HE WON'T SPEAK TO ANYONE.
EXCEPT THE HAMMER.
PERHAPS HE CAN IGNORE YOU, FREYJA...
BUT THE BOY WILL SPEAK TO HIS FATHER.
THOR!
THINE IMPERIAL ALL-FATHER ODIN HAS RETURNED TO ASGARDIA AND DEMANDS OF THEE ANSWERS!
WHAT ABSURDITY HAVE THOU ALLOWED TO BEFALL THEE HERE, BOY? HOW IS IT POSSIBLE THAT THE PRINCE OF ASGARD, THE ONE TRUE GOD OF THUNDER, THE ODINSON...

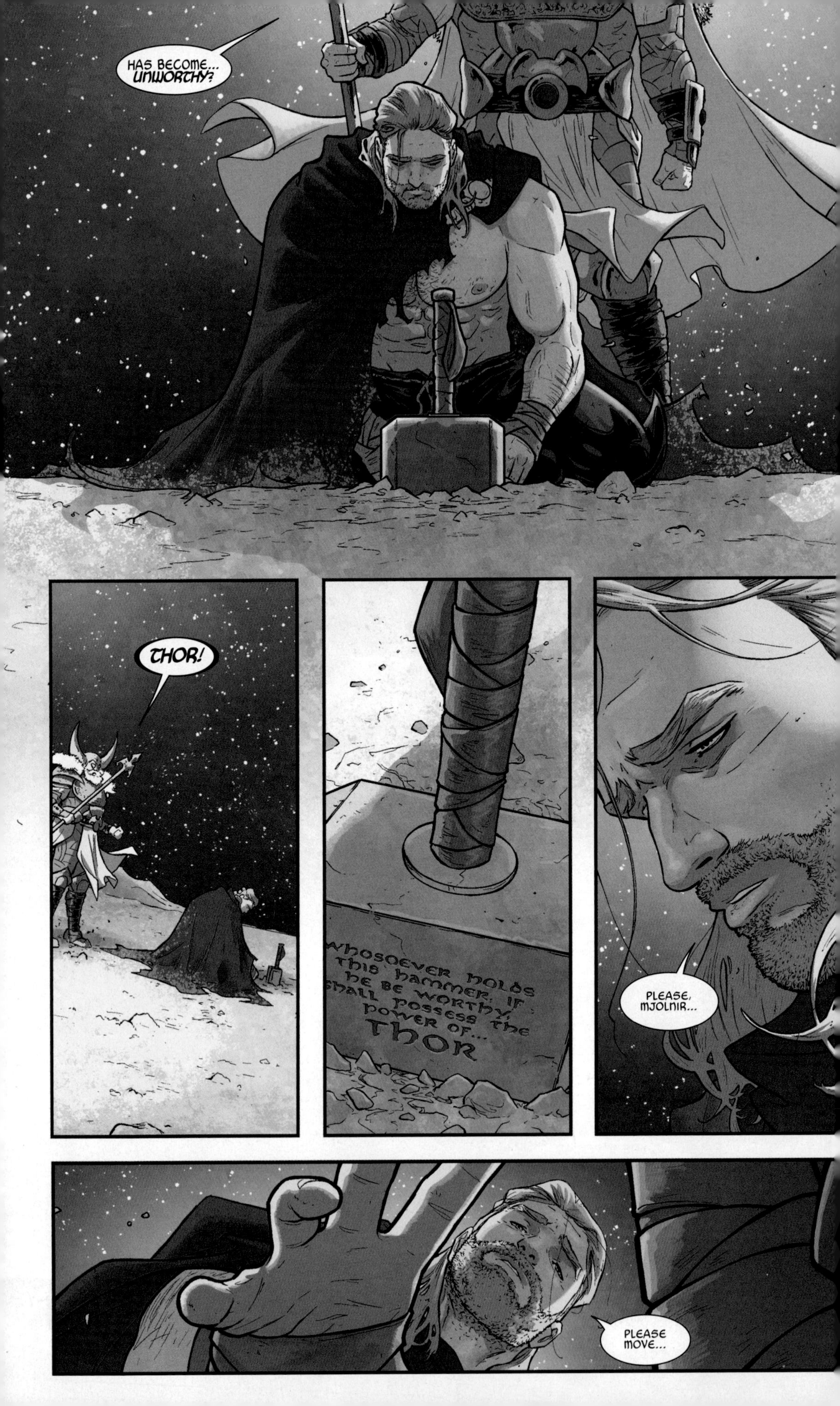
HAS BECOME... UNWORTHY?
THOR!
WHOSOEVER HOLDS THIS HAMMER, IF HE BE WORTHY, SHALL POSSESS THE POWER OF... THOR
PLEASE, MJOLNIR...
PLEASE MOVE...

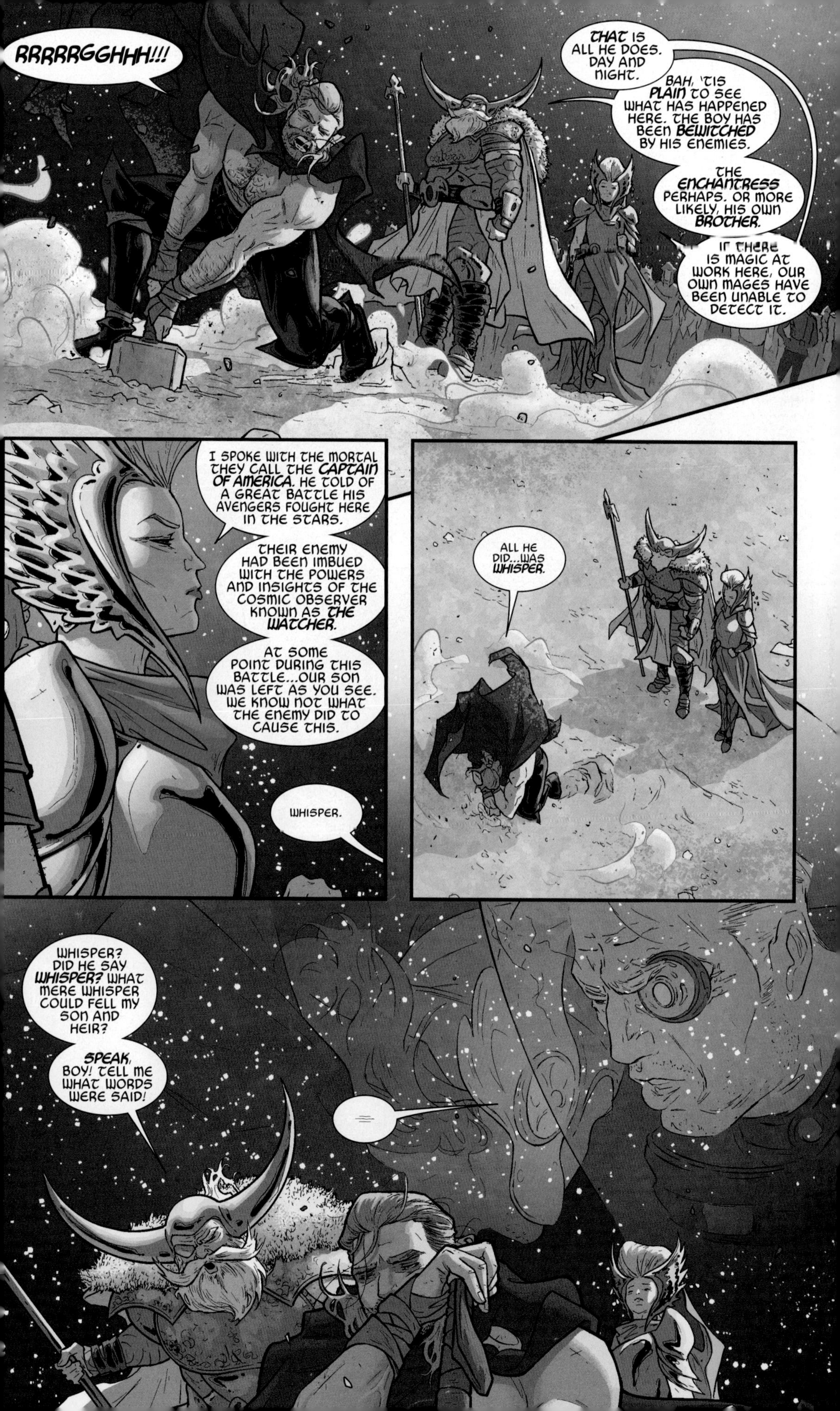
RRRRRGGHHH!!!
THAT IS ALL HE DOES. DAY AND NIGHT.
BAH, 'TIS PLAIN TO SEE WHAT HAS HAPPENED HERE. THE BOY HAS BEEN BEWITCHED BY HIS ENEMIES.
THE ENCHANTRESS PERHAPS. OR MORE LIKELY, HIS OWN BROTHER.
IF THERE IS MAGIC AT WORK HERE, OUR OWN MAGES HAVE BEEN UNABLE TO DETECT IT.
I SPOKE WITH THE MORTAL THEY CALL THE CAPTAIN OF AMERICA. HE TOLD OF A GREAT BATTLE HIS AVENGERS FOUGHT HERE IN THE STARS.
THEIR ENEMY HAD BEEN IMBUED WITH THE POWERS AND INSIGHTS OF THE COSMIC OBSERVER KNOWN AS THE WATCHER.
AT SOME POINT DURING THIS BATTLE...OUR SON WAS LEFT AS YOU SEE. WE KNOW NOT WHAT THE ENEMY DID TO CAUSE THIS.
WHISPER.
ALL HE DID...WAS WHISPER.
WHISPER? DID HE SAY WHISPER? WHAT MERE WHISPER COULD FELL MY SON AND HEIR?
SPEAK, BOY! TELL ME WHAT WORDS WERE SAID!

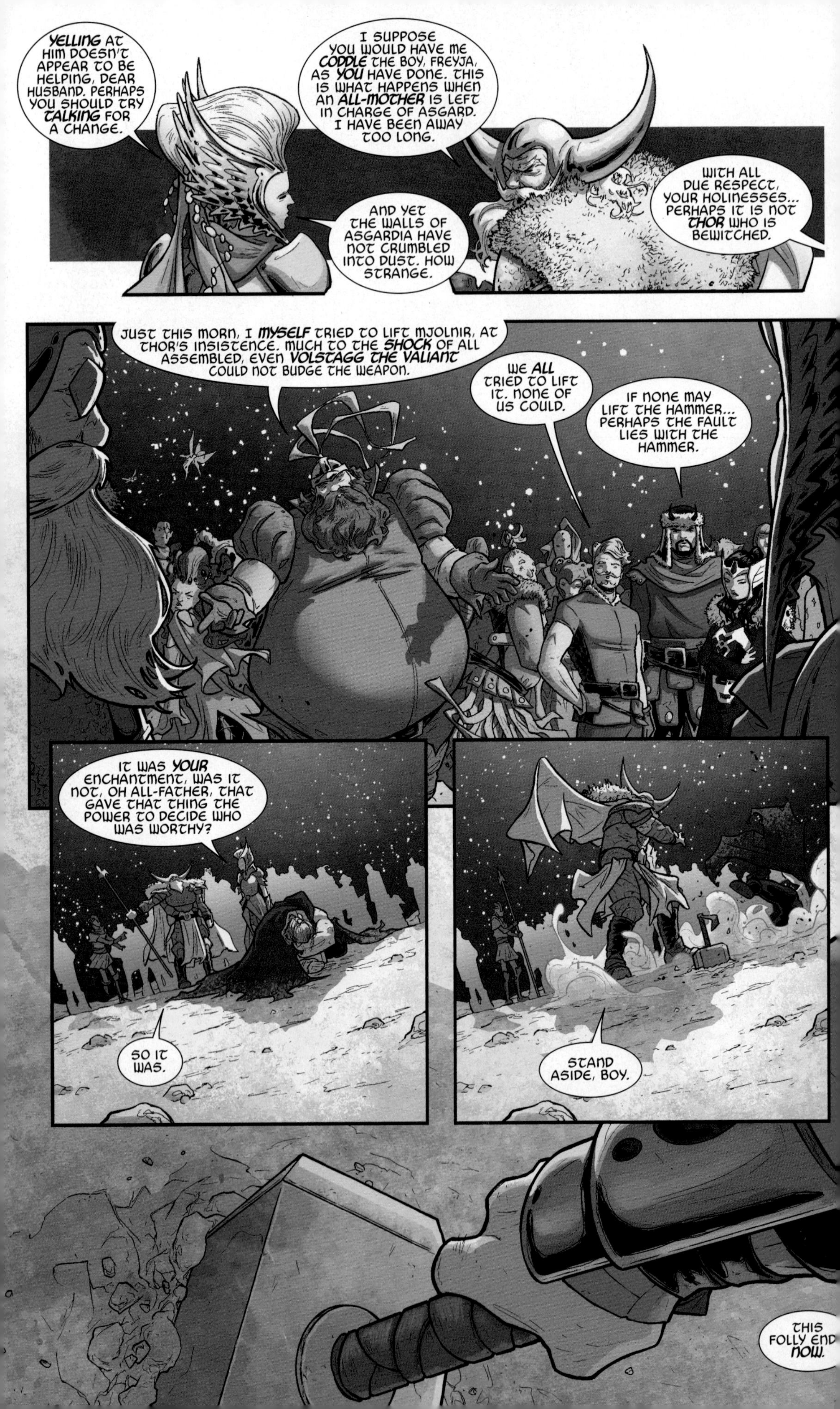
YELLING AT HIM DOESN'T APPEAR TO BE HELPING, DEAR HUSBAND. PERHAPS YOU SHOULD TRY TALKING FOR A CHANGE.
I SUPPOSE YOU WOULD HAVE ME CODDLE THE BOY, FREYJA, AS YOU HAVE DONE. THIS IS WHAT HAPPENS WHEN AN ALL-MOTHER IS LEFT IN CHARGE OF ASGARD. I HAVE BEEN AWAY TOO LONG.
AND YET THE WALLS OF ASGARDIA HAVE NOT CRUMBLED INTO DUST. HOW STRANGE.
WITH ALL DUE RESPECT, YOUR HOLINESSES... PERHAPS IT IS NOT THOR WHO IS BEWITCHED.
JUST THIS MORN, I MYSELF TRIED TO LIFT MJOLNIR, AT THOR'S INSISTENCE. MUCH TO THE SHOCK OF ALL ASSEMBLED, EVEN VOLSTAGG THE VALIANT COULD NOT BUDGE THE WEAPON.
WE ALL TRIED TO LIFT IT. NONE OF US COULD.
IF NONE MAY LIFT THE HAMMER... PERHAPS THE FAULT LIES WITH THE HAMMER.
IT WAS YOUR ENCHANTMENT, WAS IT NOT, OH ALL-FATHER, THAT GAVE THAT THING THE POWER TO DECIDE WHO WAS WORTHY?
SO IT WAS.
STAND ASIDE, BOY.
THIS FOLLY END NOW.

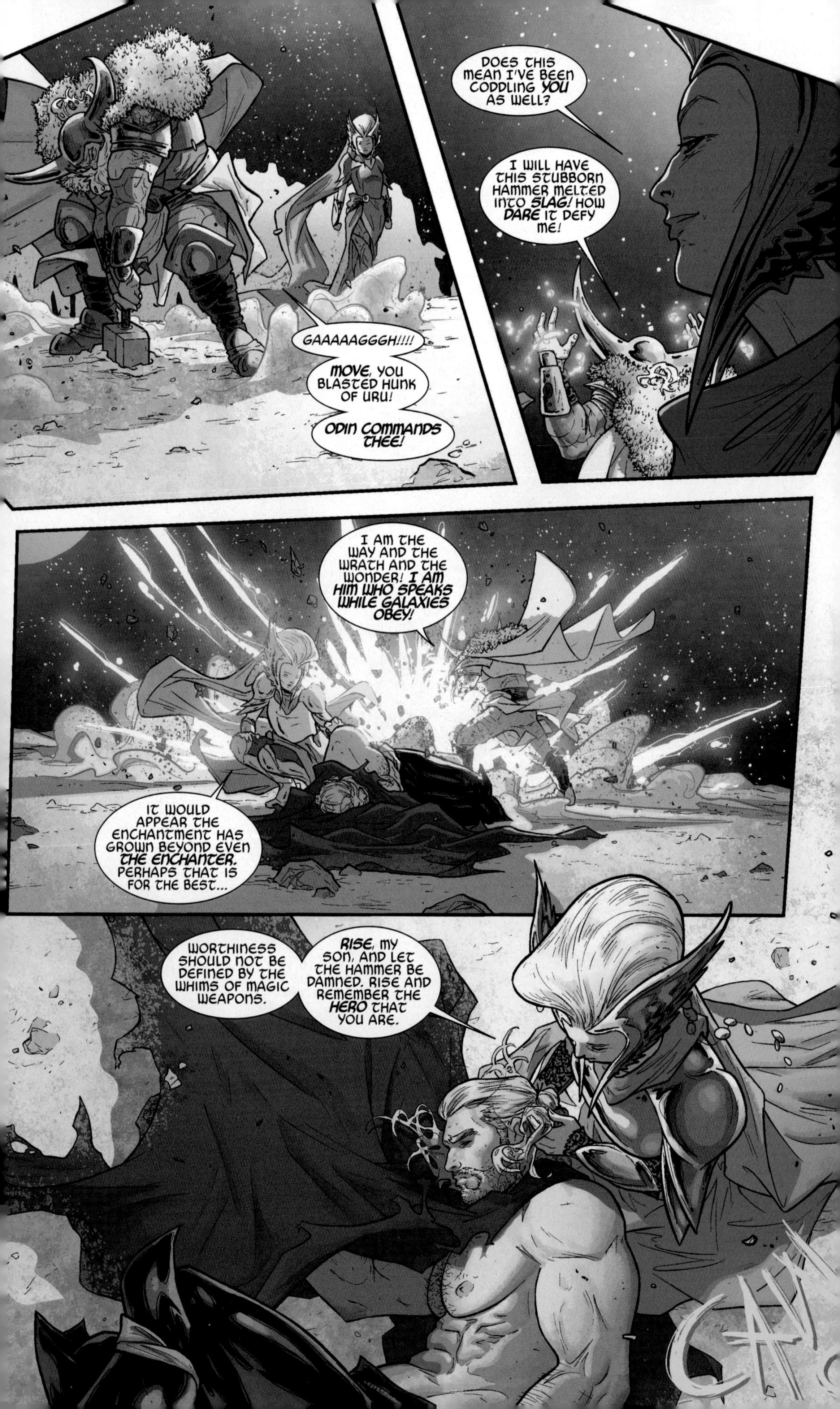
GAAAAAGGGH!!!!
MOVE, YOU BLASTED HUNK OF URU!
ODIN COMMANDS THEE!
DOES THIS MEAN I'VE BEEN CODDLING YOU AS WELL?
I WILL HAVE THIS STUBBORN HAMMER MELTED INTO SLAG! HOW DARE IT DEFY ME!
I AM THE WAY AND THE WRATH AND THE WONDER! I AM HIM WHO SPEAKS WHILE GALAXIES OBEY!
IT WOULD APPEAR THE ENCHANTMENT HAS GROWN BEYOND EVEN THE ENCHANTER. PERHAPS THAT IS FOR THE BEST...
WORTHINESS SHOULD NOT BE DEFINED BY THE WHIMS OF MAGIC WEAPONS.
RISE, MY SON, AND LET THE HAMMER BE DAMNED. RISE AND REMEMBER THE HERO THAT YOU ARE.

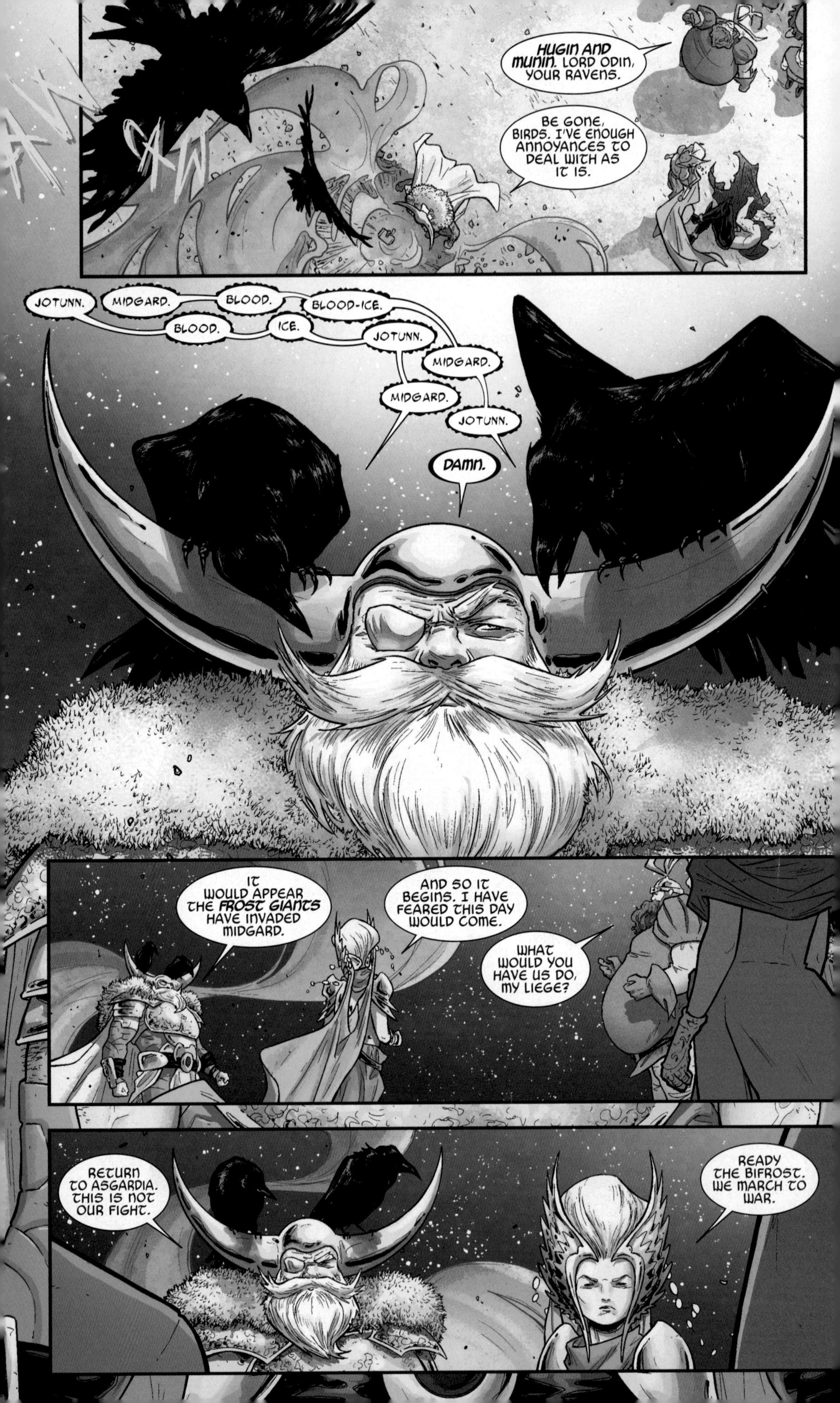
AW
AW
HUGIN AND MUNIN. LORD ODIN, YOUR RAVENS.
BE GONE, BIRDS. I'VE ENOUGH ANNOYANCES TO DEAL WITH AS IT IS.
JOTUNN.
MIDGARD.
BLOOD.
BLOOD-ICE.
BLOOD.
ICE.
JOTUNN.
MIDGARD.
MIDGARD.
JOTUNN.
DAMN.
IT WOULD APPEAR THE FROST GIANTS HAVE INVADED MIDGARD.
AND SO IT BEGINS. I HAVE FEARED THIS DAY WOULD COME.
WHAT WOULD YOU HAVE US DO, MY LIEGE?
RETURN TO ASGARDIA. THIS IS NOT OUR FIGHT.
READY THE BIFROST. WE MARCH TO WAR.

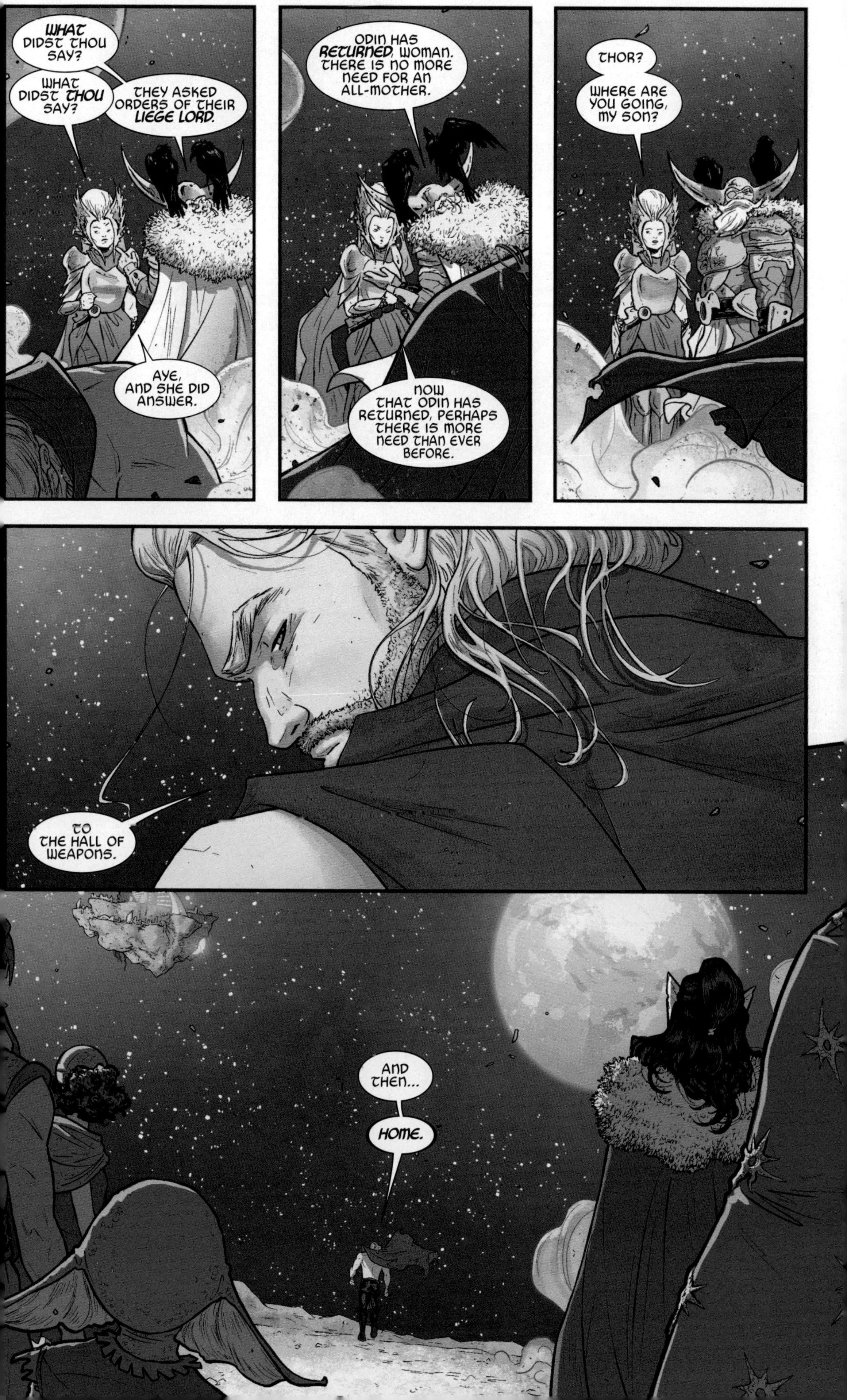
WHAT DIDST THOU SAY?
WHAT DIDST THOU SAY?
THEY ASKED ORDERS OF THEIR LIEGE LORD.
AYE, AND SHE DID ANSWER.
ODIN HAS RETURNED, WOMAN. THERE IS NO MORE NEED FOR AN ALL-MOTHER.
NOW THAT ODIN HAS RETURNED, PERHAPS THERE IS MORE NEED THAN EVER BEFORE.
THOR?
WHERE ARE YOU GOING, MY SON?
TO THE HALL OF WEAPONS.
AND THEN...
HOME.

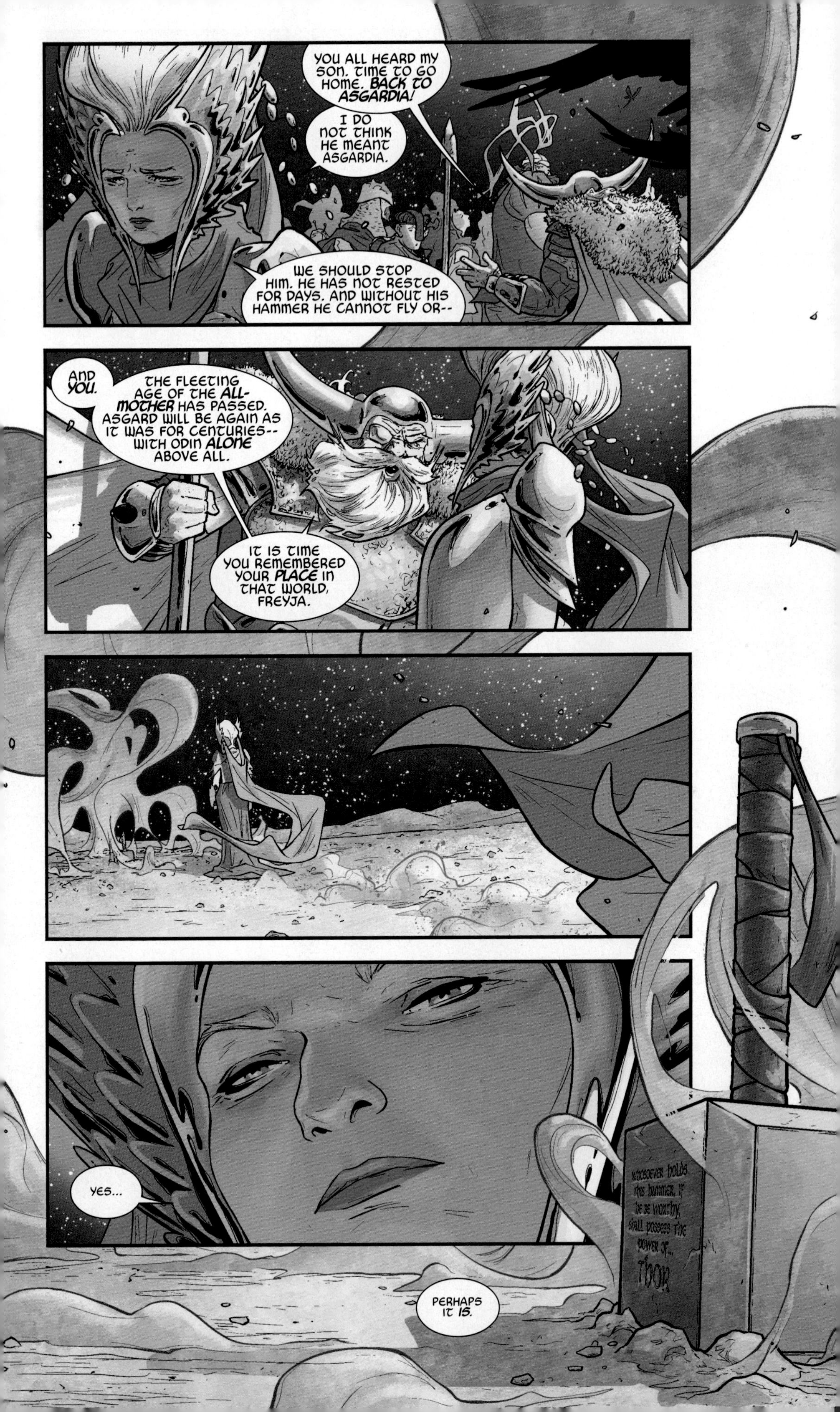
YOU ALL HEARD MY SON. TIME TO GO HOME. BACK TO ASGARDIA!
I DO NOT THINK HE MEANT ASGARDIA.
WE SHOULD STOP HIM. HE HAS NOT RESTED FOR DAYS. AND WITHOUT HIS HAMMER HE CANNOT FLY OR--
AND YOU.
THE FLEETING AGE OF THE ALL-MOTHER HAS PASSED. ASGARD WILL BE AGAIN AS IT WAS FOR CENTURIES--WITH ODIN ALONE ABOVE ALL.
IT IS TIME YOU REMEMBERED YOUR PLACE IN THAT WORLD, FREYJA.
YES...
Whosoever holds this hammer, if he be worthy, shall possess the power of... THOR
PERHAPS IT IS.

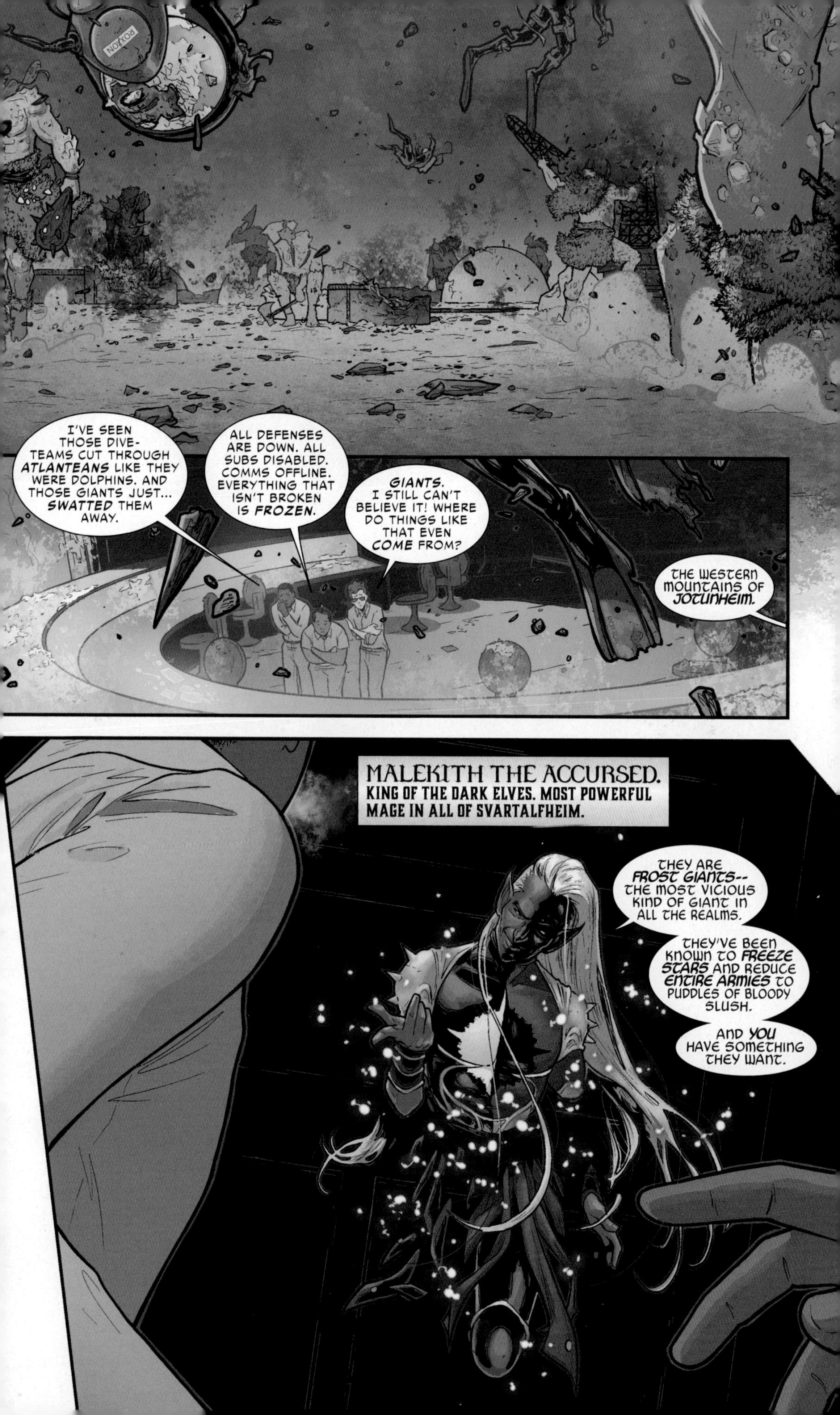
ROXXON
I'VE SEEN THOSE DIVE-TEAMS CUT THROUGH ATLANTEANS LIKE THEY WERE DOLPHINS. AND THOSE GIANTS JUST... SWATTED THEM AWAY.
ALL DEFENSES ARE DOWN. ALL SUBS DISABLED. COMMS OFFLINE. EVERYTHING THAT ISN'T BROKEN IS FROZEN.
GIANTS. I STILL CAN'T BELIEVE IT! WHERE DO THINGS LIKE THAT EVEN COME FROM?
THE WESTERN MOUNTAINS OF JOTUNHEIM.
MALEKITH THE ACCURSED.
KING OF THE DARK ELVES. MOST POWERFUL MAGE IN ALL OF SVARTALFHEIM.
THEY ARE FROST GIANTS-- THE MOST VICIOUS KIND OF GIANT IN ALL THE REALMS.
THEY'VE BEEN KNOWN TO FREEZE STARS AND REDUCE ENTIRE ARMIES TO PUDDLES OF BLOODY SLUSH.
AND YOU HAVE SOMETHING THEY WANT.

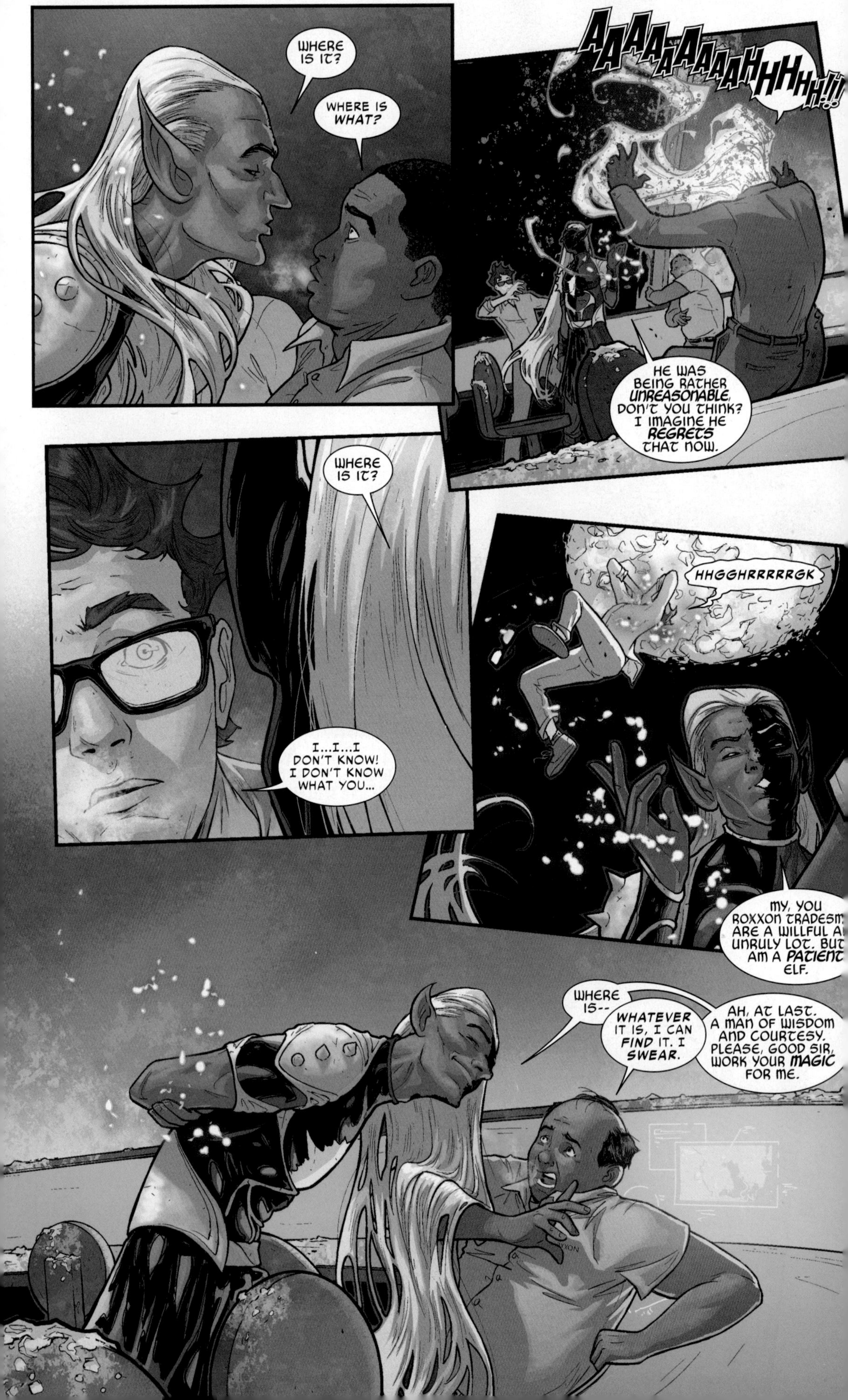

WHERE IS IT?
WHERE IS WHAT?
AAAAAAAAAAAHHHHH!!!
HE WAS BEING RATHER UNREASONABLE, DON'T YOU THINK? I IMAGINE HE REGRETS THAT NOW.
WHERE IS IT?
I...I...I DON'T KNOW! I DON'T KNOW WHAT YOU...
HHGGHRRRRRGK
MY, YOU ROXXON TRADESM ARE A WILLFUL A UNRULY LOT. BUT AM A PATIENT ELF.
WHERE IS--
WHATEVER IT IS, I CAN FIND IT. I SWEAR.
AH, AT LAST. A MAN OF WISDOM AND COURTESY. PLEASE, GOOD SIR, WORK YOUR MAGIC FOR ME.

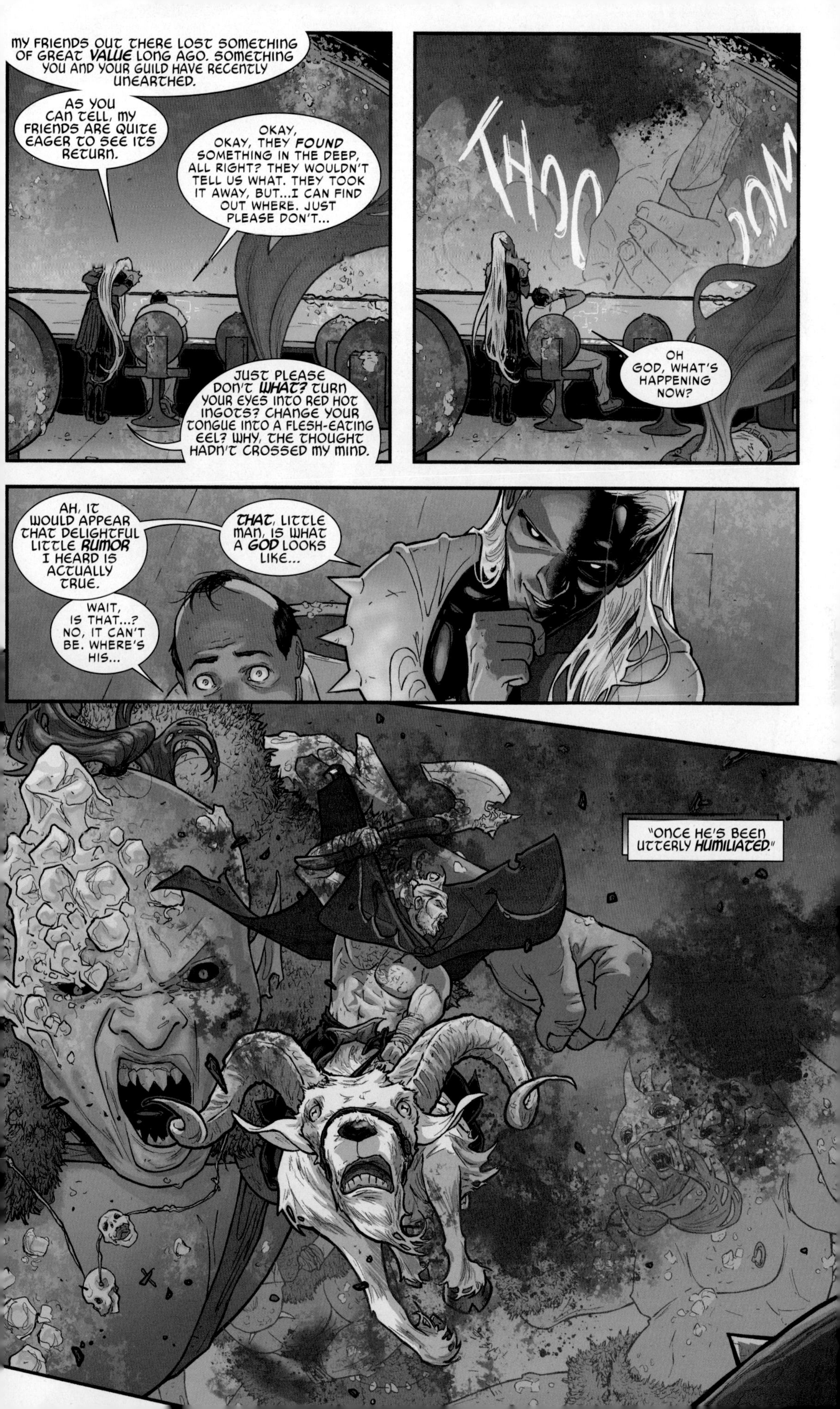

MY FRIENDS OUT THERE LOST SOMETHING OF GREAT VALUE LONG AGO. SOMETHING YOU AND YOUR GUILD HAVE RECENTLY UNEARTHED.
AS YOU CAN TELL, MY FRIENDS ARE QUITE EAGER TO SEE ITS RETURN.
OKAY, OKAY, THEY FOUND SOMETHING IN THE DEEP, ALL RIGHT? THEY WOULDN'T TELL US WHAT. THEY TOOK IT AWAY, BUT...I CAN FIND OUT WHERE. JUST PLEASE DON'T...
JUST PLEASE DON'T WHAT? TURN YOUR EYES INTO RED HOT INGOTS? CHANGE YOUR TONGUE INTO A FLESH-EATING EEL? WHY, THE THOUGHT HADN'T CROSSED MY MIND.
OH GOD, WHAT'S HAPPENING NOW?
AH, IT WOULD APPEAR THAT DELIGHTFUL LITTLE RUMOR I HEARD IS ACTUALLY TRUE.
THAT, LITTLE MAN, IS WHAT A GOD LOOKS LIKE...
WAIT, IS THAT...? NO, IT CAN'T BE. WHERE'S HIS...
"ONCE HE'S BEEN UTTERLY HUMILIATED."

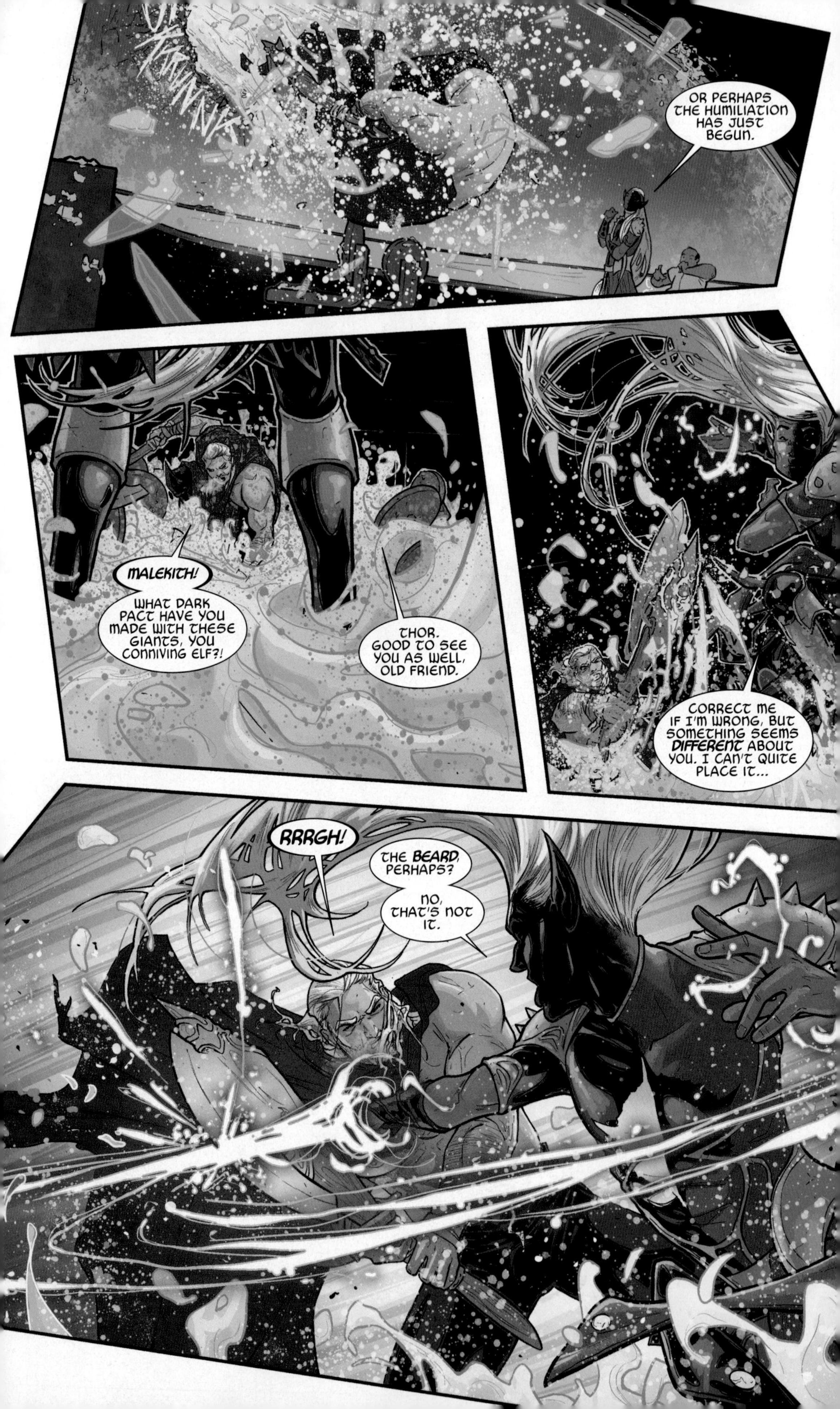

KRAWNNK
OR PERHAPS THE HUMILIATION HAS JUST BEGUN.
MALEKITH!
WHAT DARK PACT HAVE YOU MADE WITH THESE GIANTS, YOU CONNIVING ELF?!
THOR. GOOD TO SEE YOU AS WELL, OLD FRIEND.
CORRECT ME IF I'M WRONG, BUT SOMETHING SEEMS DIFFERENT ABOUT YOU. I CAN'T QUITE PLACE IT...
RRRGH!
THE BEARD, PERHAPS?
NO, THAT'S NOT IT.

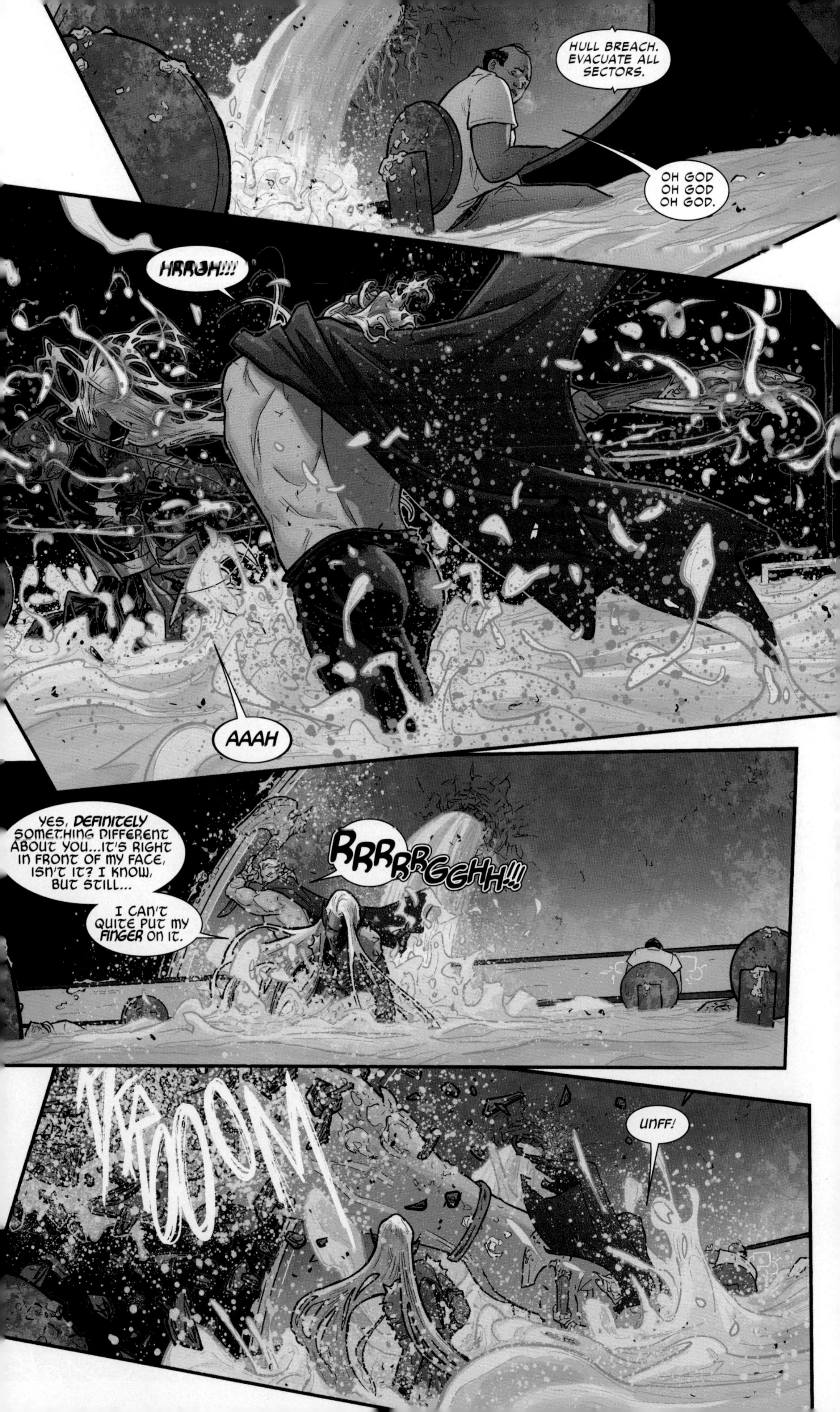
HULL BREACH. EVACUATE ALL SECTORS.
OH GOD OH GOD OH GOD.
HRRGH!!!
AAAH
YES, DEFINITELY SOMETHING DIFFERENT ABOUT YOU...IT'S RIGHT IN FRONT OF MY FACE, ISN'T IT? I KNOW, BUT STILL...
I CAN'T QUITE PUT MY FINGER ON IT.
BRRRRRGGHH!!!
KRAOOOM
UNFF!

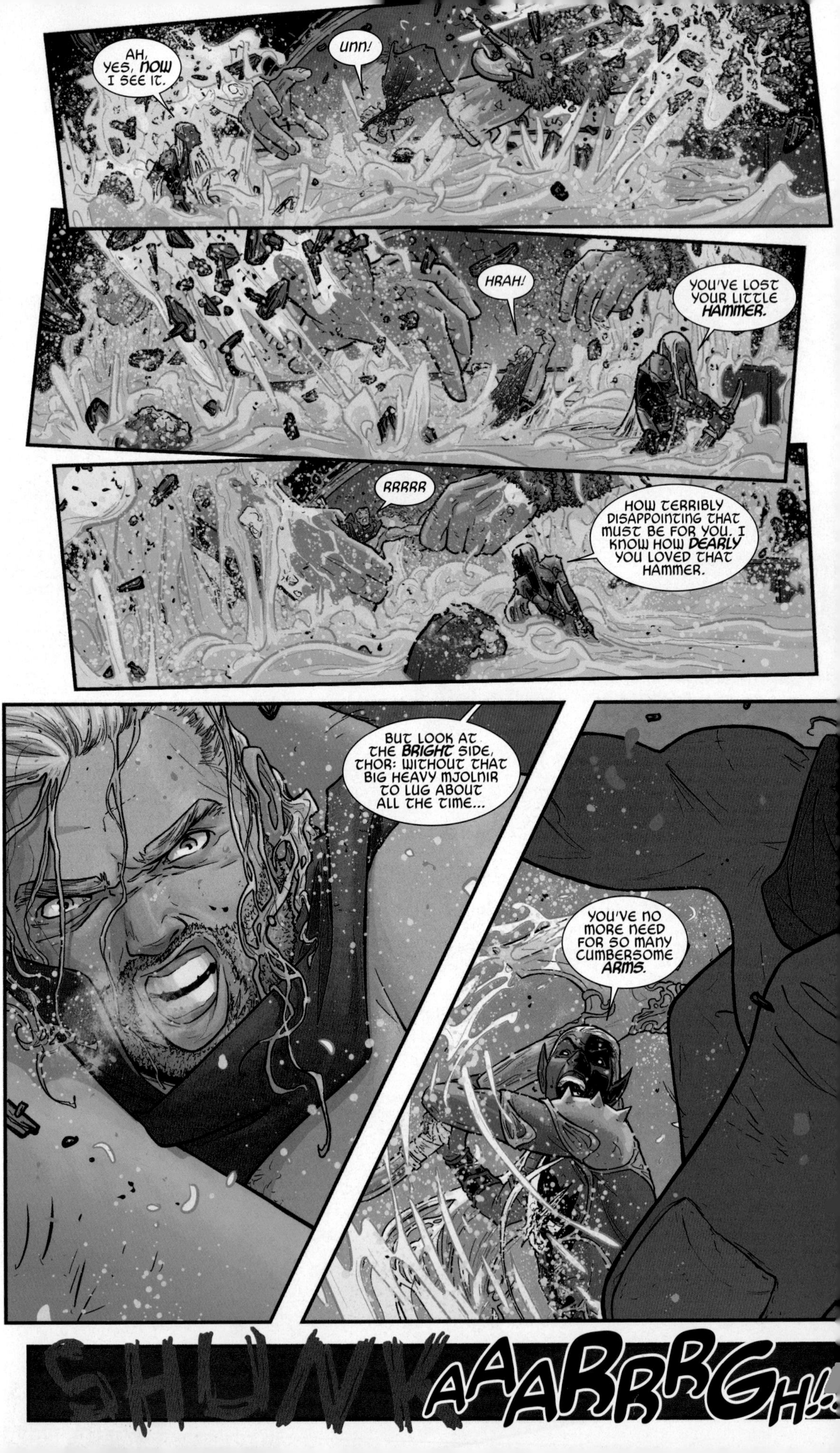
AH, YES, NOW I SEE IT.
UNN!
HRAH!
YOU'VE LOST YOUR LITTLE HAMMER.
RRRRR
HOW TERRIBLY DISAPPOINTING THAT MUST BE FOR YOU. I KNOW HOW DEARLY YOU LOVED THAT HAMMER.
BUT LOOK AT THE BRIGHT SIDE, THOR: WITHOUT THAT BIG HEAVY MJOLNIR TO LUG ABOUT ALL THE TIME...
YOU'VE NO MORE NEED FOR SO MANY CUMBERSOME ARMS.
SHUNK
AAARRRGH!

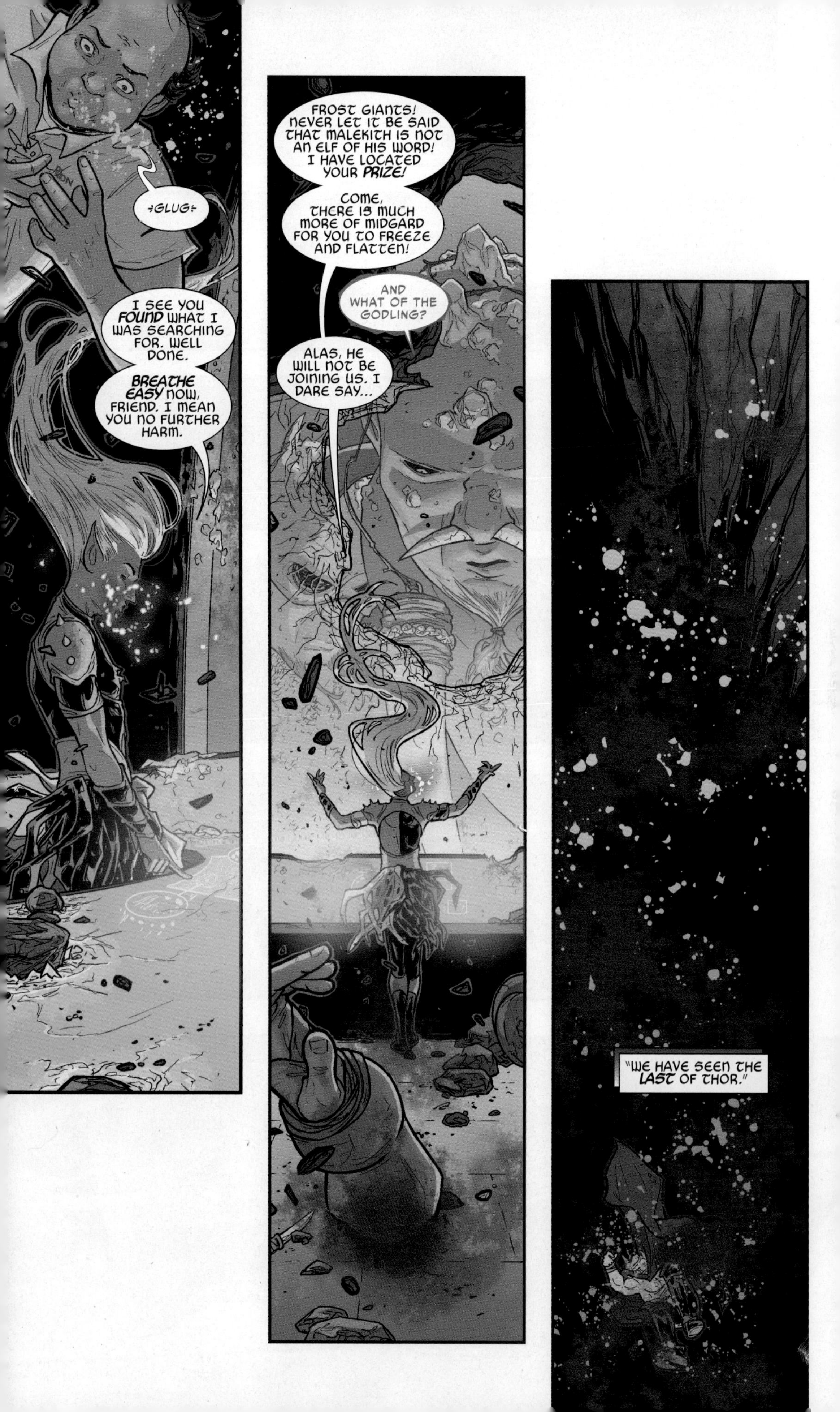

-GLUG-
I SEE YOU FOUND WHAT I WAS SEARCHING FOR. WELL DONE.
BREATHE EASY NOW, FRIEND. I MEAN YOU NO FURTHER HARM.
FROST GIANTS! NEVER LET IT BE SAID THAT MALEKITH IS NOT AN ELF OF HIS WORD! I HAVE LOCATED YOUR PRIZE!
COME, THERE IS MUCH MORE OF MIDGARD FOR YOU TO FREEZE AND FLATTEN!
AND WHAT OF THE GODLING?
ALAS, HE WILL NOT BE JOINING US. I DARE SAY...
"WE HAVE SEEN THE LAST OF THOR."

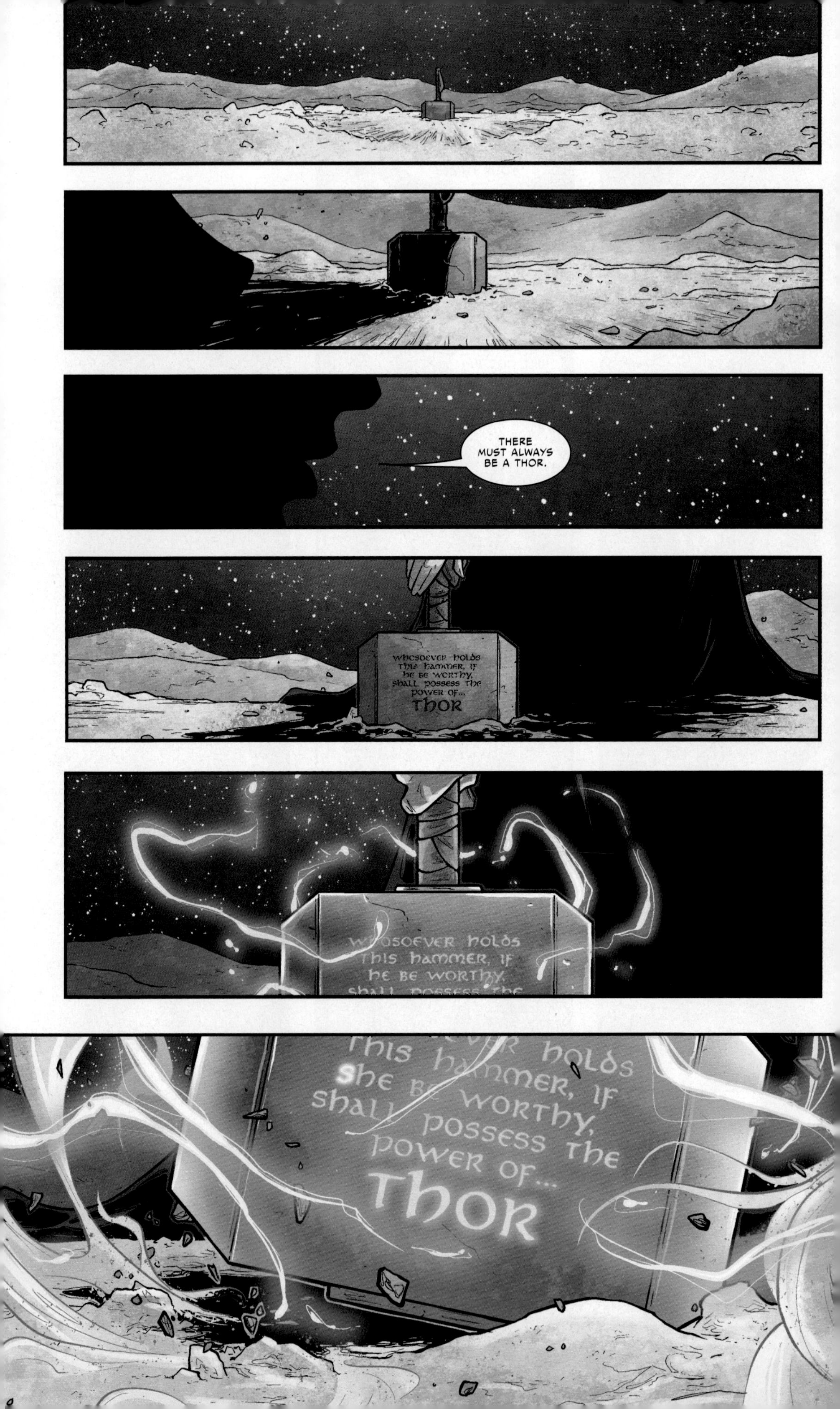
THERE MUST ALWAYS BE A THOR.
WHOSOEVER HOLDS THIS HAMMER, IF HE BE WORTHY, SHALL POSSESS THE POWER OF... THOR
WHOSOEVER HOLDS THIS HAMMER, IF HE BE WORTHY,
THIS HAMMER, IF SHE BE WORTHY, SHALL POSSESS THE POWER OF... THOR

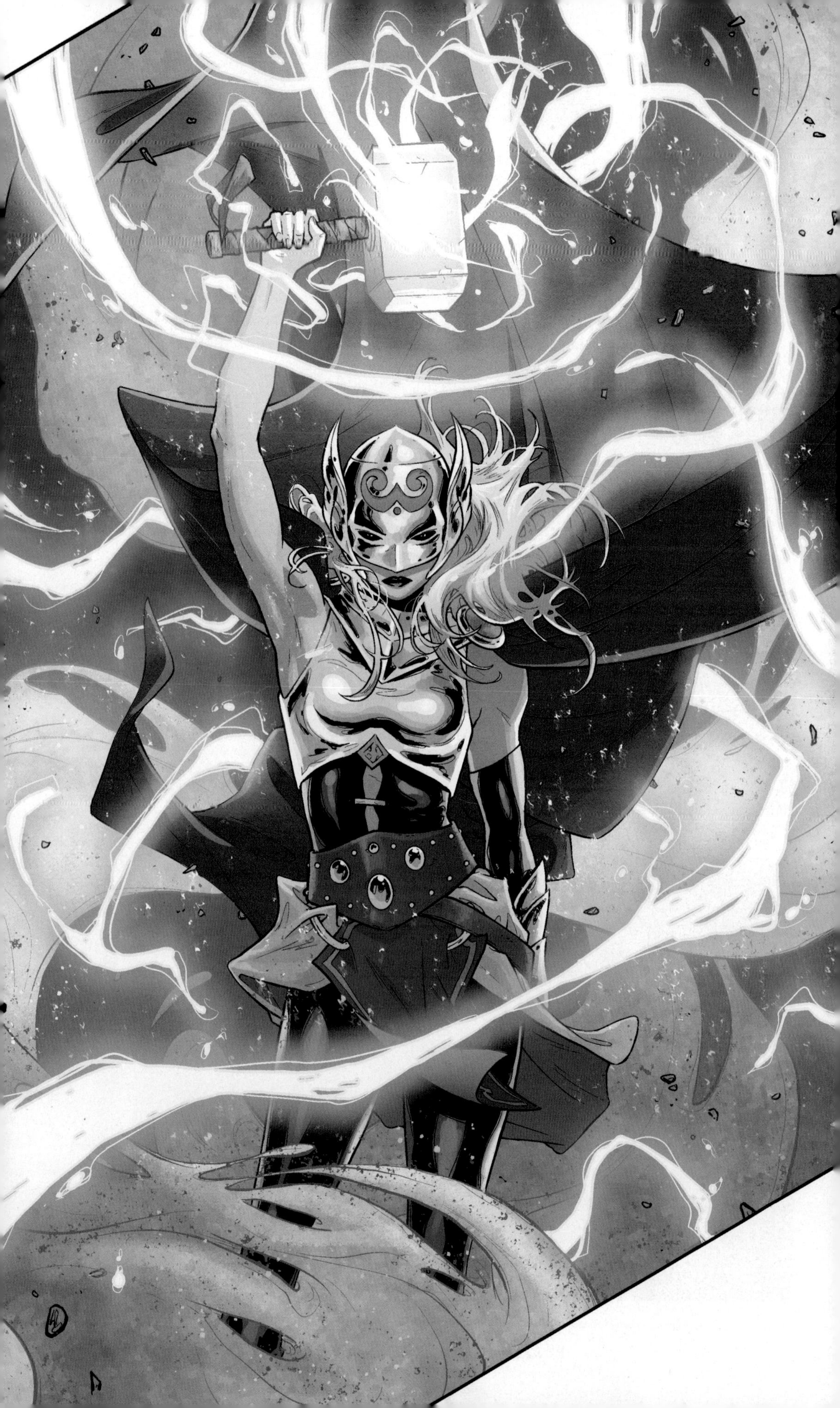

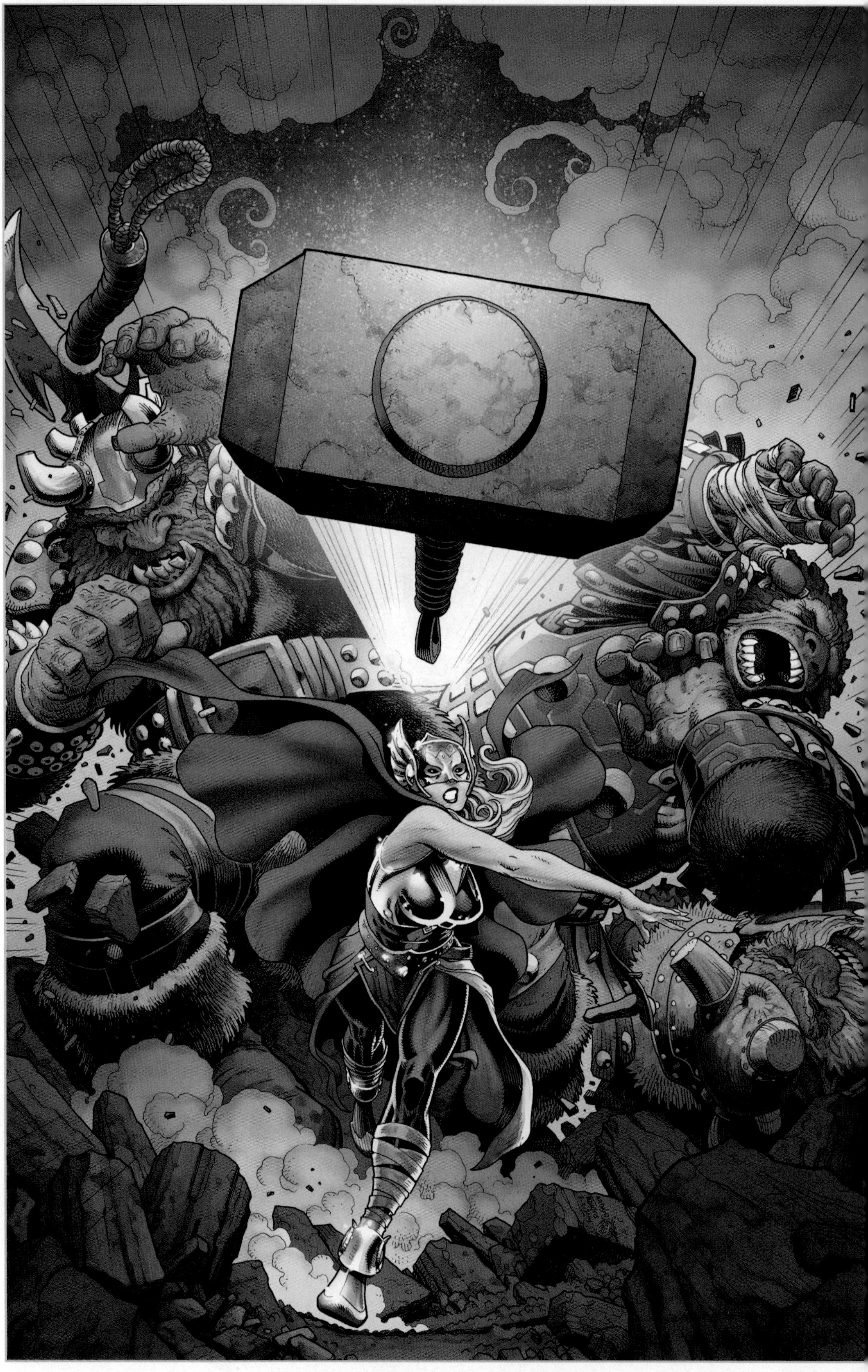

THOR # 1 VARIANT
BY **ARTHUR ADAMS & PETER STEIGERWALD**

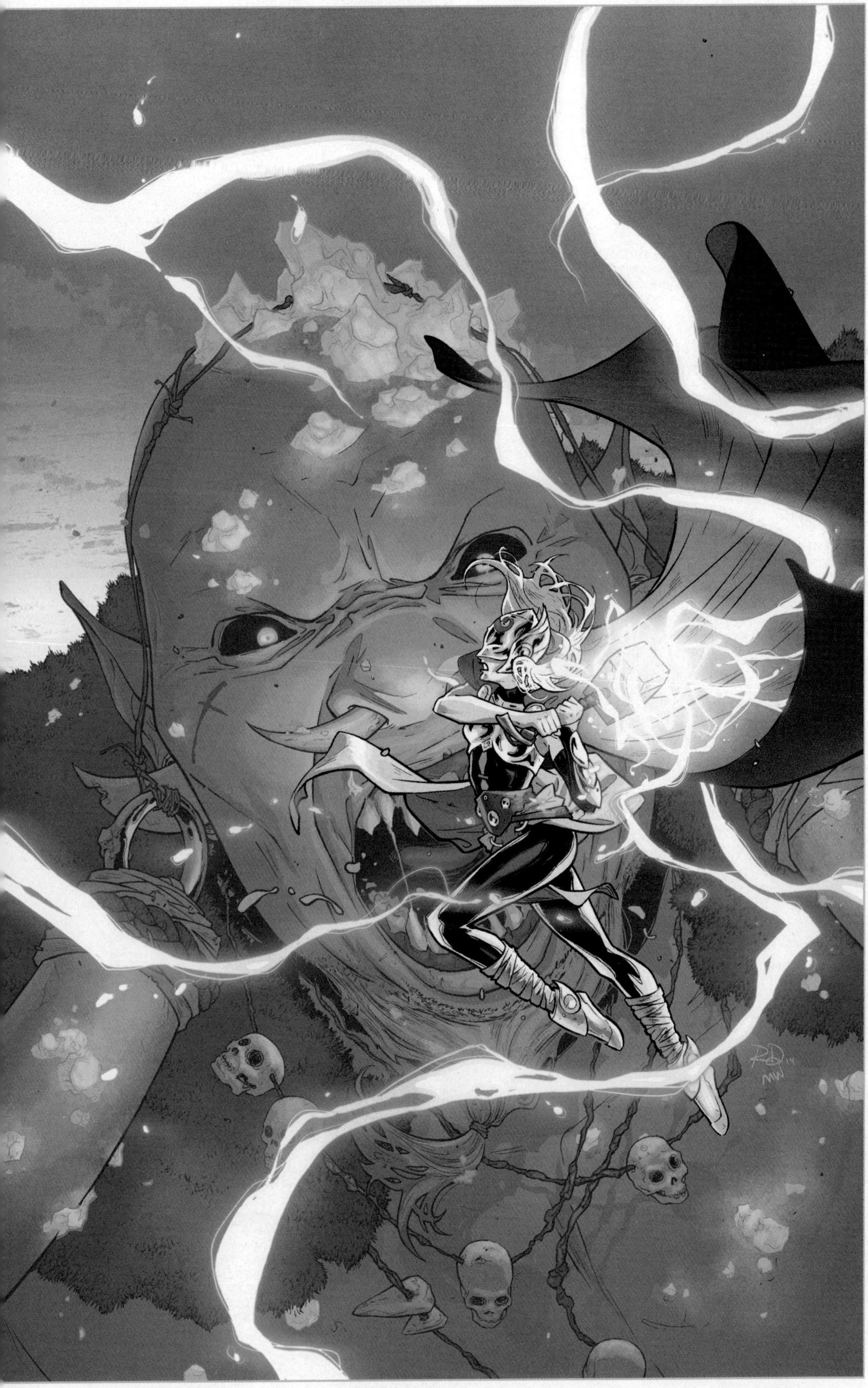

2

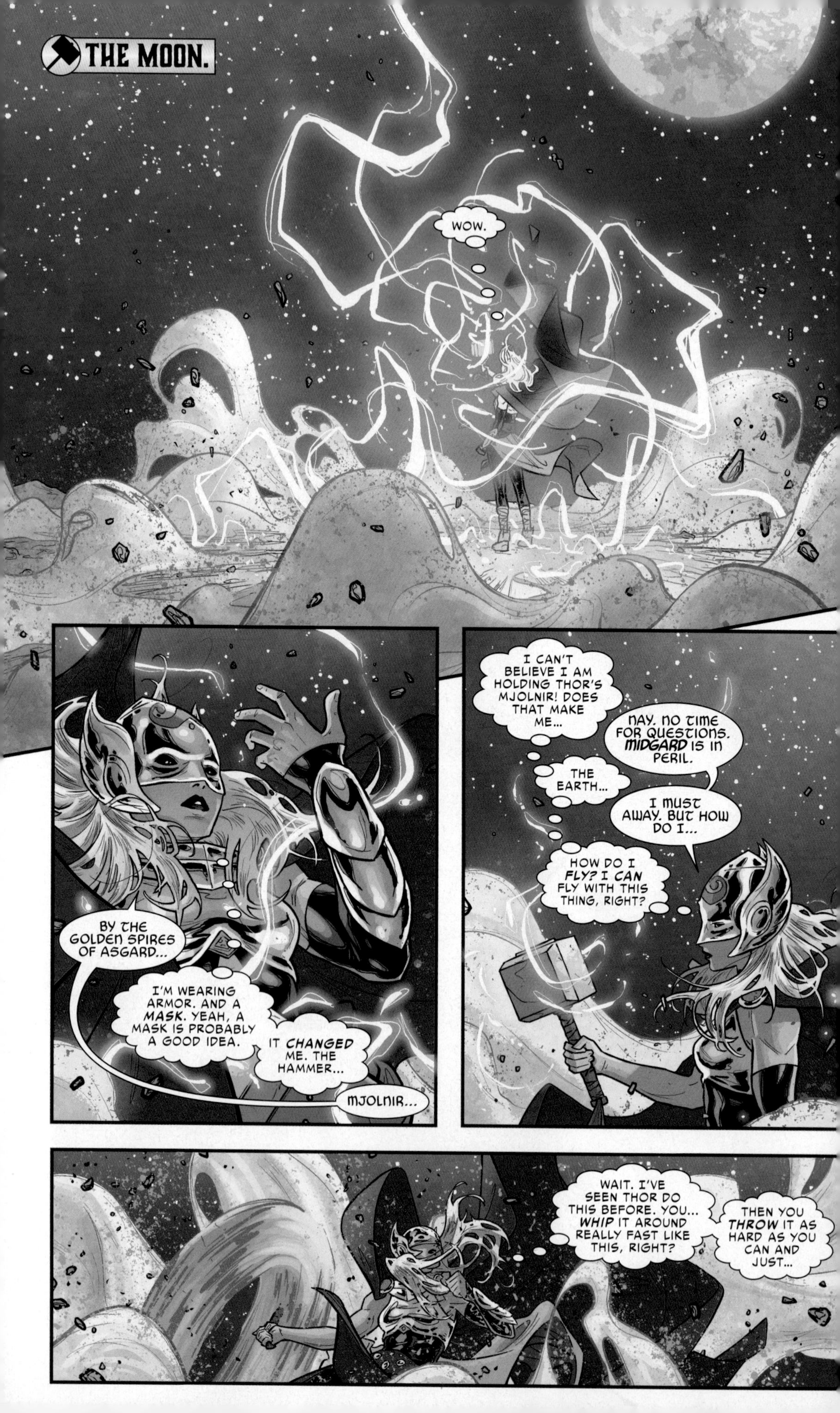
THE MOON.
WOW.
BY THE GOLDEN SPIRES OF ASGARD...
MJOLNIR...
IT CHANGED ME. THE HAMMER...
I'M WEARING ARMOR. AND A MASK. YEAH, A MASK IS PROBABLY A GOOD IDEA.
I CAN'T BELIEVE I AM HOLDING THOR'S MJOLNIR! DOES THAT MAKE ME...
NAY. NO TIME FOR QUESTIONS. MIDGARD IS IN PERIL.
THE EARTH...
I MUST AWAY. BUT HOW DO I...
HOW DO I FLY? I CAN FLY WITH THIS THING, RIGHT?
WAIT. I'VE SEEN THOR DO THIS BEFORE. YOU... WHIP IT AROUND REALLY FAST LIKE THIS, RIGHT?
THEN YOU THROW IT AS HARD AS YOU CAN AND JUST...

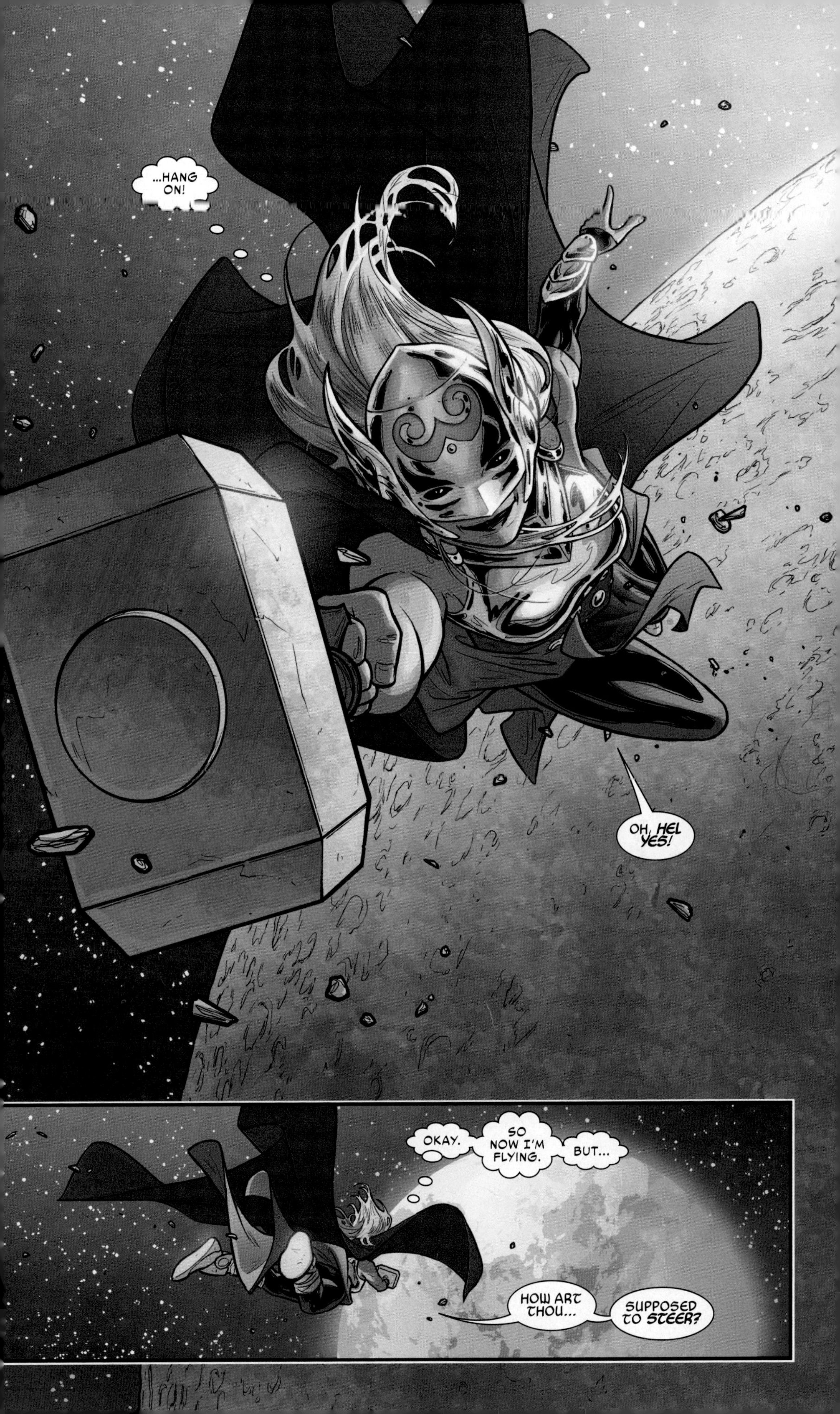
...HANG ON!
OH, HEL YES!
OKAY.
SO NOW I'M FLYING.
BUT...
HOW ART THOU...
SUPPOSED TO STEER?

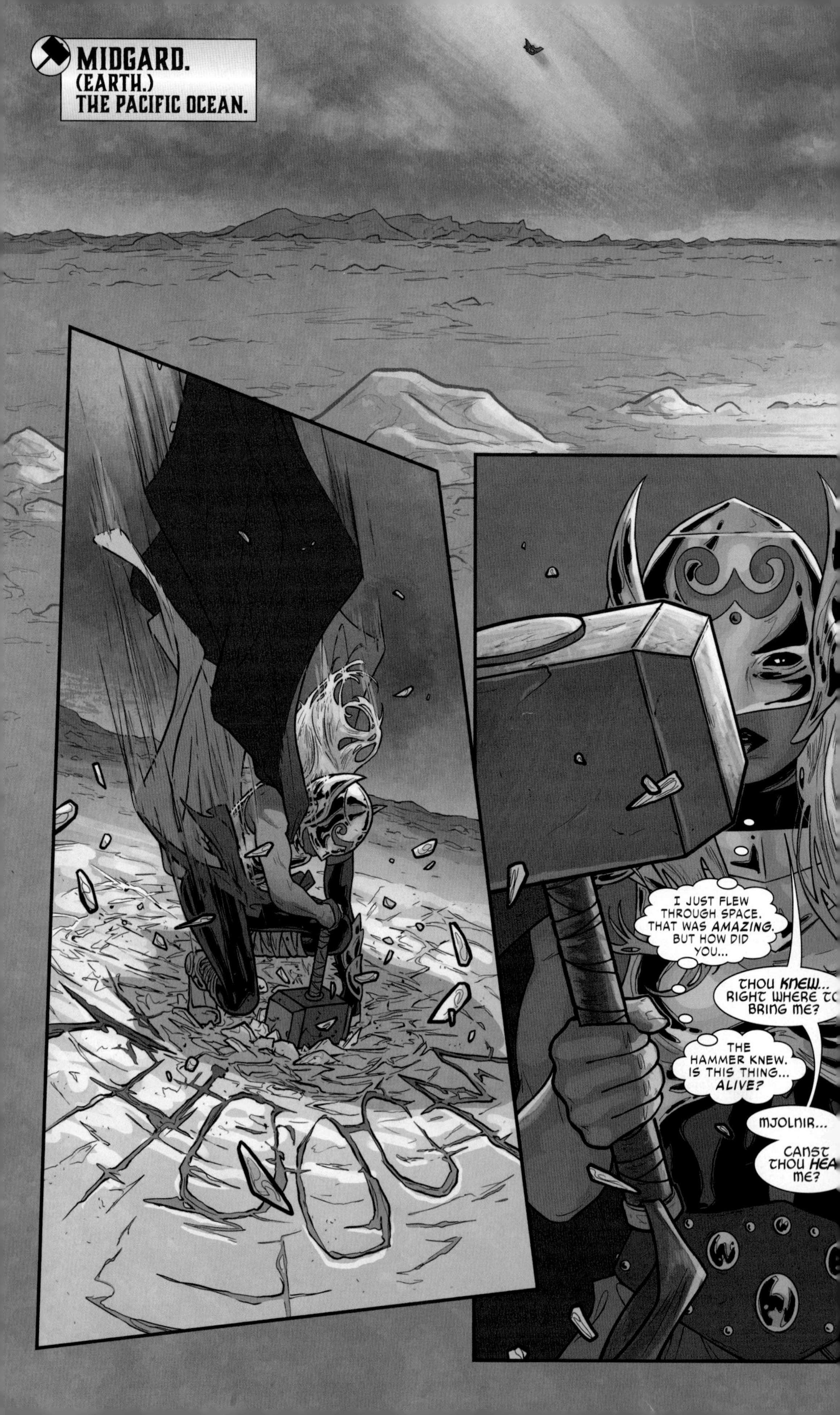
MIDGARD.
(EARTH.)
THE PACIFIC OCEAN.
I JUST FLEW THROUGH SPACE. THAT WAS AMAZING. BUT HOW DID YOU...
THOU KNEW... RIGHT WHERE TO BRING ME?
THE HAMMER KNEW. IS THIS THING... ALIVE?
MJOLNIR...
CANST THOU HEAR ME?

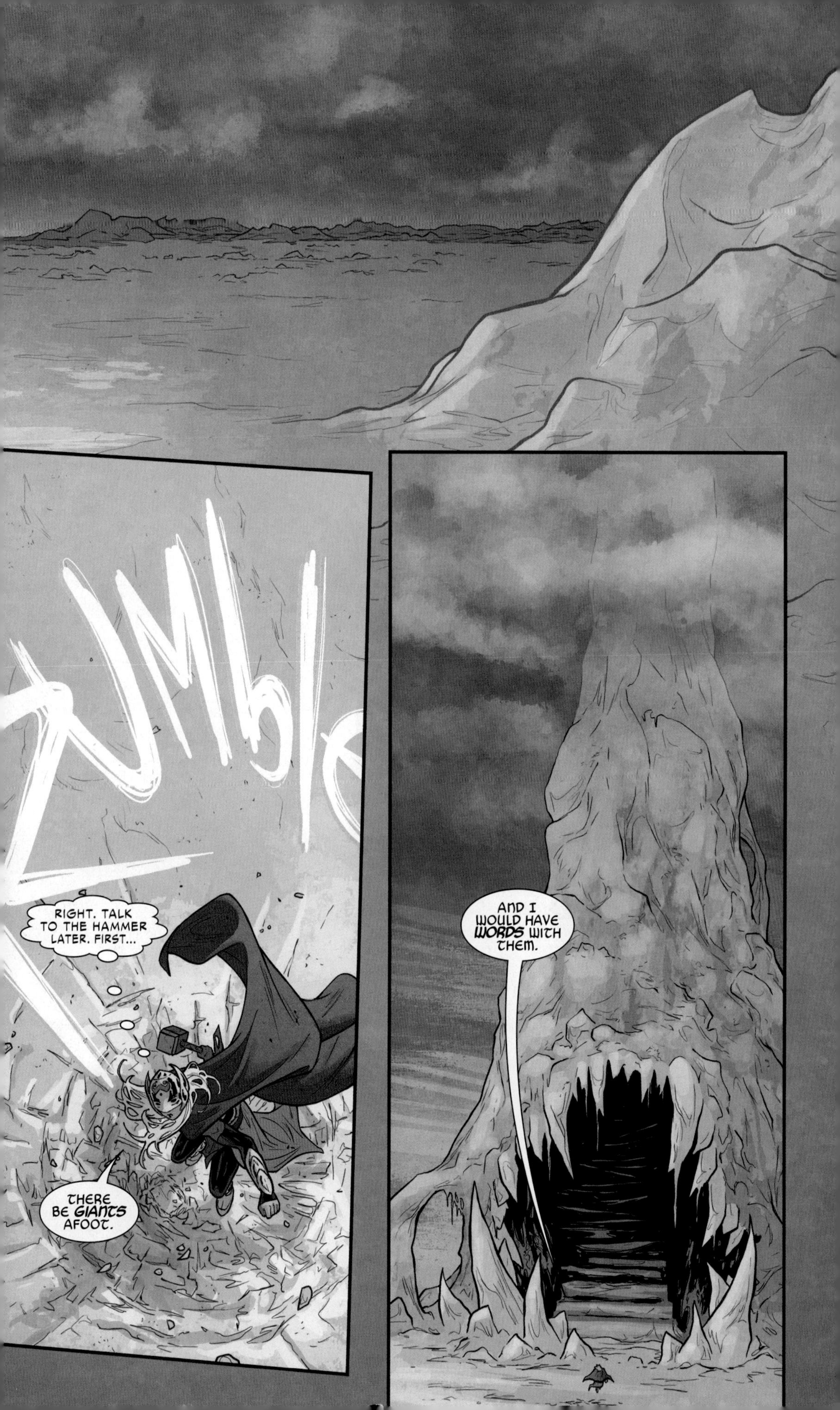
RIGHT. TALK TO THE HAMMER LATER. FIRST...
THERE BE GIANTS AFOOT.
AND I WOULD HAVE WORDS WITH THEM.

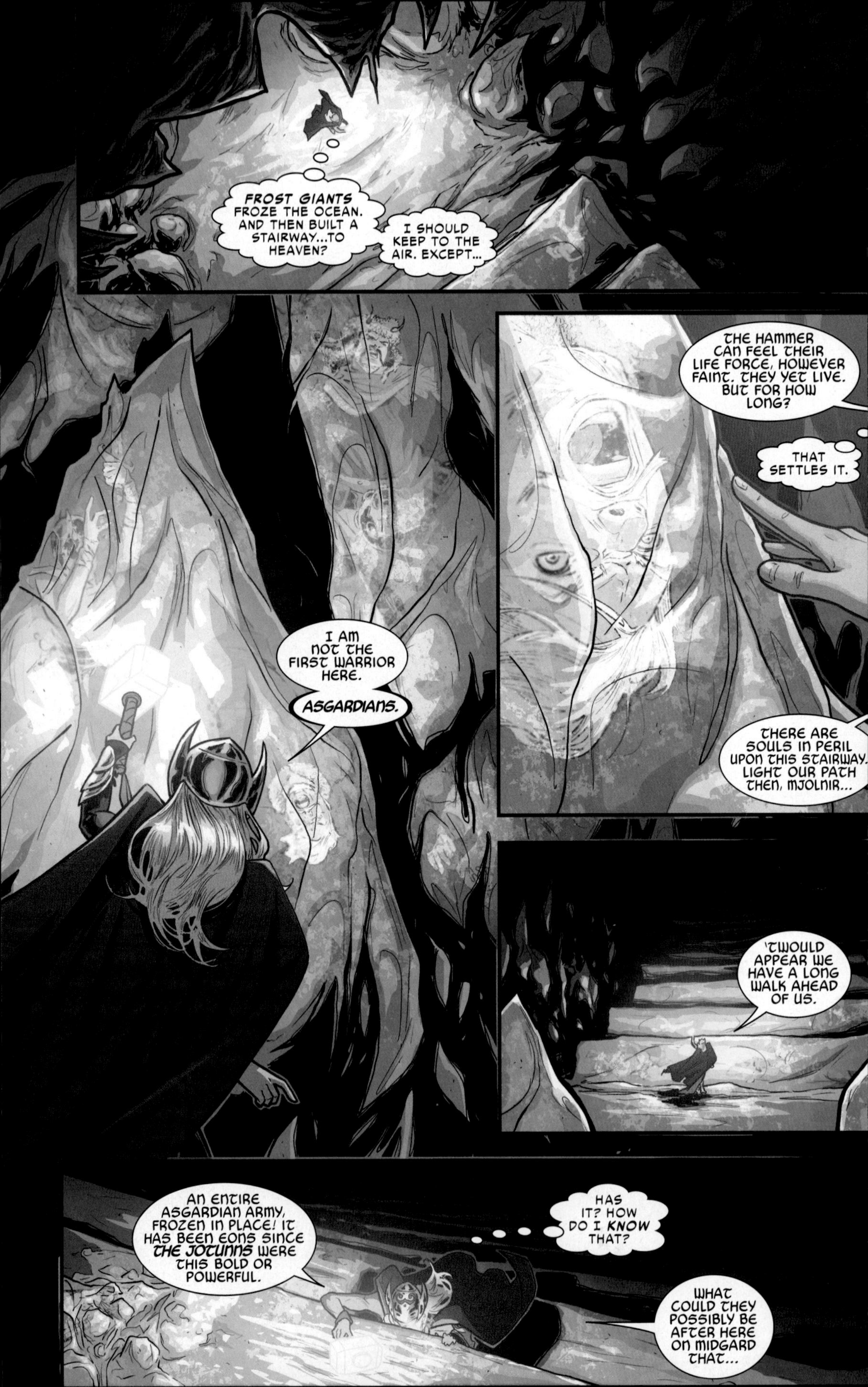
FROST GIANTS FROZE THE OCEAN. AND THEN BUILT A STAIRWAY...TO HEAVEN?
I SHOULD KEEP TO THE AIR. EXCEPT...
I AM NOT THE FIRST WARRIOR HERE.
ASGARDIANS.
THE HAMMER CAN FEEL THEIR LIFE FORCE, HOWEVER FAINT. THEY YET LIVE. BUT FOR HOW LONG?
THAT SETTLES IT.
THERE ARE SOULS IN PERIL UPON THIS STAIRWAY. LIGHT OUR PATH THEN, MJOLNIR...
'TWOULD APPEAR WE HAVE A LONG WALK AHEAD OF US.
AN ENTIRE ASGARDIAN ARMY, FROZEN IN PLACE! IT HAS BEEN EONS SINCE THE JOTUNNS WERE THIS BOLD OR POWERFUL.
HAS IT? HOW DO I KNOW THAT?
WHAT COULD THEY POSSIBLY BE AFTER HERE ON MIDGARD THAT...

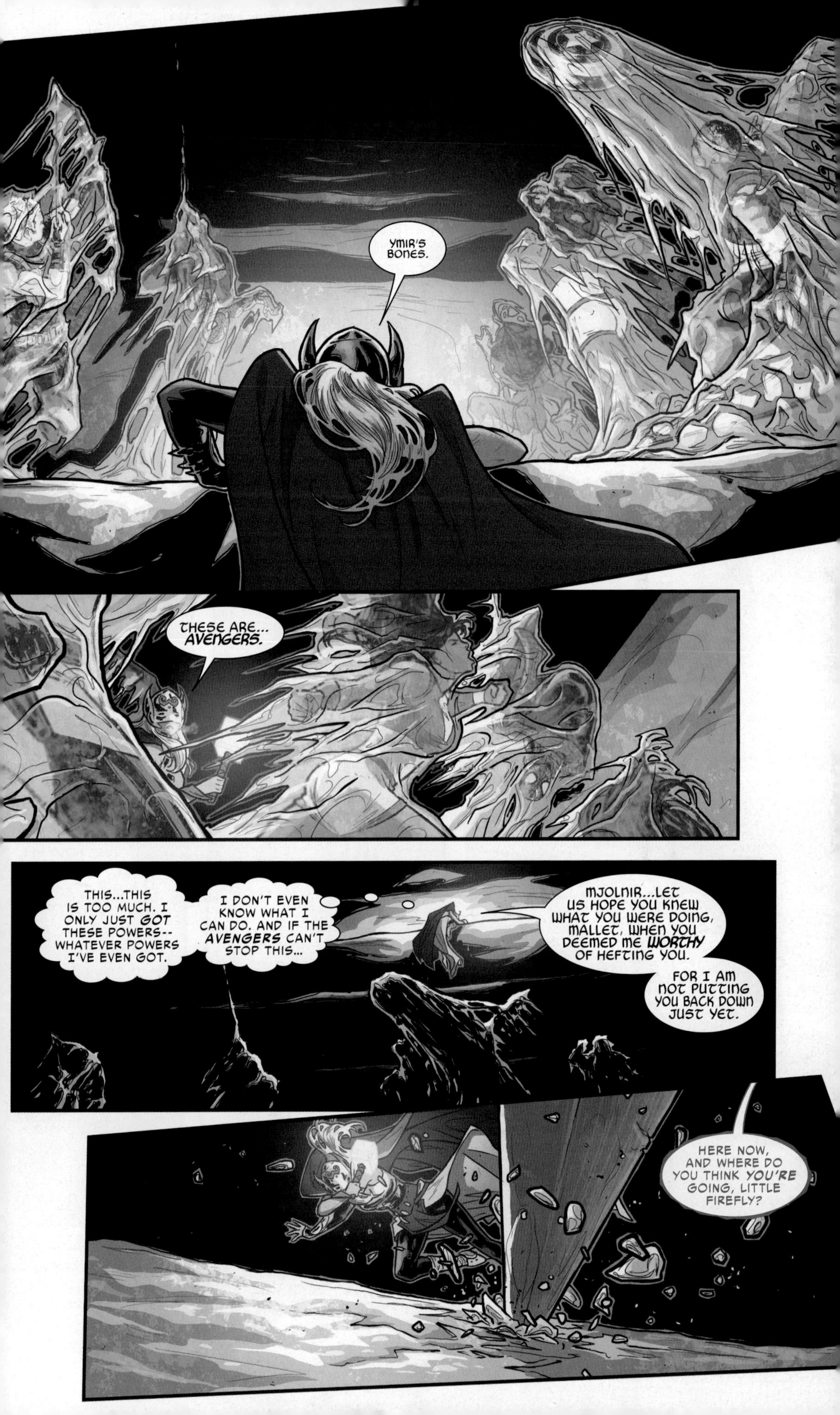
YMIR'S BONES.
THESE ARE... AVENGERS.
THIS...THIS IS TOO MUCH. I ONLY JUST GOT THESE POWERS-- WHATEVER POWERS I'VE EVEN GOT.
I DON'T EVEN KNOW WHAT I CAN DO. AND IF THE AVENGERS CAN'T STOP THIS...
MJOLNIR...LET US HOPE YOU KNEW WHAT YOU WERE DOING, MALLET, WHEN YOU DEEMED ME WORTHY OF HEFTING YOU.
FOR I AM NOT PUTTING YOU BACK DOWN JUST YET.
HERE NOW, AND WHERE DO YOU THINK YOU'RE GOING, LITTLE FIREFLY?

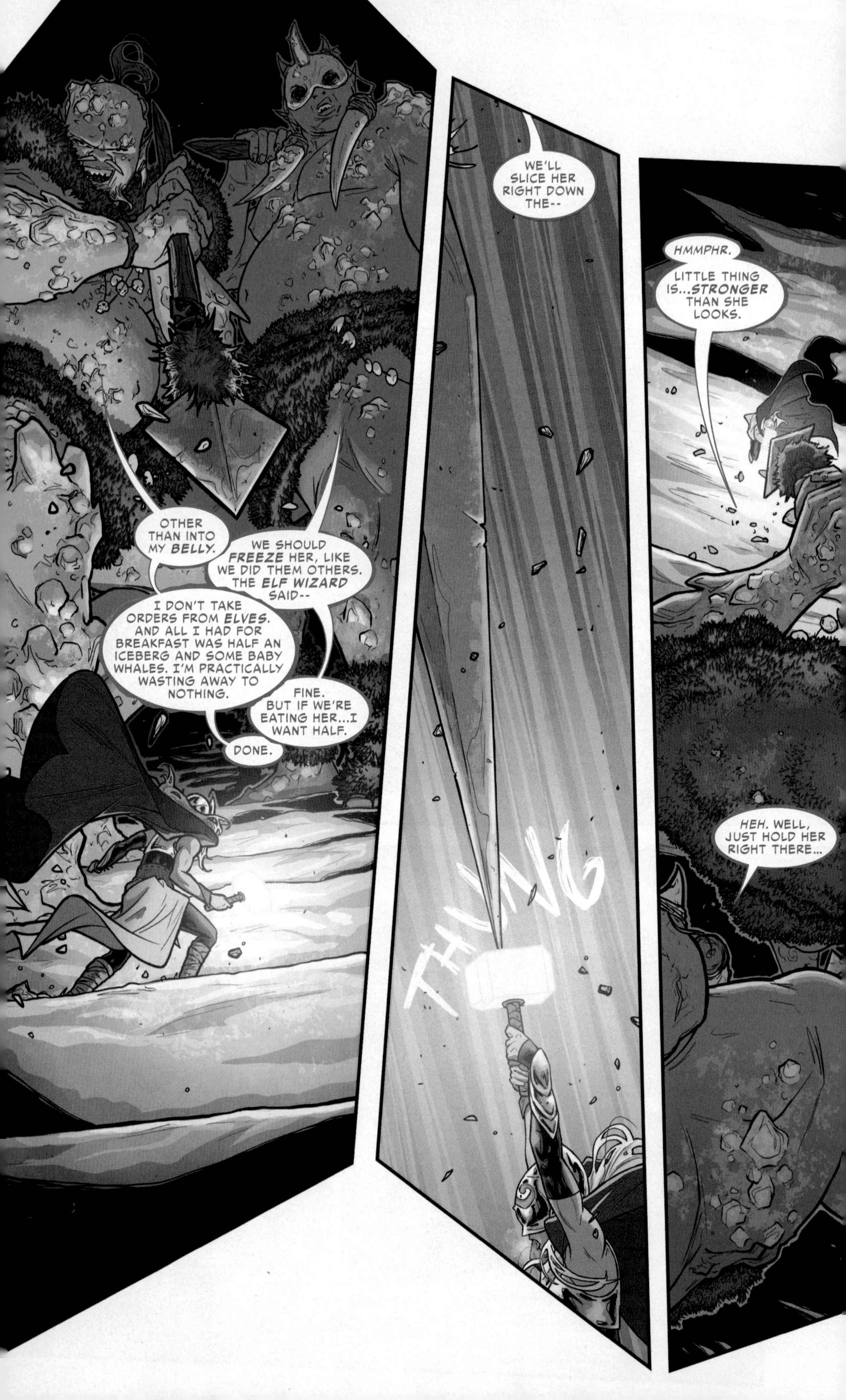

OTHER THAN INTO MY BELLY.
WE SHOULD FREEZE HER, LIKE WE DID THEM OTHERS. THE ELF WIZARD SAID--
I DON'T TAKE ORDERS FROM ELVES. AND ALL I HAD FOR BREAKFAST WAS HALF AN ICEBERG AND SOME BABY WHALES. I'M PRACTICALLY WASTING AWAY TO NOTHING.
FINE. BUT IF WE'RE EATING HER...I WANT HALF.
DONE.
WE'LL SLICE HER RIGHT DOWN THE--
THUNG
HMMPHR.
LITTLE THING IS...STRONGER THAN SHE LOOKS.
HEH. WELL, JUST HOLD HER RIGHT THERE...

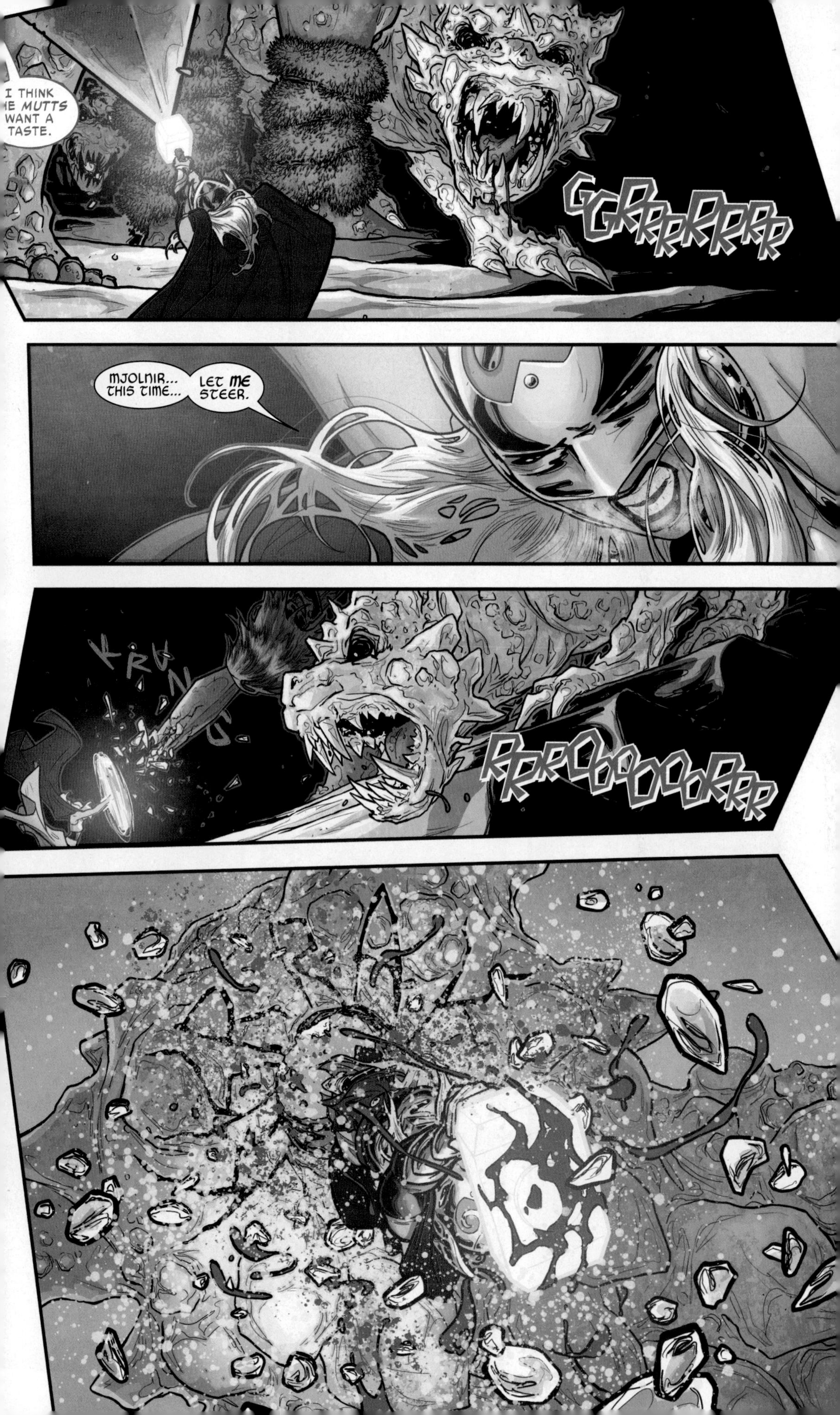

I THINK
E MUTTS
WANT A
TASTE.
GGRRRRRRRRR
MJOLNIR... THIS TIME...
LET ME STEER.
KRUNG
RRRROOOOOORRRR

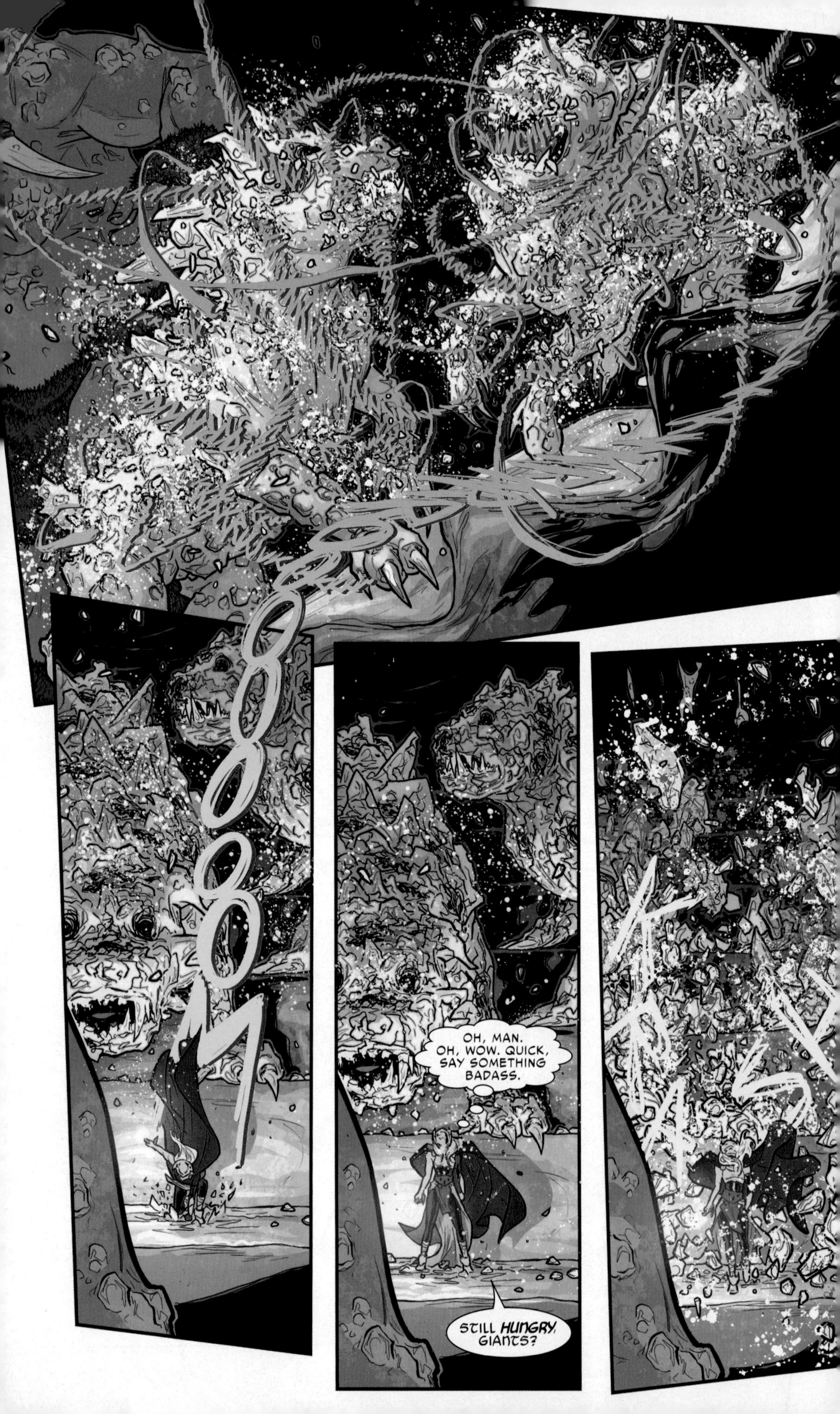
OH, MAN.
OH, WOW. QUICK, SAY SOMETHING BADASS.
STILL HUNGRY, GIANTS?

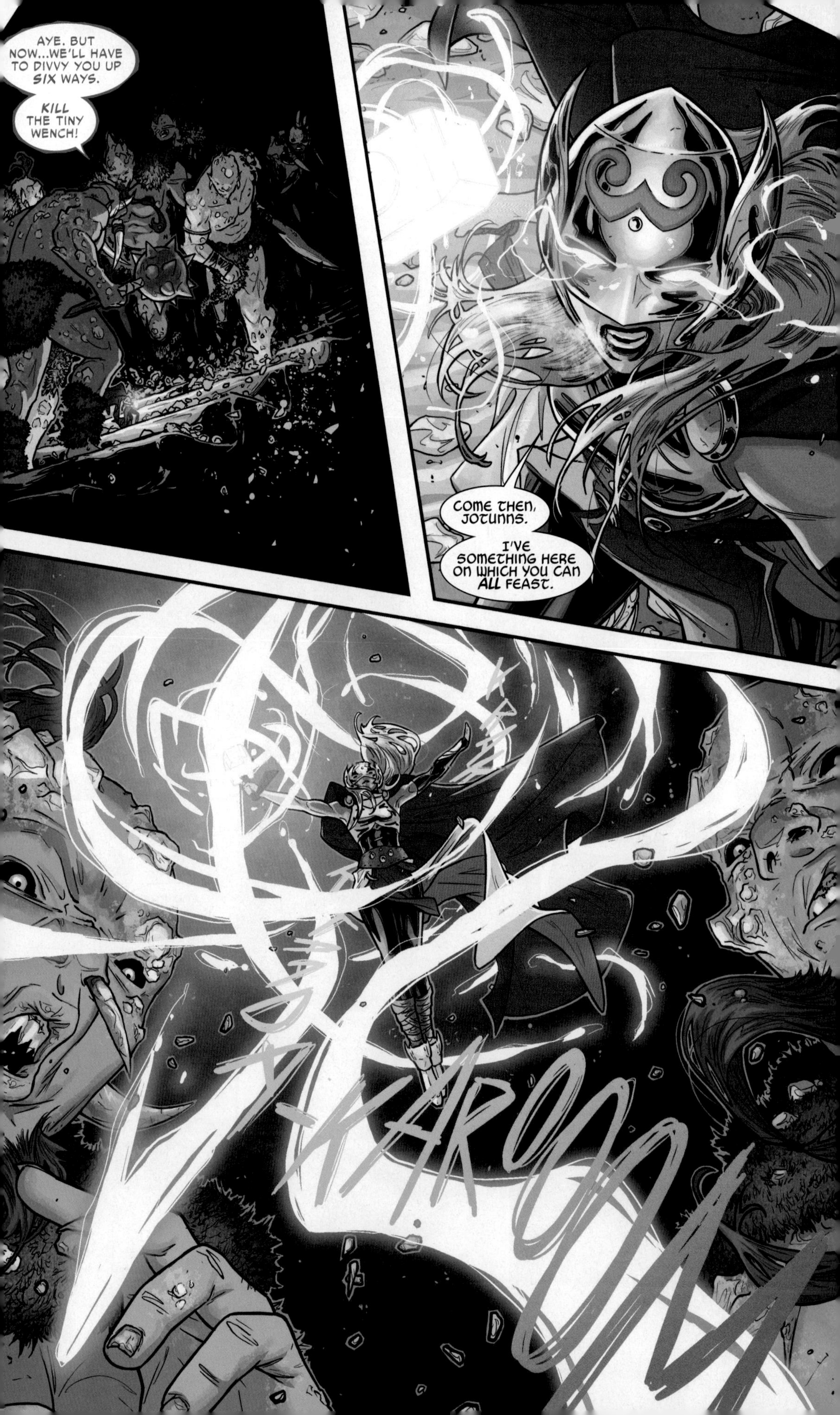
AYE. BUT NOW...WE'LL HAVE TO DIVVY YOU UP SIX WAYS.
KILL THE TINY WENCH!
COME THEN, JOTUNNS.
I'VE SOMETHING HERE ON WHICH YOU CAN ALL FEAST.

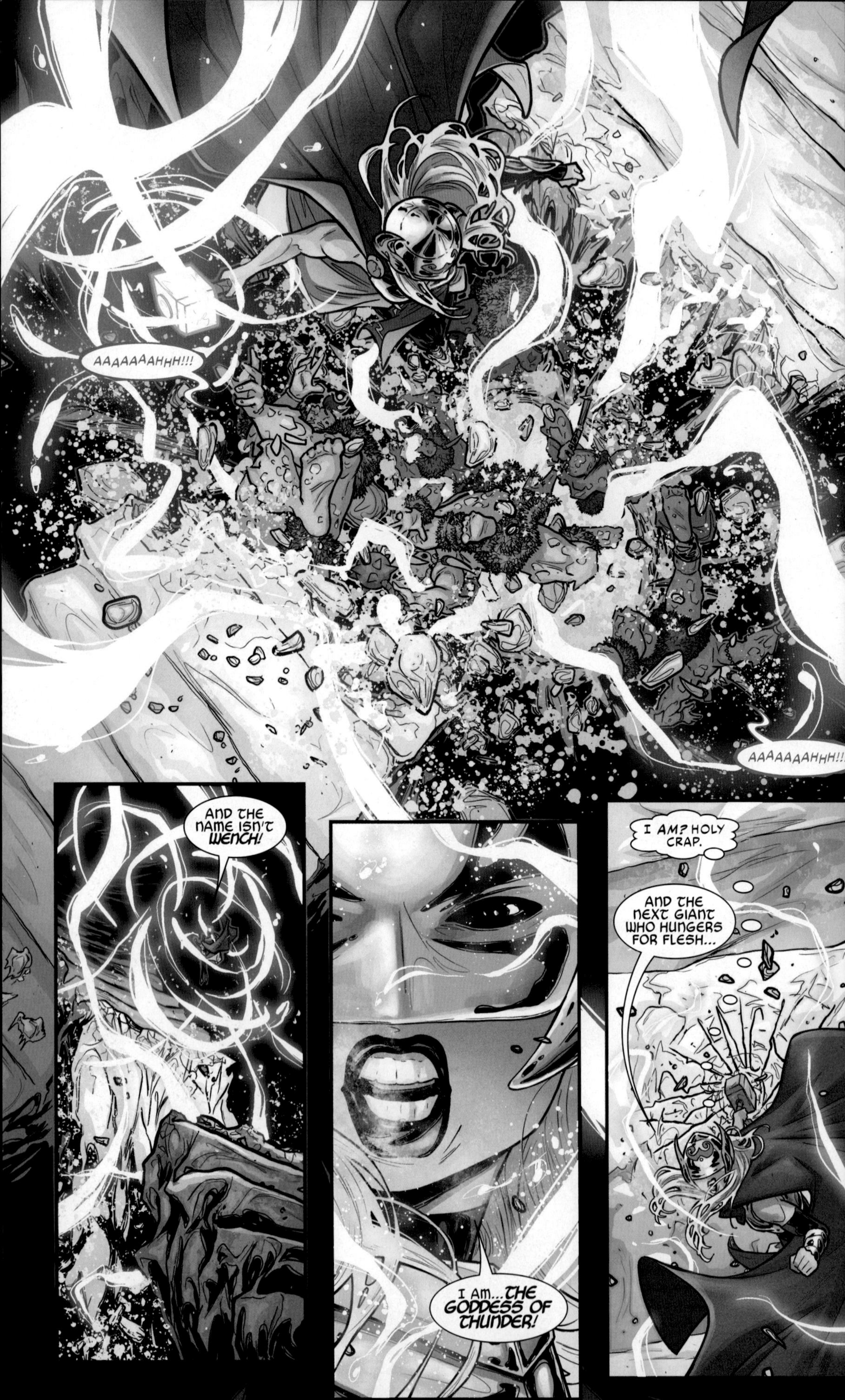
AAAAAAAHHH!!!
AAAAAAAHHH!!!
AND THE NAME ISN'T WENCH!
I AM... THE GODDESS OF THUNDER!
I AM? HOLY CRAP.
AND THE NEXT GIANT WHO HUNGERS FOR FLESH...

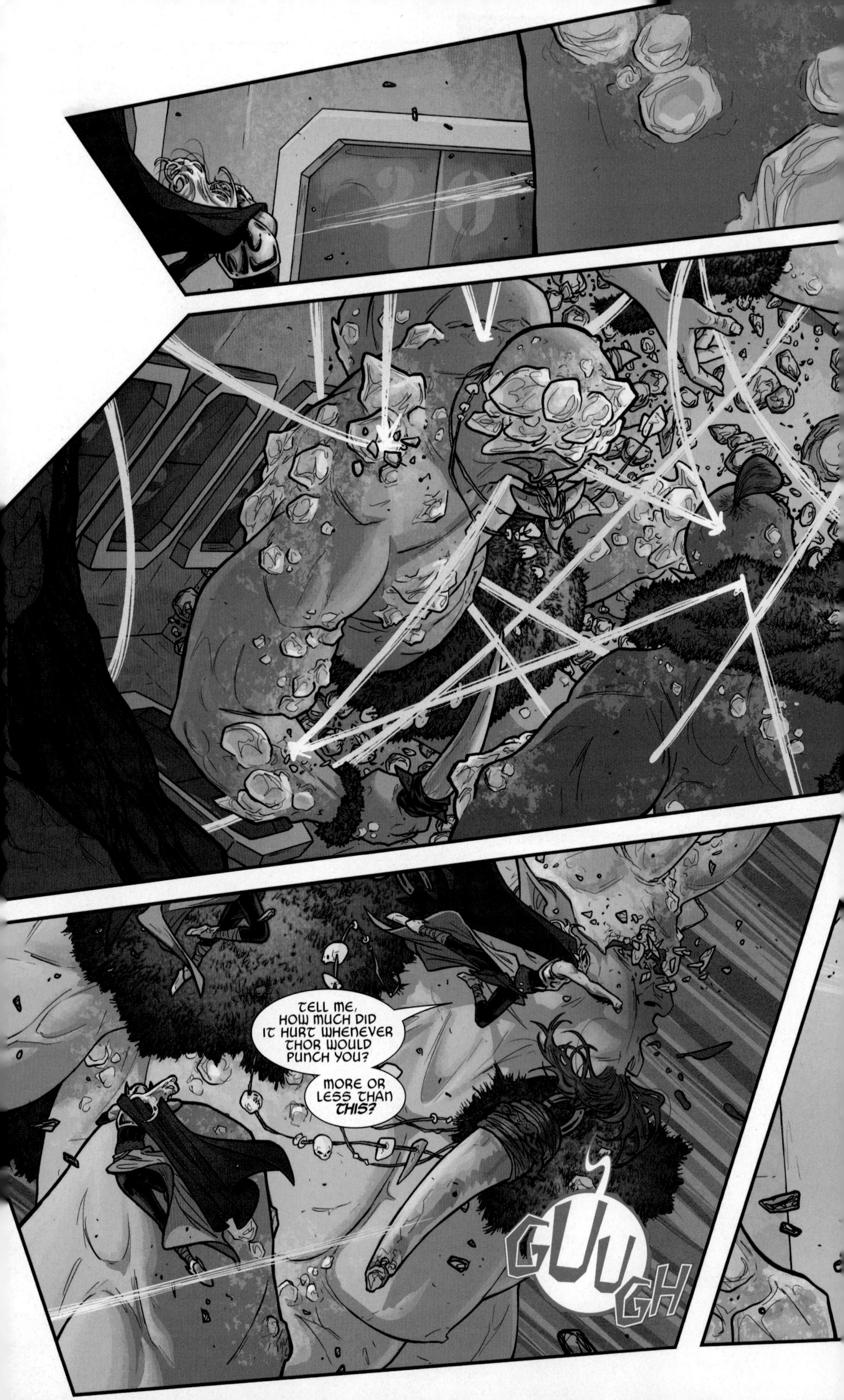
TELL ME, HOW MUCH DID IT HURT WHENEVER THOR WOULD PUNCH YOU?
MORE OR LESS THAN THIS?
GUUGH

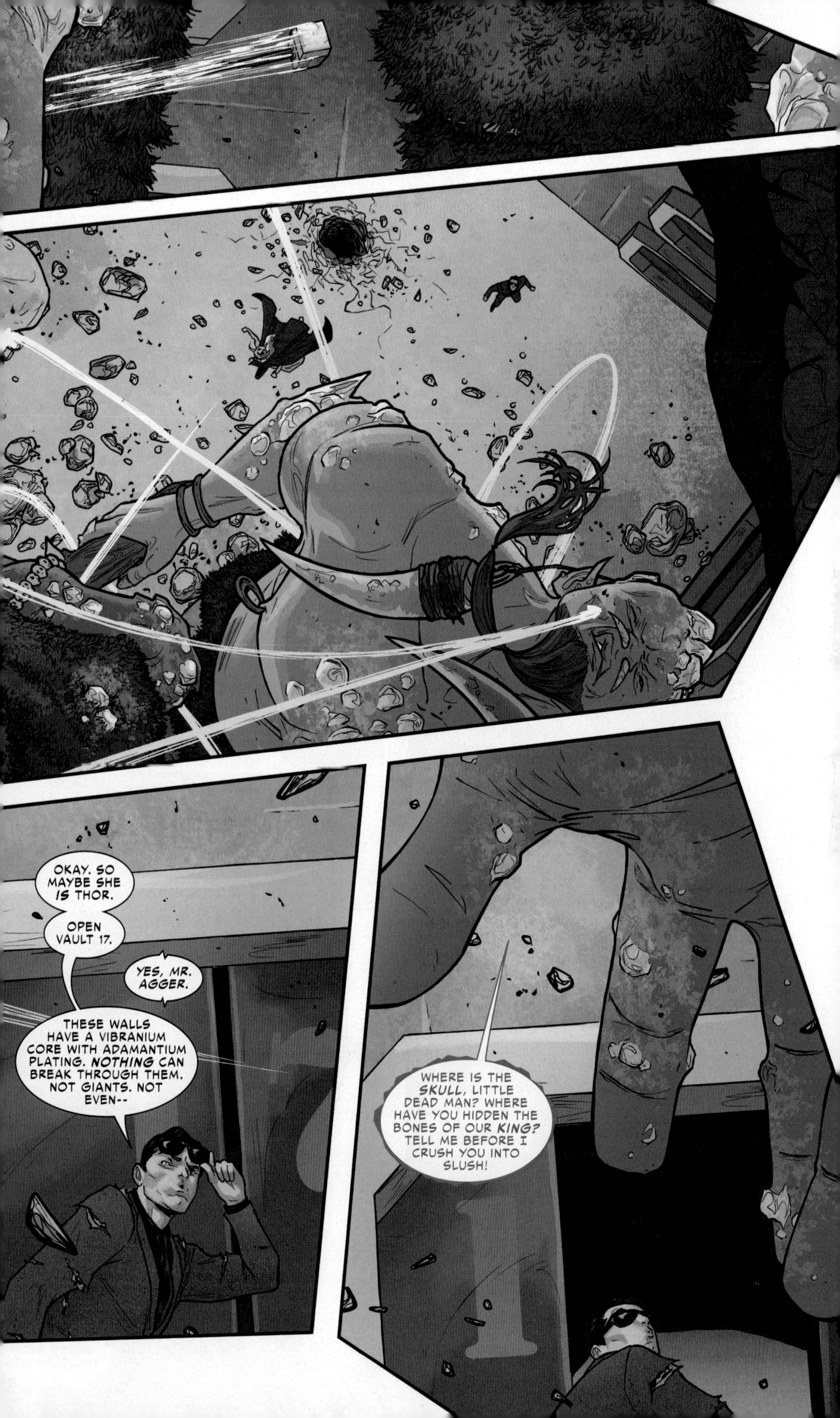

OKAY. SO MAYBE SHE *IS* THOR.
OPEN VAULT 17.
YES, MR. AGGER.
THESE WALLS HAVE A VIBRANIUM CORE WITH ADAMANTIUM PLATING. *NOTHING* CAN BREAK THROUGH THEM. NOT GIANTS. NOT EVEN--
WHERE IS THE *SKULL*, LITTLE DEAD MAN? WHERE HAVE YOU HIDDEN THE BONES OF OUR *KING?* TELL ME BEFORE I CRUSH YOU INTO SLUSH!

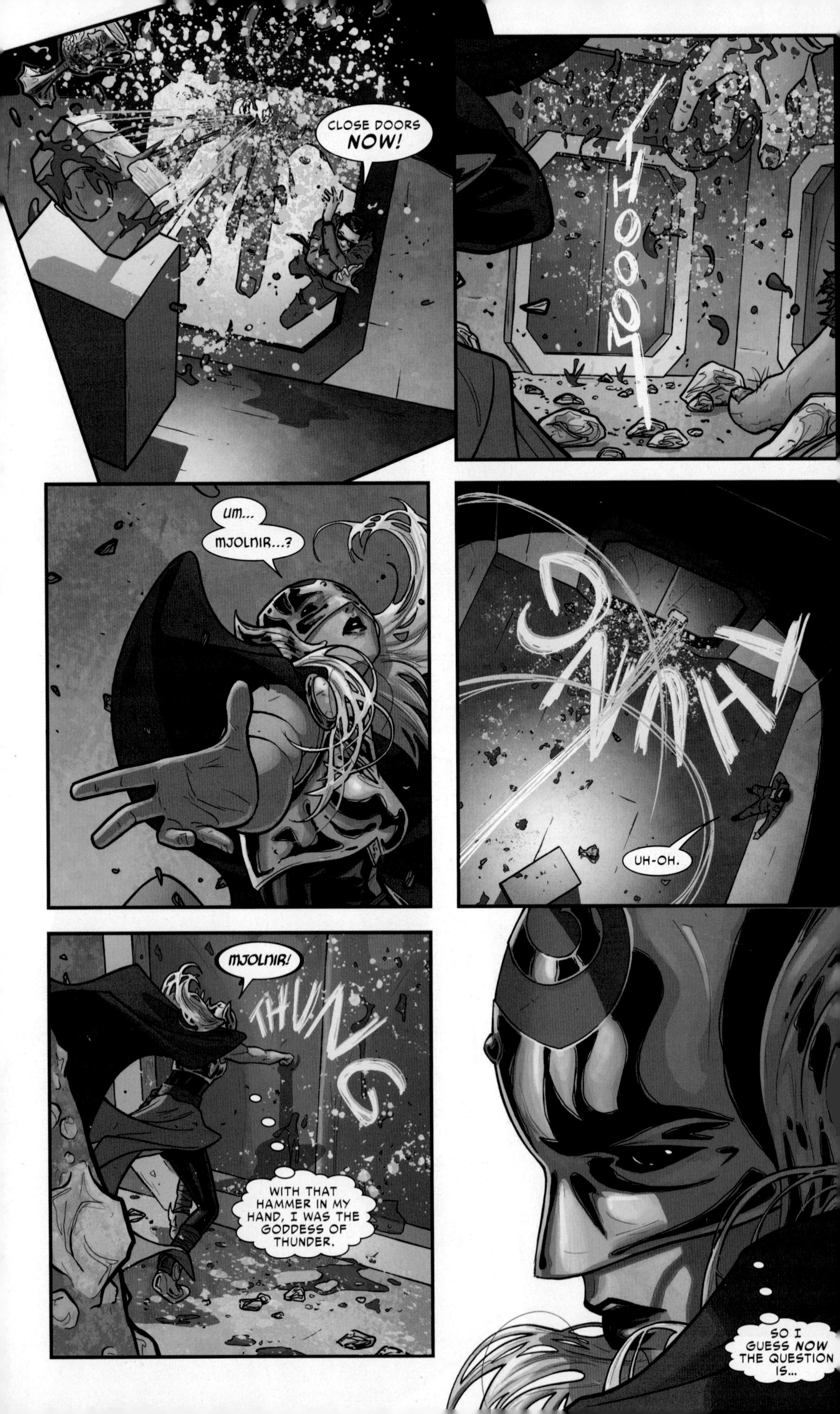
CLOSE DOORS NOW!
THOOOOOM
UM...
MJOLNIR...?
UH-OH.
MJOLNIR!
THUNG
WITH THAT HAMMER IN MY HAND, I WAS THE GODDESS OF THUNDER.
SO I GUESS NOW THE QUESTION IS...

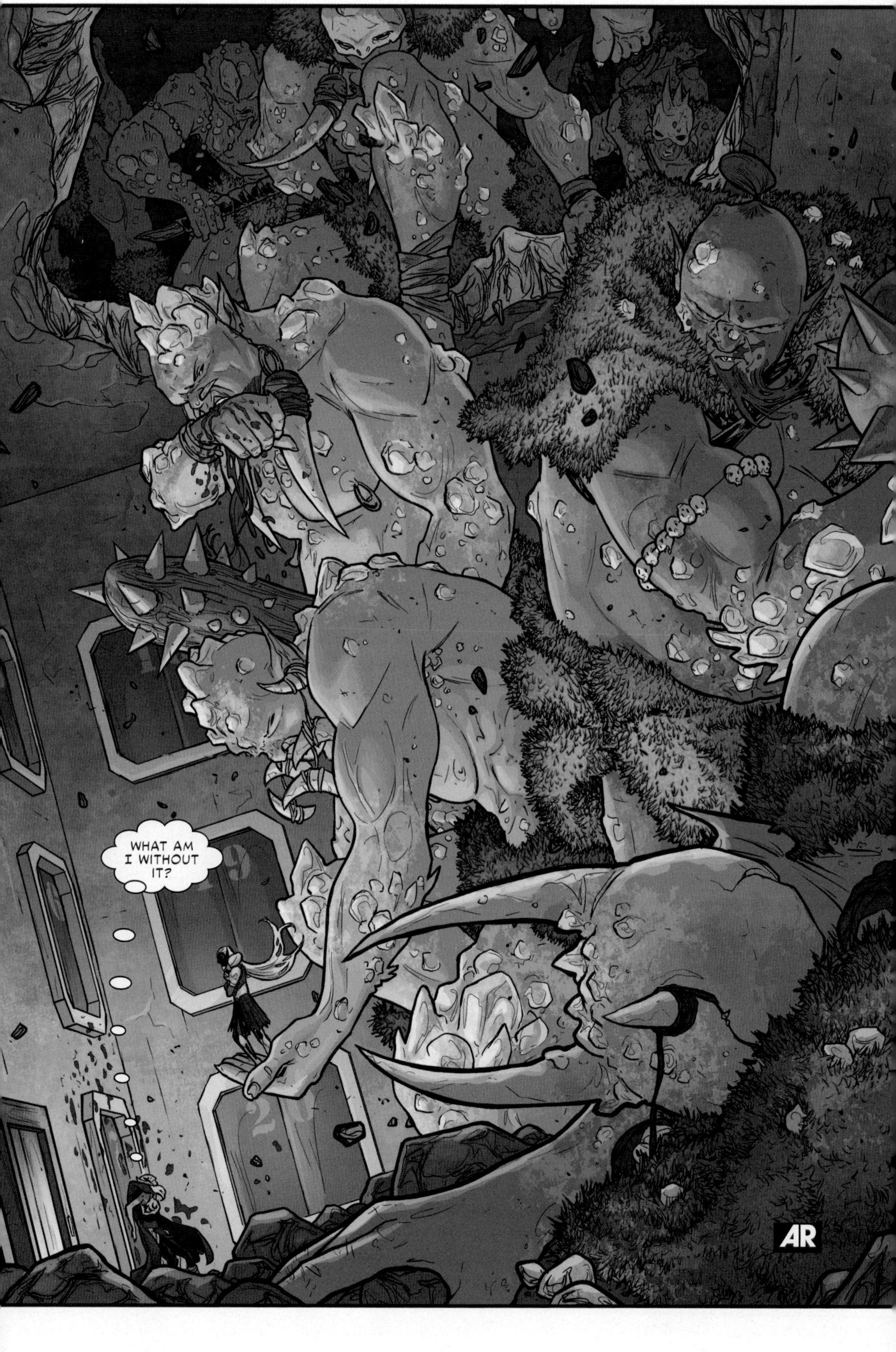

WHAT AM I WITHOUT IT?
AR

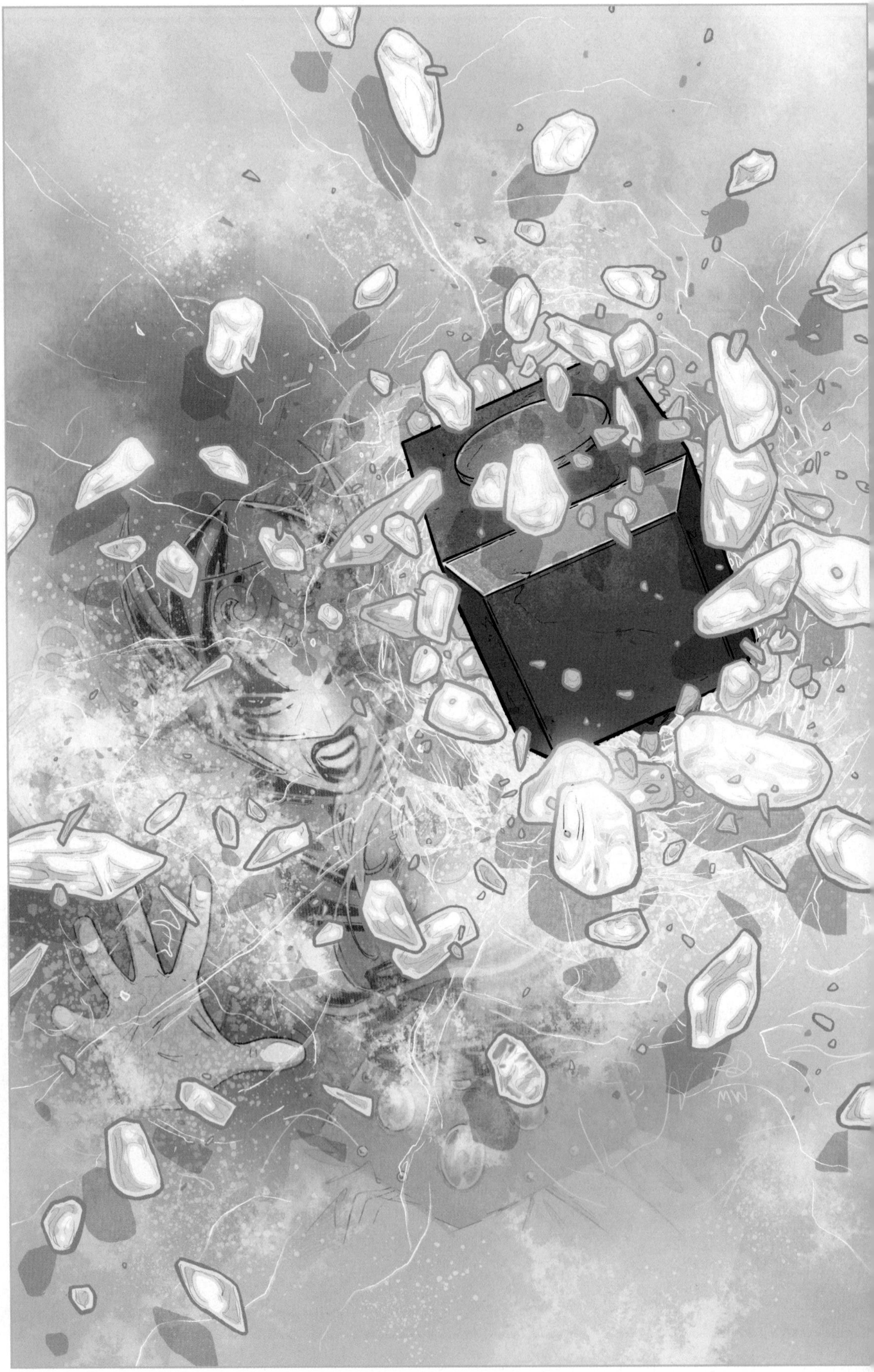

— 3 —

"TODAY IS THE *ONLY* HOLIDAY WE CELEBRATE HERE IN *JOTUNHEIM.*

"TODAY WE MARK THE COMING OF THE *MOTHER STORM.*

DAYS AGO. THE CITADEL OF UTGARD. IN THE MOUNTAINS OF JOTUNHEIM, REALM OF GIANTS.

"IT ROARS DOWN OUT OF THE VOID, JUST AS IT HAS FOR UNTOLD EONS. A BLIZZARD THE SIZE OF A GALAXY, WITH WINDS THAT SNUFF OUT STARS LIKE FLICKERING CANDLES.

"AND ONCE THE MOTHER STORM IS AT ITS FIERCEST...ONCE THAT HOWLING, MURDEROUS HURRICANE OF ICE AND COLD HAS ENVELOPED THIS ENTIRE REALM IN ITS *HOLY FURY...*

"INTO THAT FURY... WE HURL OUR *CHILDREN.*"

THOSE WHO SURVIVE THE STORM TO FIND THEIR WAY HOME ARE GREETED AS WARRIORS AND AWARDED THEIR FIRST WARCICLE.

THOSE WHO DON'T...ARE NEVER SPOKEN OF AGAIN.

SUCH IS THE WAY IT HAS *ALWAYS* BEEN, EVER SINCE THE FIRST OF THE JOTNAR ROSE OUT OF THE RIME. SUCH IS THE WAY OF THE *FROST GIANTS.*

BUT THAT WAY, I NOW FEAR...

...IS *DOOMED.*

SKRYMIR. **GUARDIAN OF UTGARD.**

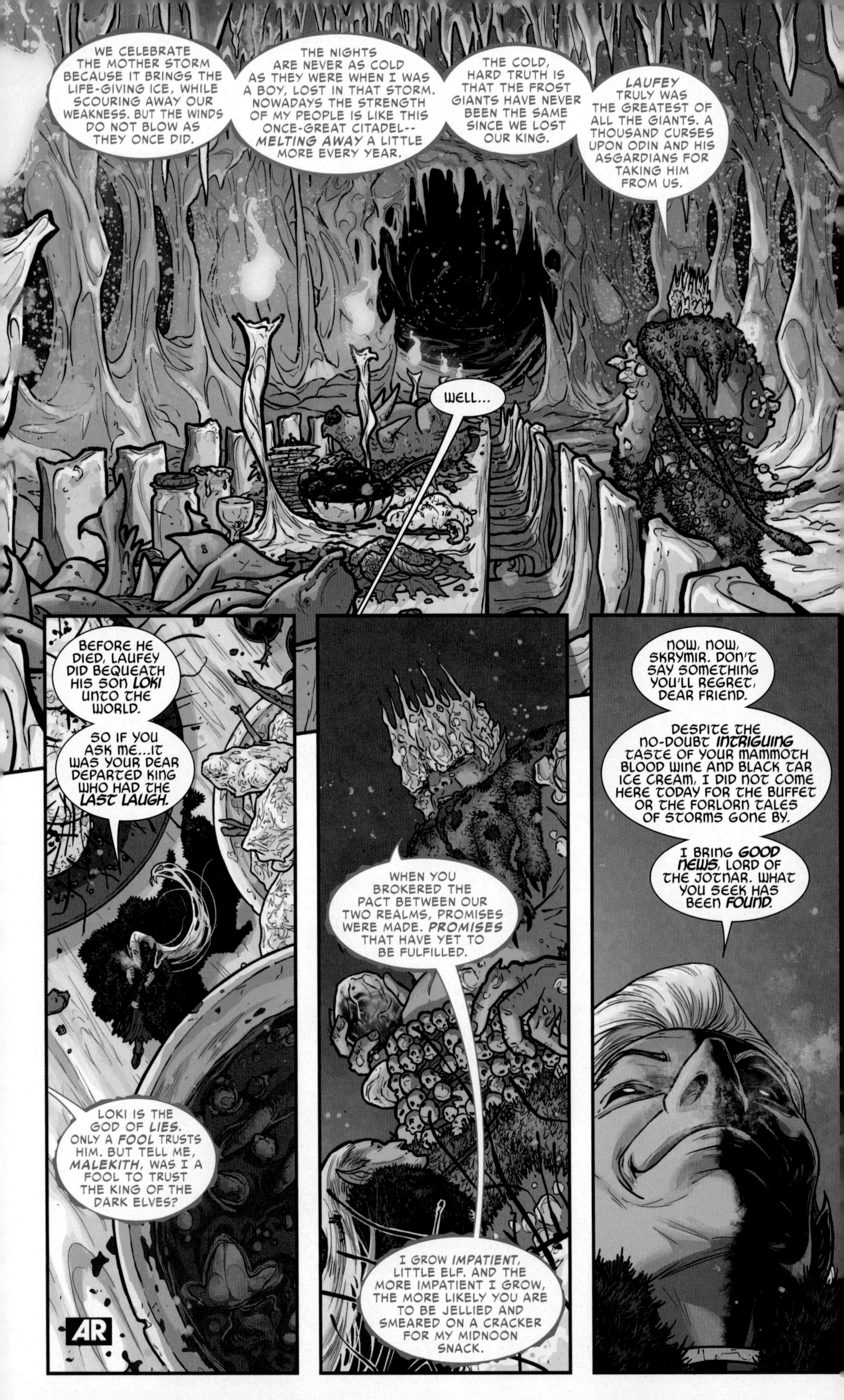
WE CELEBRATE THE MOTHER STORM BECAUSE IT BRINGS THE LIFE-GIVING ICE, WHILE SCOURING AWAY OUR WEAKNESS. BUT THE WINDS DO NOT BLOW AS THEY ONCE DID.
THE NIGHTS ARE NEVER AS COLD AS THEY WERE WHEN I WAS A BOY, LOST IN THAT STORM. NOWADAYS THE STRENGTH OF MY PEOPLE IS LIKE THIS ONCE-GREAT CITADEL-- *MELTING AWAY* A LITTLE MORE EVERY YEAR.
THE COLD, HARD TRUTH IS THAT THE FROST GIANTS HAVE NEVER BEEN THE SAME SINCE WE LOST OUR KING.
LAUFEY TRULY WAS THE GREATEST OF ALL THE GIANTS. A THOUSAND CURSES UPON ODIN AND HIS ASGARDIANS FOR TAKING HIM FROM US.
WELL...
BEFORE HE DIED, LAUFEY DID BEQUEATH HIS SON *LOKI* UNTO THE WORLD.
SO IF YOU ASK ME...IT WAS YOUR DEAR DEPARTED KING WHO HAD THE *LAST LAUGH.*
LOKI IS THE GOD OF *LIES*. ONLY A *FOOL* TRUSTS HIM. BUT TELL ME, *MALEKITH*, WAS I A FOOL TO TRUST THE KING OF THE DARK ELVES?
WHEN YOU BROKERED THE PACT BETWEEN OUR TWO REALMS, PROMISES WERE MADE. *PROMISES* THAT HAVE YET TO BE FULFILLED.
I GROW *IMPATIENT*, LITTLE ELF. AND THE MORE IMPATIENT I GROW, THE MORE LIKELY YOU ARE TO BE JELLIED AND SMEARED ON A CRACKER FOR MY MIDNOON SNACK.
NOW, NOW, SKRYMIR. DON'T SAY SOMETHING YOU'LL REGRET, DEAR FRIEND.
DESPITE THE NO-DOUBT *INTRIGUING* TASTE OF YOUR MAMMOTH BLOOD WINE AND BLACK TAR ICE CREAM, I DID NOT COME HERE TODAY FOR THE BUFFET OR THE FORLORN TALES OF STORMS GONE BY.
I BRING *GOOD NEWS*, LORD OF THE JOTNAR. WHAT YOU SEEK HAS BEEN *FOUND*.
AR

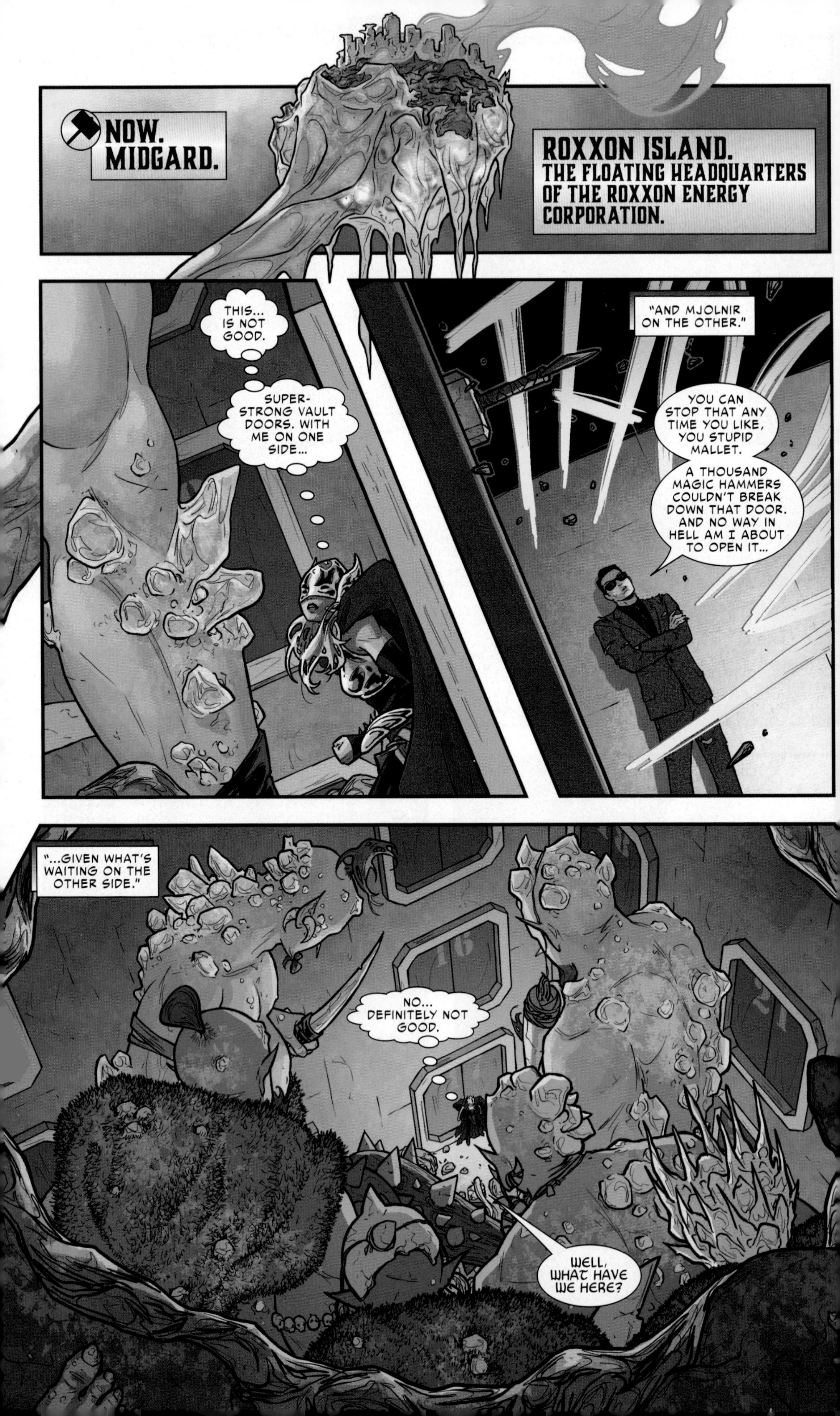
NOW. MIDGARD.
ROXXON ISLAND. THE FLOATING HEADQUARTERS OF THE ROXXON ENERGY CORPORATION.
THIS... IS NOT GOOD.
SUPER-STRONG VAULT DOORS. WITH ME ON ONE SIDE...
"AND MJOLNIR ON THE OTHER."
YOU CAN STOP THAT ANY TIME YOU LIKE, YOU STUPID MALLET.
A THOUSAND MAGIC HAMMERS COULDN'T BREAK DOWN THAT DOOR. AND NO WAY IN HELL AM I ABOUT TO OPEN IT...
"...GIVEN WHAT'S WAITING ON THE OTHER SIDE."
NO... DEFINITELY NOT GOOD.
WELL, WHAT HAVE WE HERE?

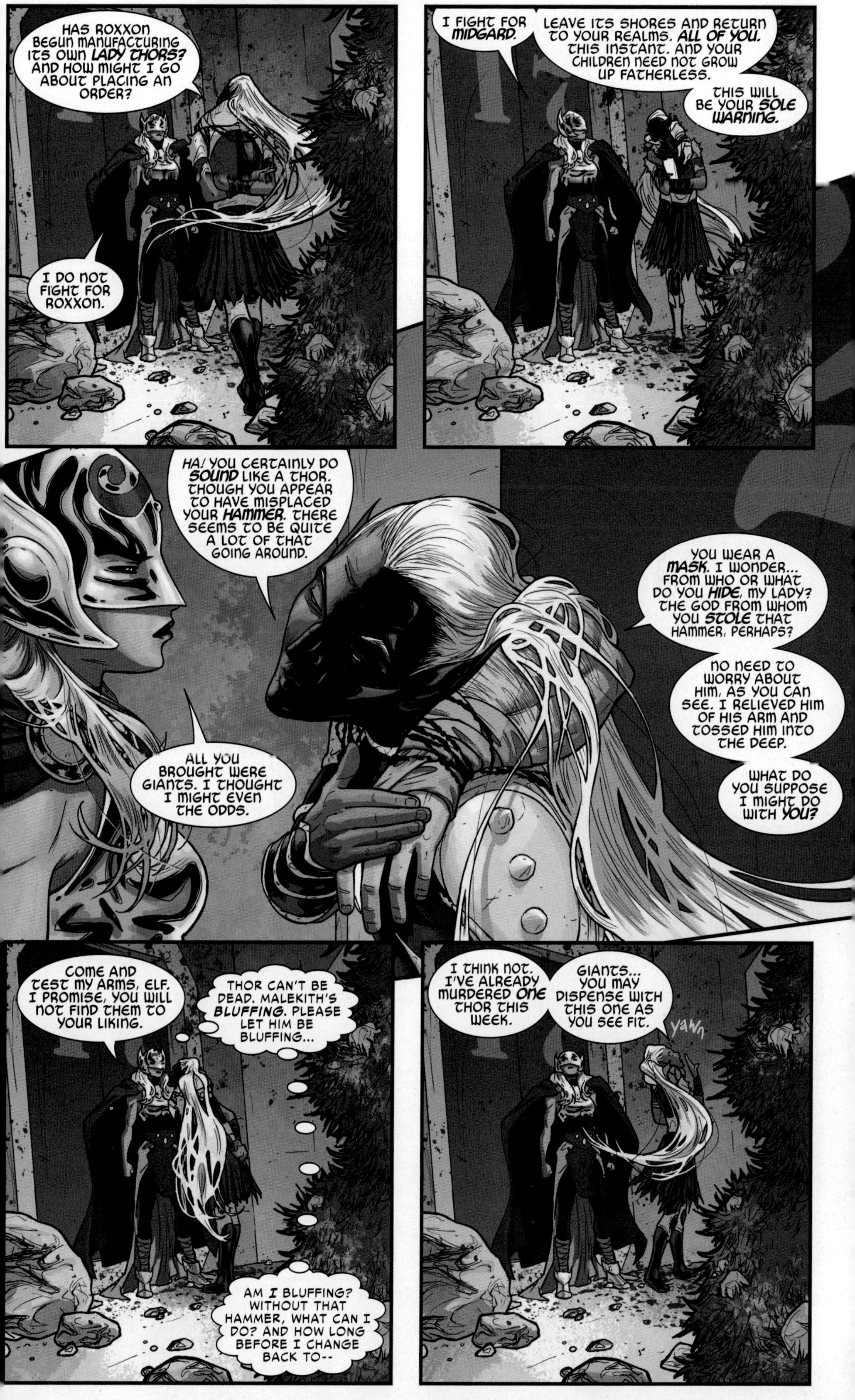
HAS ROXXON BEGUN MANUFACTURING ITS OWN LADY THORS? AND HOW MIGHT I GO ABOUT PLACING AN ORDER?
I DO NOT FIGHT FOR ROXXON.
I FIGHT FOR MIDGARD.
LEAVE ITS SHORES AND RETURN TO YOUR REALMS. ALL OF YOU. THIS INSTANT. AND YOUR CHILDREN NEED NOT GROW UP FATHERLESS.
THIS WILL BE YOUR SOLE WARNING.
HA! YOU CERTAINLY DO SOUND LIKE A THOR. THOUGH YOU APPEAR TO HAVE MISPLACED YOUR HAMMER. THERE SEEMS TO BE QUITE A LOT OF THAT GOING AROUND.
ALL YOU BROUGHT WERE GIANTS. I THOUGHT I MIGHT EVEN THE ODDS.
YOU WEAR A MASK. I WONDER... FROM WHO OR WHAT DO YOU HIDE, MY LADY? THE GOD FROM WHOM YOU STOLE THAT HAMMER, PERHAPS?
NO NEED TO WORRY ABOUT HIM, AS YOU CAN SEE. I RELIEVED HIM OF HIS ARM AND TOSSED HIM INTO THE DEEP.
WHAT DO YOU SUPPOSE I MIGHT DO WITH YOU?
COME AND TEST MY ARMS, ELF. I PROMISE, YOU WILL NOT FIND THEM TO YOUR LIKING.
THOR CAN'T BE DEAD. MALEKITH'S BLUFFING. PLEASE LET HIM BE BLUFFING...
AM I BLUFFING? WITHOUT THAT HAMMER, WHAT CAN I DO? AND HOW LONG BEFORE I CHANGE BACK TO--
I THINK NOT. I'VE ALREADY MURDERED ONE THOR THIS WEEK.
GIANTS... YOU MAY DISPENSE WITH THIS ONE AS YOU SEE FIT.
YAWN

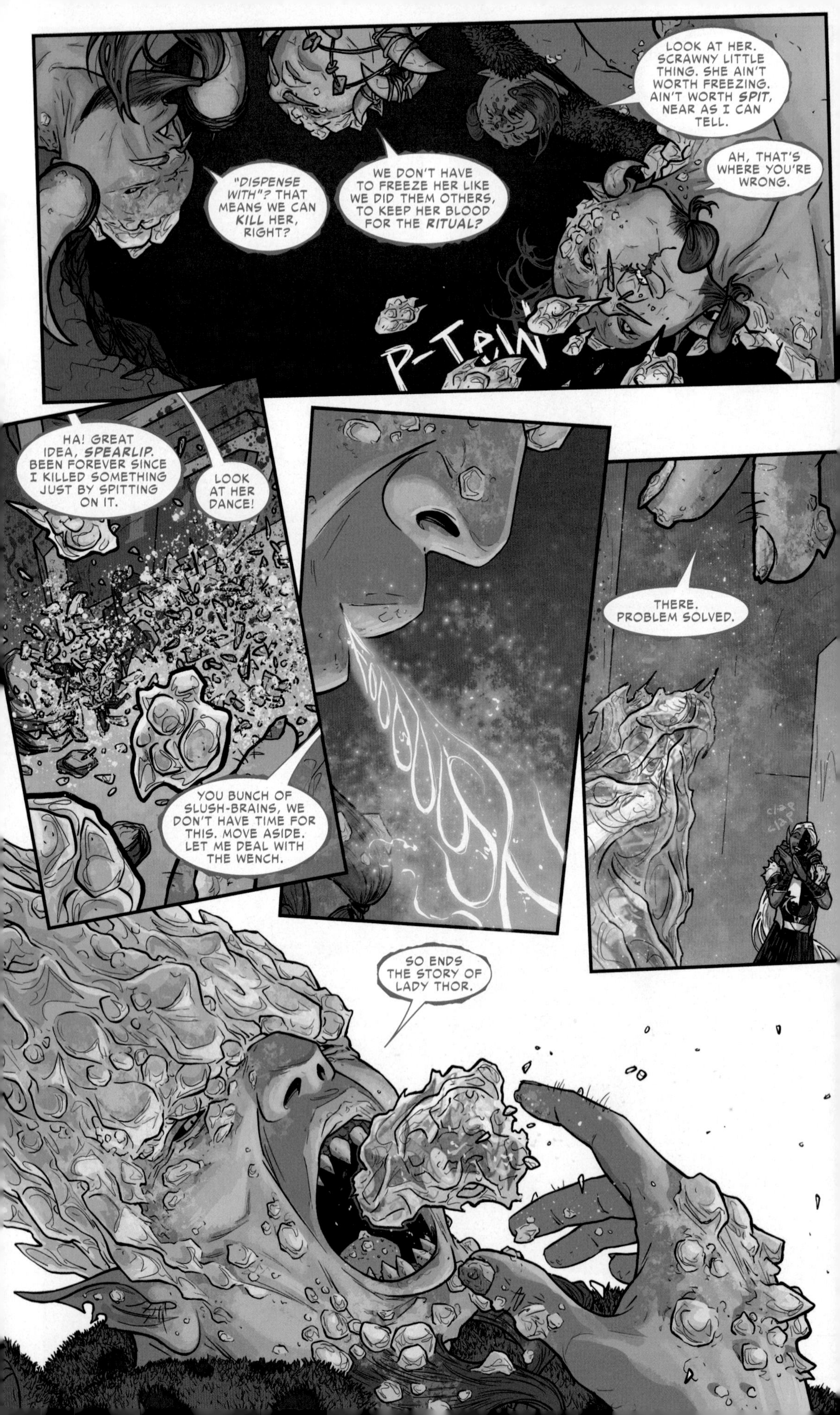

"DISPENSE WITH"? THAT MEANS WE CAN KILL HER, RIGHT?
WE DON'T HAVE TO FREEZE HER LIKE WE DID THEM OTHERS, TO KEEP HER BLOOD FOR THE RITUAL?
LOOK AT HER. SCRAWNY LITTLE THING. SHE AIN'T WORTH FREEZING. AIN'T WORTH SPIT, NEAR AS I CAN TELL.
AH, THAT'S WHERE YOU'RE WRONG.
P-TEW
HA! GREAT IDEA, SPEARLIP. BEEN FOREVER SINCE I KILLED SOMETHING JUST BY SPITTING ON IT.
LOOK AT HER DANCE!
YOU BUNCH OF SLUSH-BRAINS, WE DON'T HAVE TIME FOR THIS. MOVE ASIDE. LET ME DEAL WITH THE WENCH.
THERE. PROBLEM SOLVED.
clap clap
SO ENDS THE STORY OF LADY THOR.

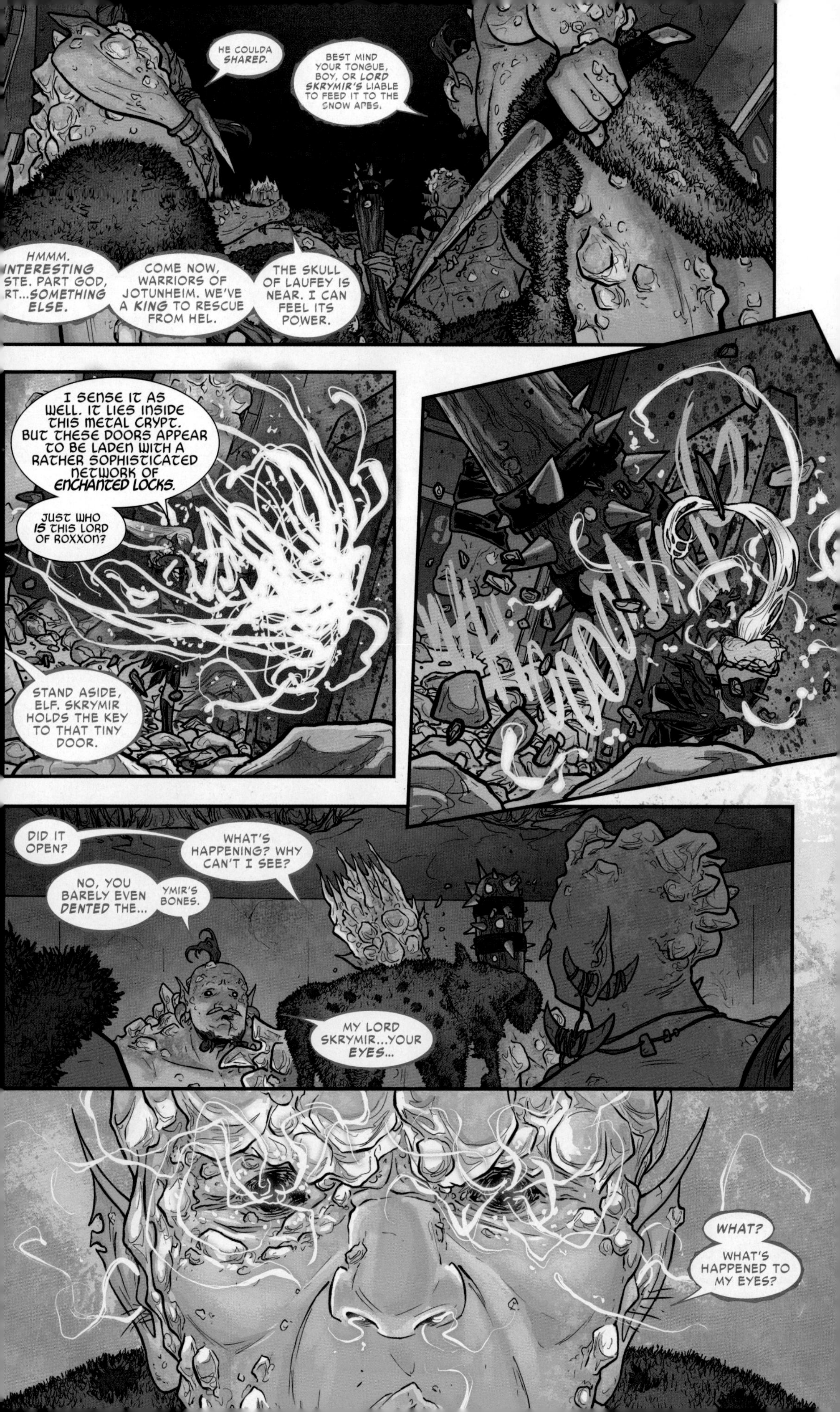

HE COULDA *SHARED.*
BEST MIND YOUR TONGUE, BOY, OR *LORD SKRYMIR'S* LIABLE TO FEED IT TO THE SNOW APES.
HMMM. *INTERESTING* STE. PART GOD, RT...*SOMETHING ELSE.*
COME NOW, WARRIORS OF JOTUNHEIM. WE'VE A *KING* TO RESCUE FROM HEL.
THE SKULL OF LAUFEY IS NEAR. I CAN FEEL ITS POWER.
I SENSE IT AS WELL. IT LIES INSIDE THIS METAL CRYPT. BUT THESE DOORS APPEAR TO BE LADEN WITH A RATHER SOPHISTICATED NETWORK OF *ENCHANTED LOCKS.*
JUST WHO *IS* THIS LORD OF ROXXON?
STAND ASIDE, ELF. SKRYMIR HOLDS THE KEY TO THAT TINY DOOR.
DID IT OPEN?
WHAT'S HAPPENING? WHY CAN'T I SEE?
NO, YOU BARELY EVEN *DENTED* THE...
YMIR'S BONES.
MY LORD SKRYMIR...YOUR *EYES*...
WHAT?
WHAT'S HAPPENED TO MY EYES?

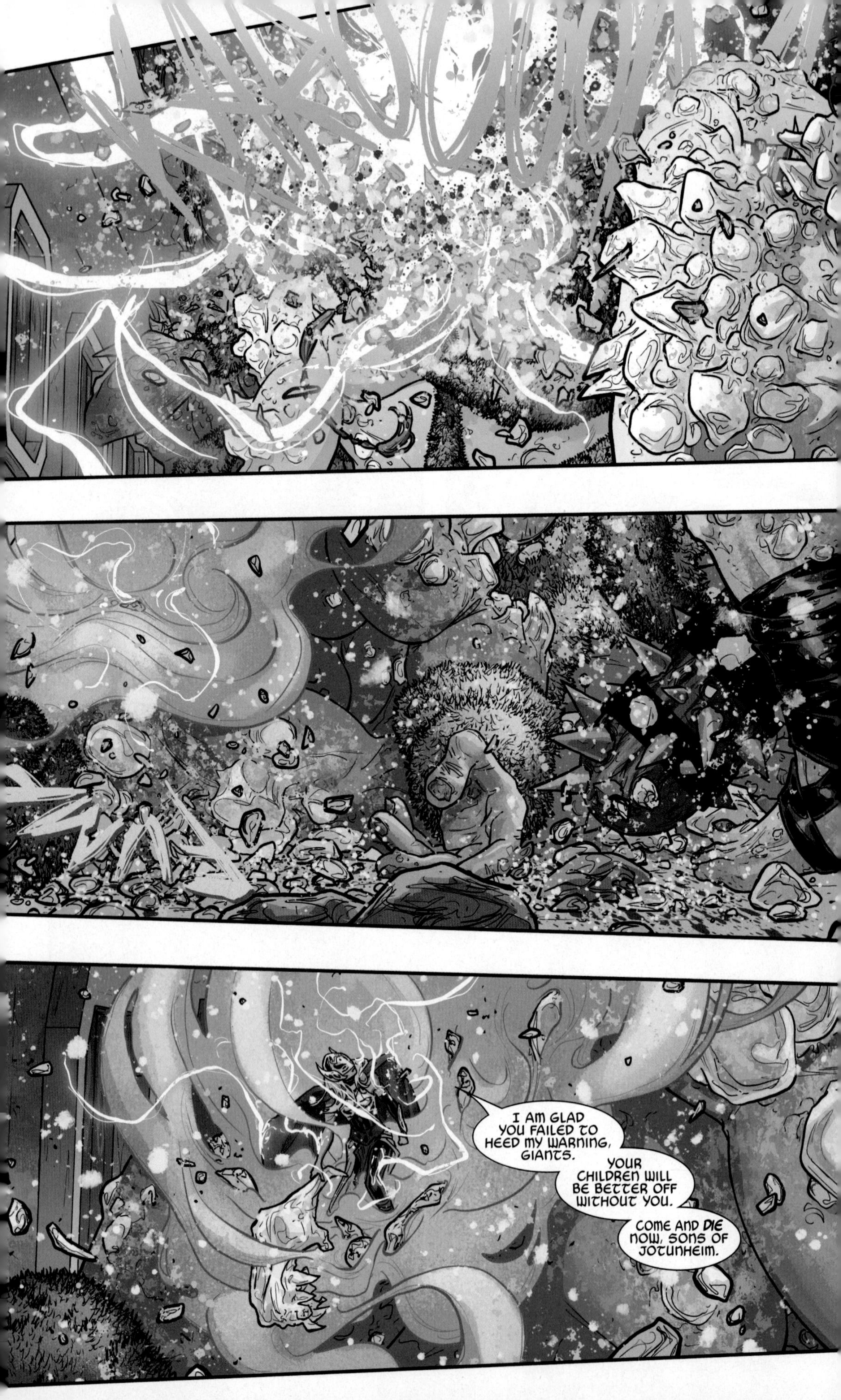
I AM GLAD YOU FAILED TO HEED MY WARNING, GIANTS.
YOUR CHILDREN WILL BE BETTER OFF WITHOUT YOU.
COME AND **DIE** NOW, SONS OF JOTUNHEIM.

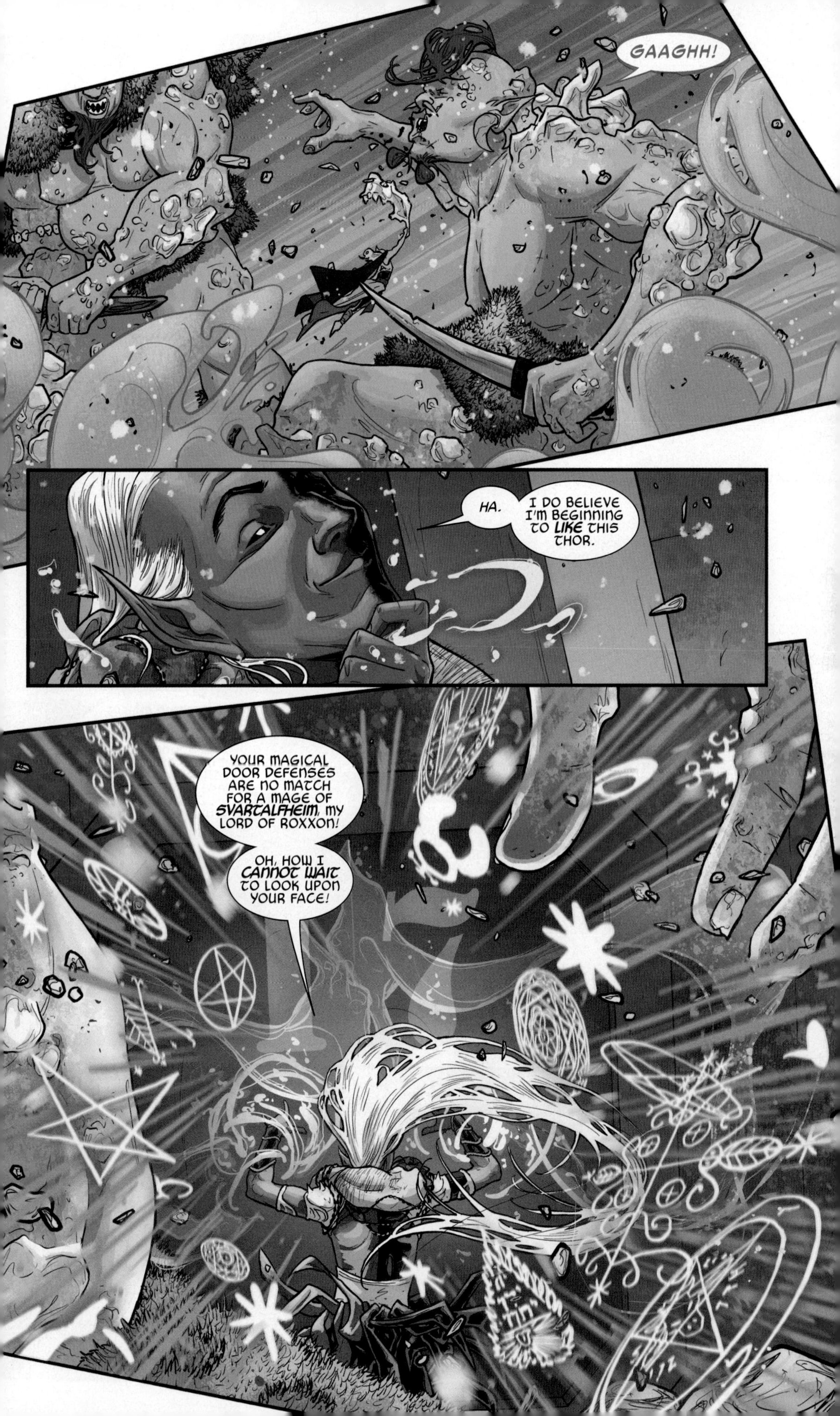
GAAGHH!
HA.
I DO BELIEVE I'M BEGINNING TO LIKE THIS THOR.
YOUR MAGICAL DOOR DEFENSES ARE NO MATCH FOR A MAGE OF SVARTALFHEIM, MY LORD OF ROXXON!
OH, HOW I CANNOT WAIT TO LOOK UPON YOUR FACE!

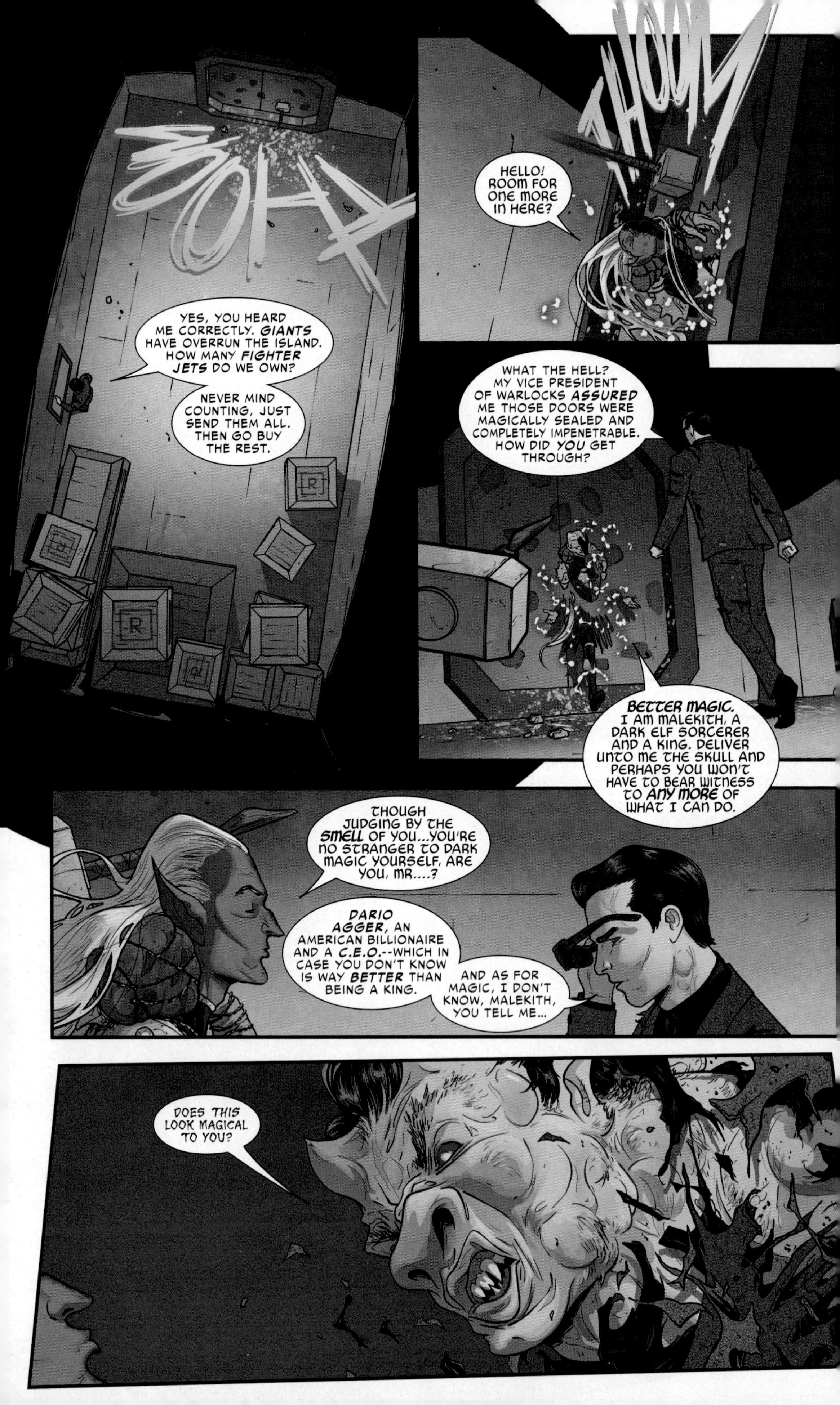
WOOM
YES, YOU HEARD ME CORRECTLY. GIANTS HAVE OVERRUN THE ISLAND. HOW MANY FIGHTER JETS DO WE OWN?
NEVER MIND COUNTING, JUST SEND THEM ALL. THEN GO BUY THE REST.
THOOM
HELLO! ROOM FOR ONE MORE IN HERE?
WHAT THE HELL? MY VICE PRESIDENT OF WARLOCKS ASSURED ME THOSE DOORS WERE MAGICALLY SEALED AND COMPLETELY IMPENETRABLE. HOW DID YOU GET THROUGH?
BETTER MAGIC. I AM MALEKITH, A DARK ELF SORCERER AND A KING. DELIVER UNTO ME THE SKULL AND PERHAPS YOU WON'T HAVE TO BEAR WITNESS TO ANY MORE OF WHAT I CAN DO.
THOUGH JUDGING BY THE SMELL OF YOU...YOU'RE NO STRANGER TO DARK MAGIC YOURSELF, ARE YOU, MR....?
DARIO AGGER, AN AMERICAN BILLIONAIRE AND A C.E.O.--WHICH IN CASE YOU DON'T KNOW IS WAY BETTER THAN BEING A KING.
AND AS FOR MAGIC, I DON'T KNOW, MALEKITH, YOU TELL ME...
DOES THIS LOOK MAGICAL TO YOU?

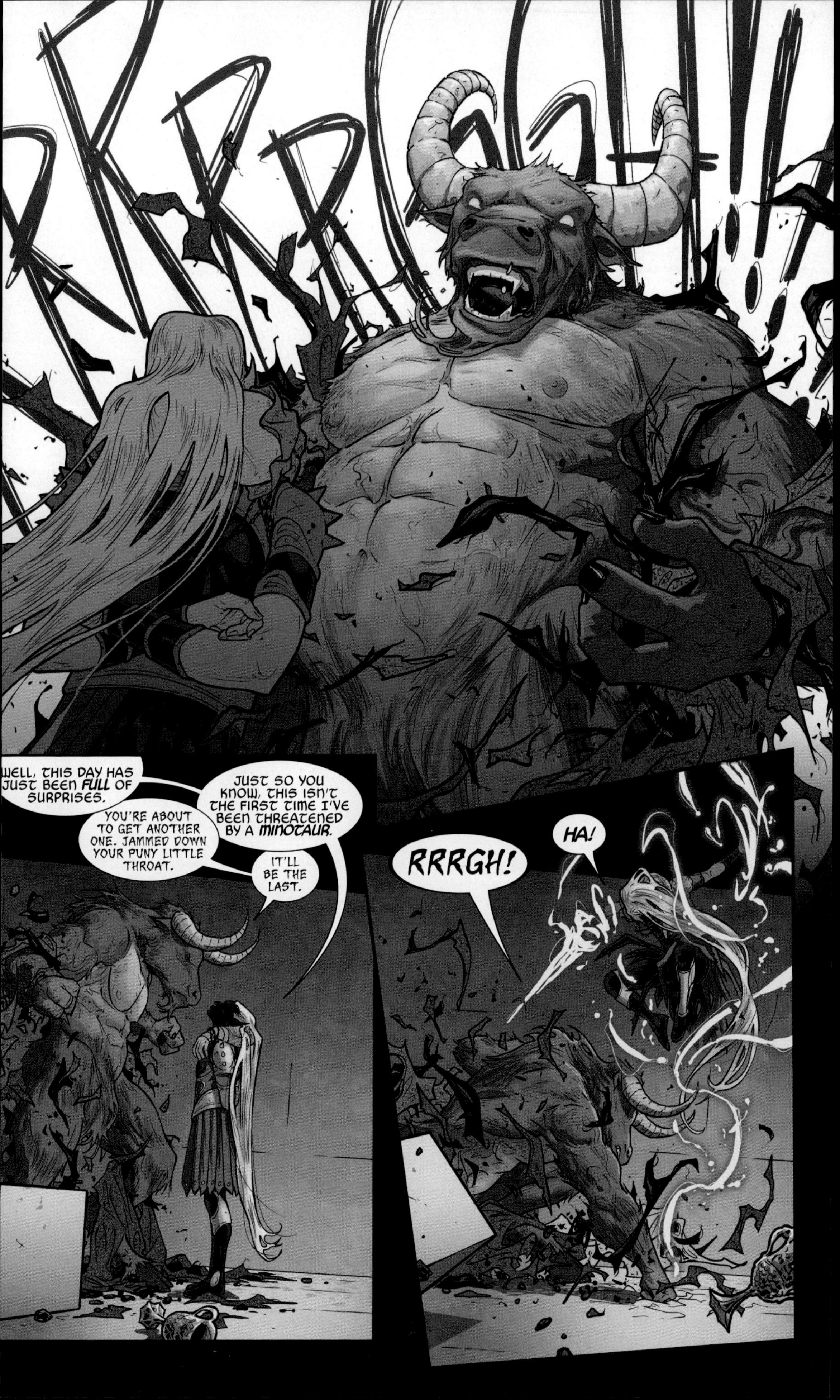

WELL, THIS DAY HAS JUST BEEN **FULL** OF SURPRISES.
JUST SO YOU KNOW, THIS ISN'T THE FIRST TIME I'VE BEEN THREATENED BY A **MINOTAUR**.
YOU'RE ABOUT TO GET ANOTHER ONE. JAMMED DOWN YOUR PUNY LITTLE THROAT.
IT'LL BE THE LAST.
RRRGH!
HA!

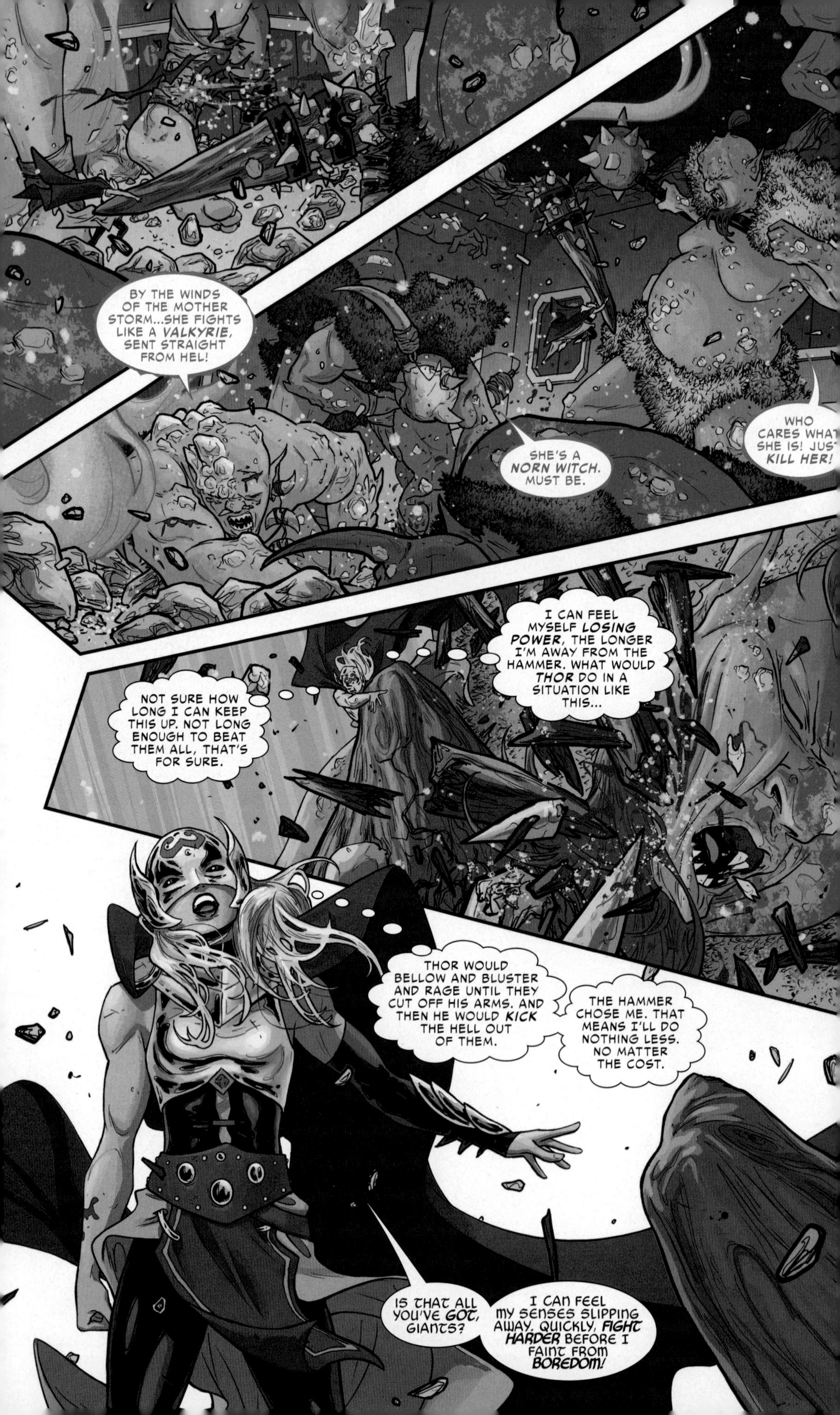
BY THE WINDS OF THE MOTHER STORM...SHE FIGHTS LIKE A VALKYRIE, SENT STRAIGHT FROM HEL!
SHE'S A NORN WITCH. MUST BE.
WHO CARES WHAT SHE IS! JUST KILL HER!
NOT SURE HOW LONG I CAN KEEP THIS UP. NOT LONG ENOUGH TO BEAT THEM ALL, THAT'S FOR SURE.
I CAN FEEL MYSELF LOSING POWER, THE LONGER I'M AWAY FROM THE HAMMER. WHAT WOULD THOR DO IN A SITUATION LIKE THIS...
THOR WOULD BELLOW AND BLUSTER AND RAGE UNTIL THEY CUT OFF HIS ARMS. AND THEN HE WOULD KICK THE HELL OUT OF THEM.
THE HAMMER CHOSE ME. THAT MEANS I'LL DO NOTHING LESS. NO MATTER THE COST.
IS THAT ALL YOU'VE GOT, GIANTS?
I CAN FEEL MY SENSES SLIPPING AWAY. QUICKLY, FIGHT HARDER BEFORE I FAINT FROM BOREDOM!

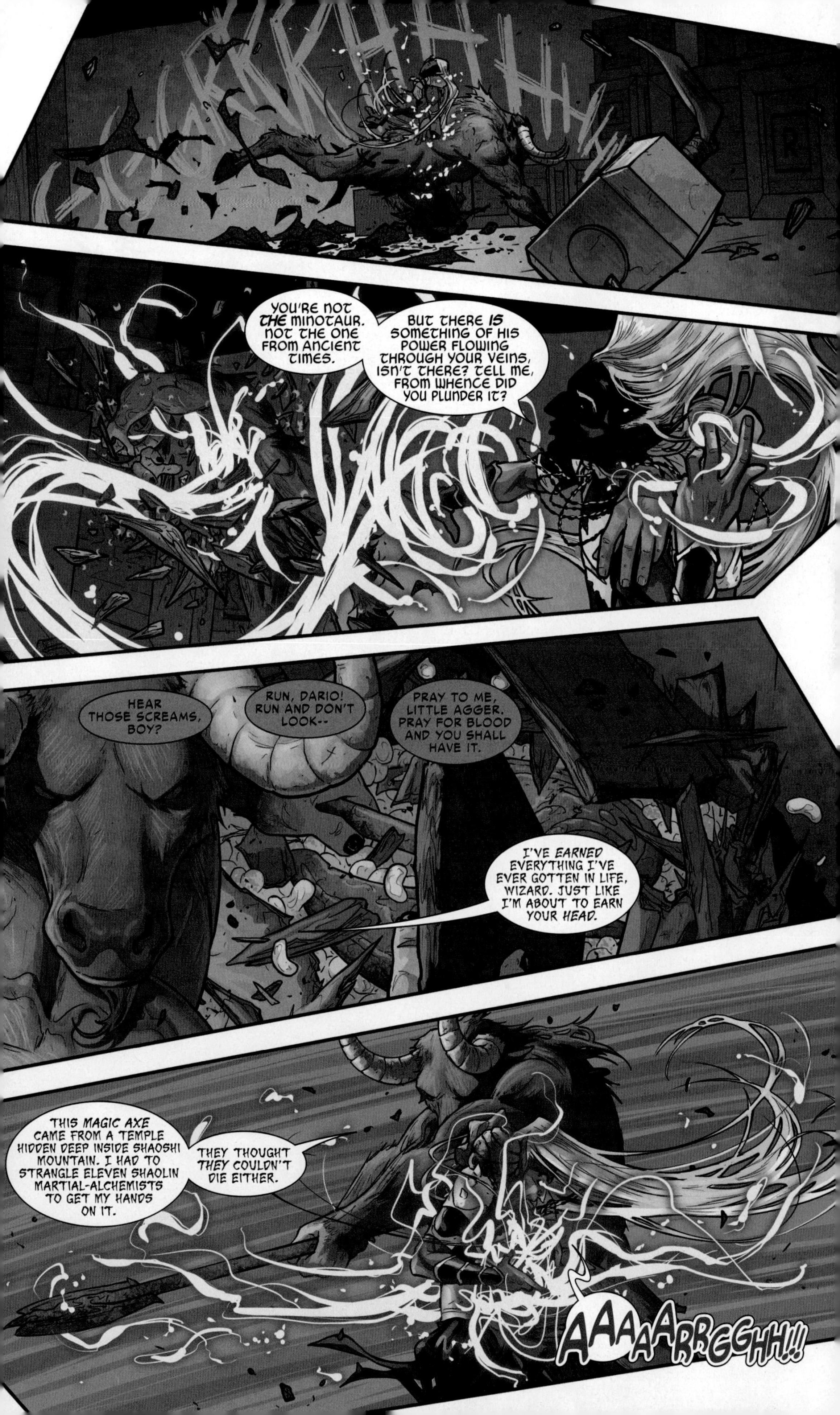
YOU'RE NOT *THE* MINOTAUR. NOT THE ONE FROM ANCIENT TIMES.
BUT THERE *IS* SOMETHING OF HIS POWER FLOWING THROUGH YOUR VEINS, ISN'T THERE? TELL ME, FROM WHENCE DID YOU PLUNDER IT?
HEAR THOSE SCREAMS, BOY?
RUN, DARIO! RUN AND DON'T LOOK--
PRAY TO ME, LITTLE AGGER. PRAY FOR BLOOD AND YOU SHALL HAVE IT.
I'VE *EARNED* EVERYTHING I'VE EVER GOTTEN IN LIFE, WIZARD. JUST LIKE I'M ABOUT TO EARN YOUR *HEAD*.
THIS *MAGIC AXE* CAME FROM A TEMPLE HIDDEN DEEP INSIDE SHAOSHI MOUNTAIN. I HAD TO STRANGLE ELEVEN SHAOLIN MARTIAL-ALCHEMISTS TO GET MY HANDS ON IT.
THEY THOUGHT *THEY* COULDN'T DIE EITHER.
AAAAARRGGHH!!!

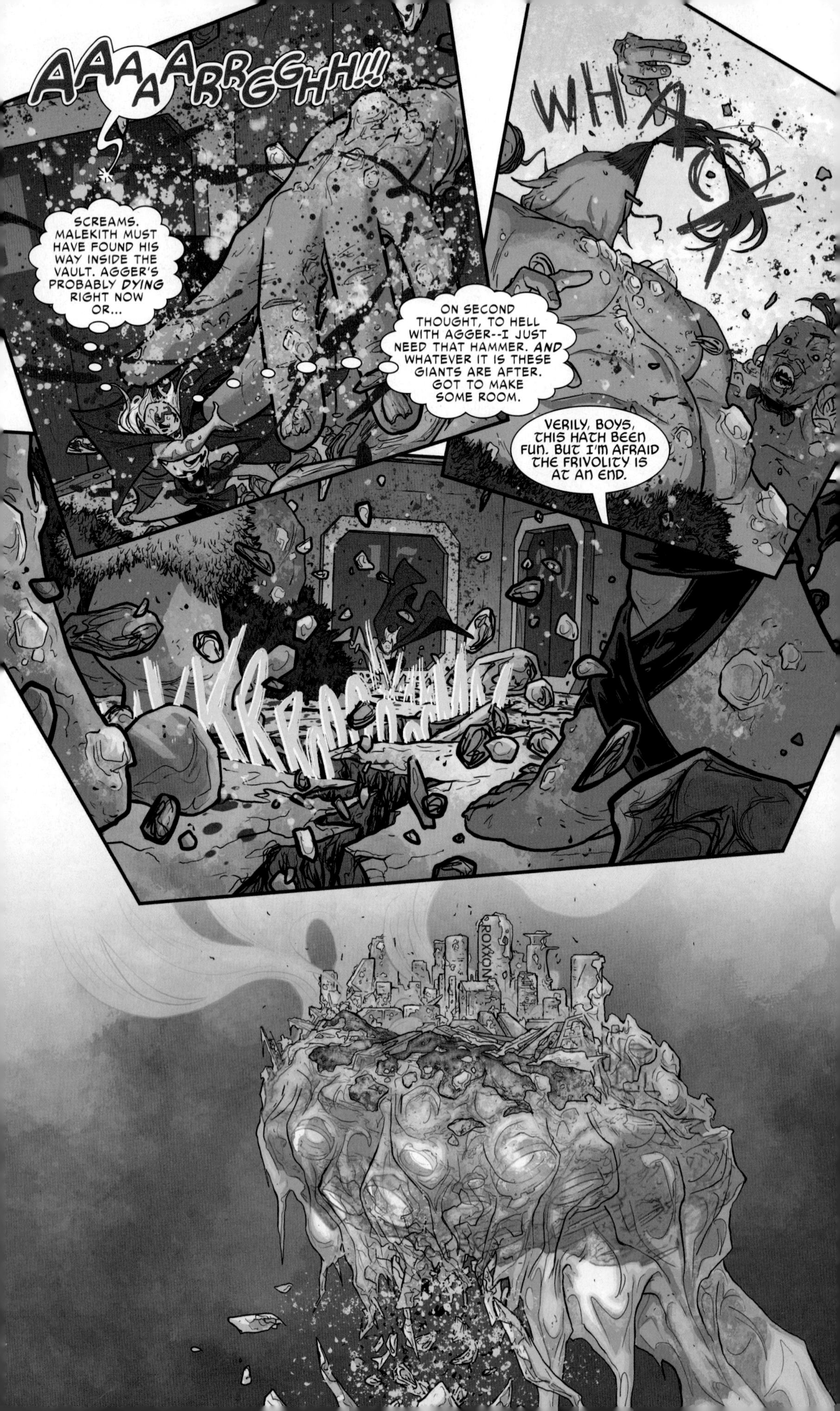
AAAAARRGGHH!!!
SCREAMS. MALEKITH MUST HAVE FOUND HIS WAY INSIDE THE VAULT. AGGER'S PROBABLY *DYING* RIGHT NOW OR...
ON SECOND THOUGHT, TO HELL WITH AGGER--I JUST NEED THAT HAMMER. *AND* WHATEVER IT IS THESE GIANTS ARE AFTER. GOT TO MAKE SOME ROOM.
WHA
VERILY, BOYS, THIS HATH BEEN FUN. BUT I'M AFRAID THE FRIVOLITY IS AT AN END.
ROXXON

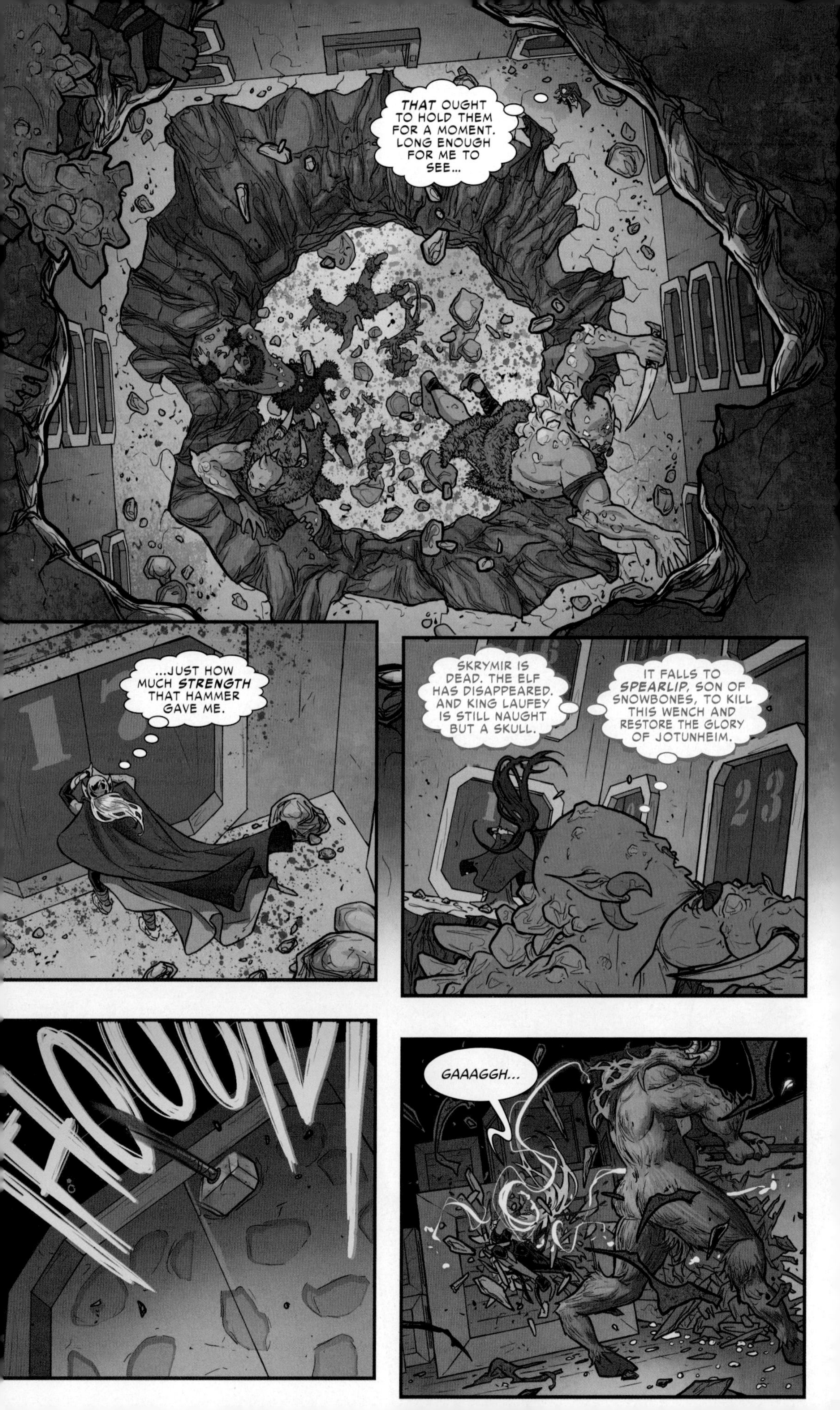
THAT OUGHT TO HOLD THEM FOR A MOMENT. LONG ENOUGH FOR ME TO SEE...
...JUST HOW MUCH STRENGTH THAT HAMMER GAVE ME.
SKRYMIR IS DEAD. THE ELF HAS DISAPPEARED. AND KING LAUFEY IS STILL NAUGHT BUT A SKULL.
IT FALLS TO SPEARLIP, SON OF SNOWBONES, TO KILL THIS WENCH AND RESTORE THE GLORY OF JOTUNHEIM.
GAAAGGH...

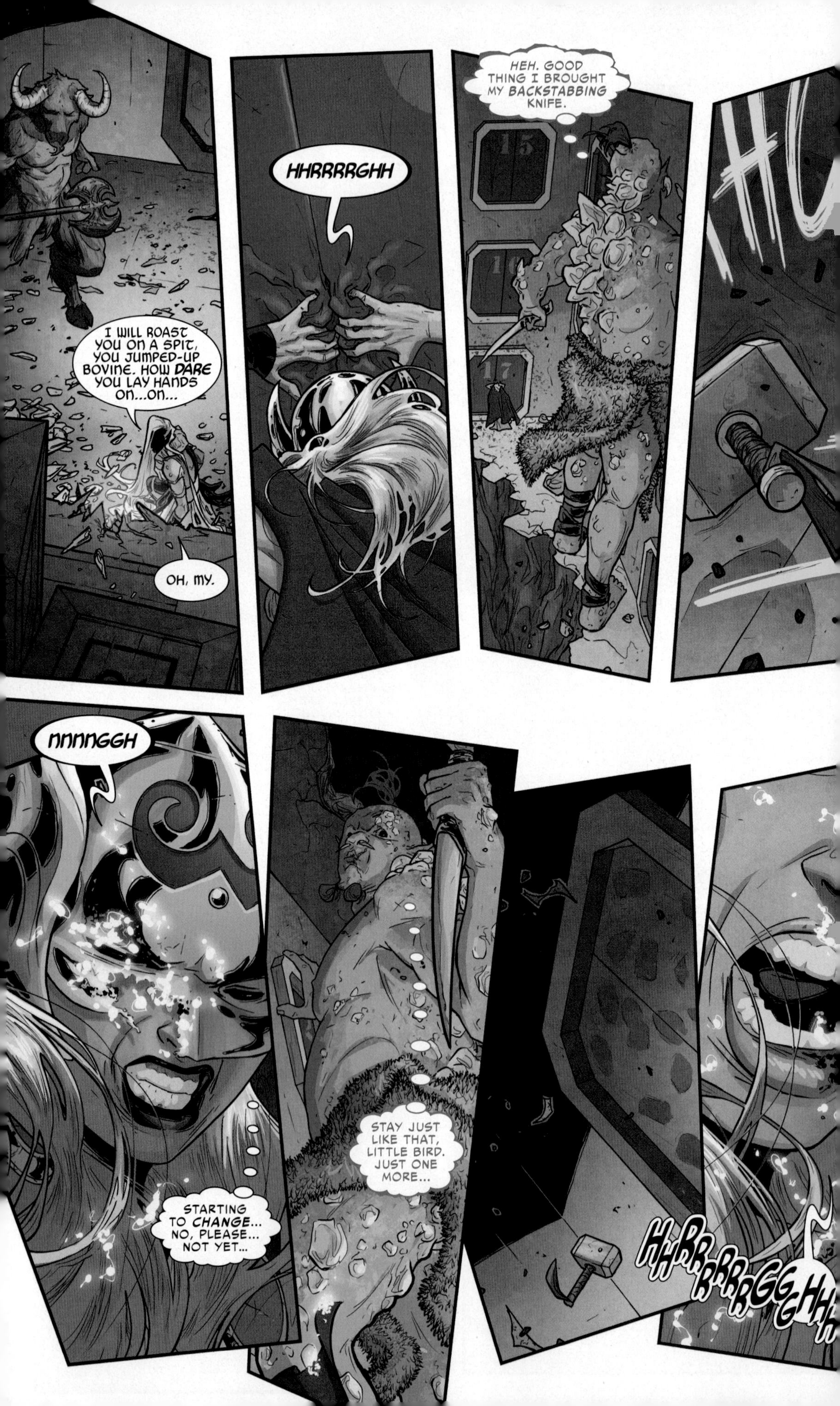
I WILL ROAST YOU ON A SPIT, YOU JUMPED-UP BOVINE. HOW DARE YOU LAY HANDS ON...ON...
OH, MY.
HHRRRRGHH
HEH. GOOD THING I BROUGHT MY BACKSTABBING KNIFE.
NNNNGGH
STARTING TO CHANGE... NO, PLEASE... NOT YET...
STAY JUST LIKE THAT, LITTLE BIRD. JUST ONE MORE...
HHRRRRRRGGGHHH

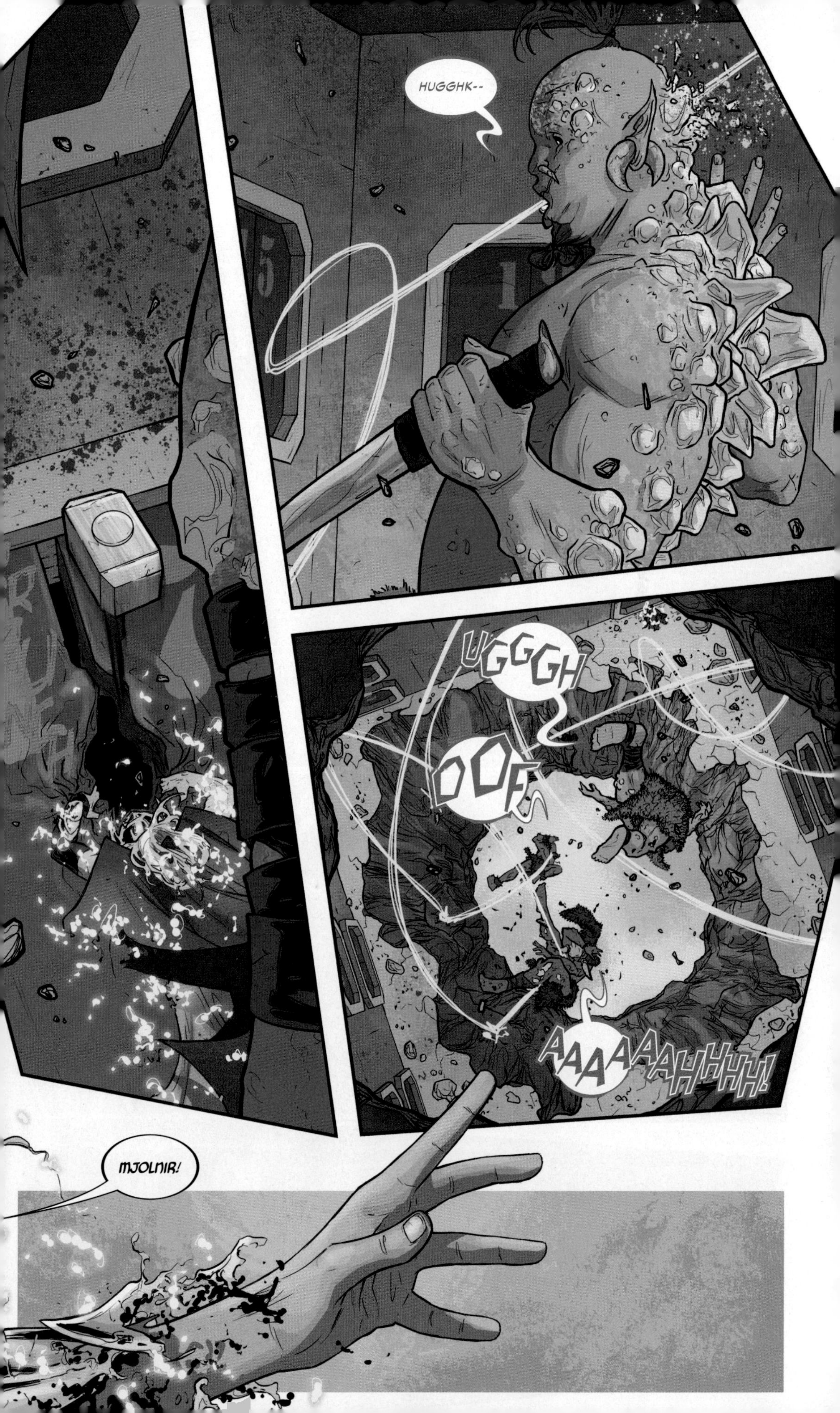
HUGGHK--
UGGGH
OOF
AAAAAAHHHH!
MJOLNIR!

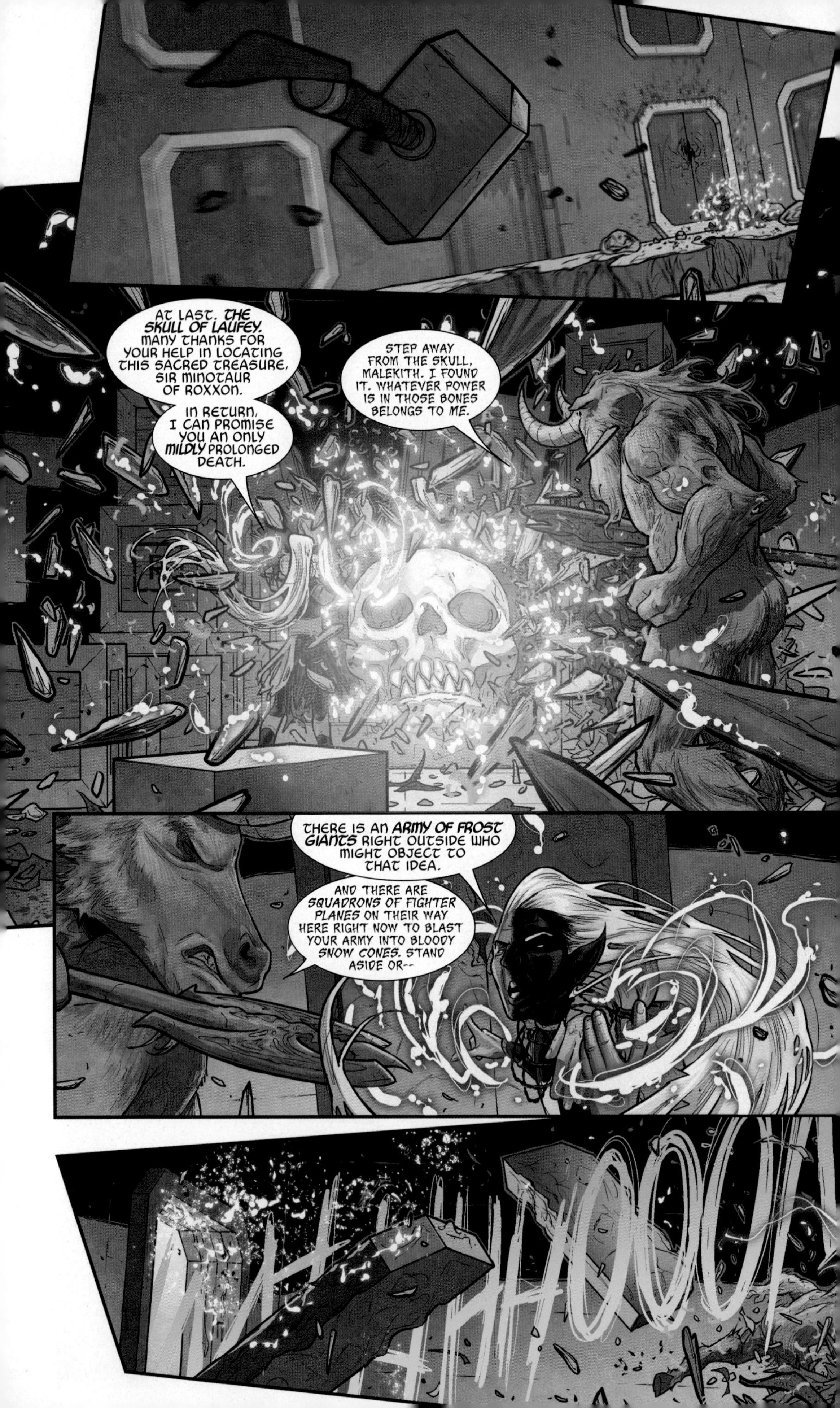

AT LAST. ***THE SKULL OF LAUFEY.*** MANY THANKS FOR YOUR HELP IN LOCATING THIS SACRED TREASURE, SIR MINOTAUR OF ROXXON.
IN RETURN, I CAN PROMISE YOU AN ONLY ***MILDLY*** PROLONGED DEATH.
STEP AWAY FROM THE SKULL, MALEKITH. I FOUND IT. WHATEVER POWER IS IN THOSE BONES BELONGS TO *ME*.
THERE IS AN ***ARMY OF FROST GIANTS*** RIGHT OUTSIDE WHO MIGHT OBJECT TO THAT IDEA.
AND THERE ARE ***SQUADRONS OF FIGHTER PLANES*** ON THEIR WAY HERE RIGHT NOW TO BLAST YOUR ARMY INTO BLOODY SNOW CONES. STAND ASIDE OR--
WHHHOOO!

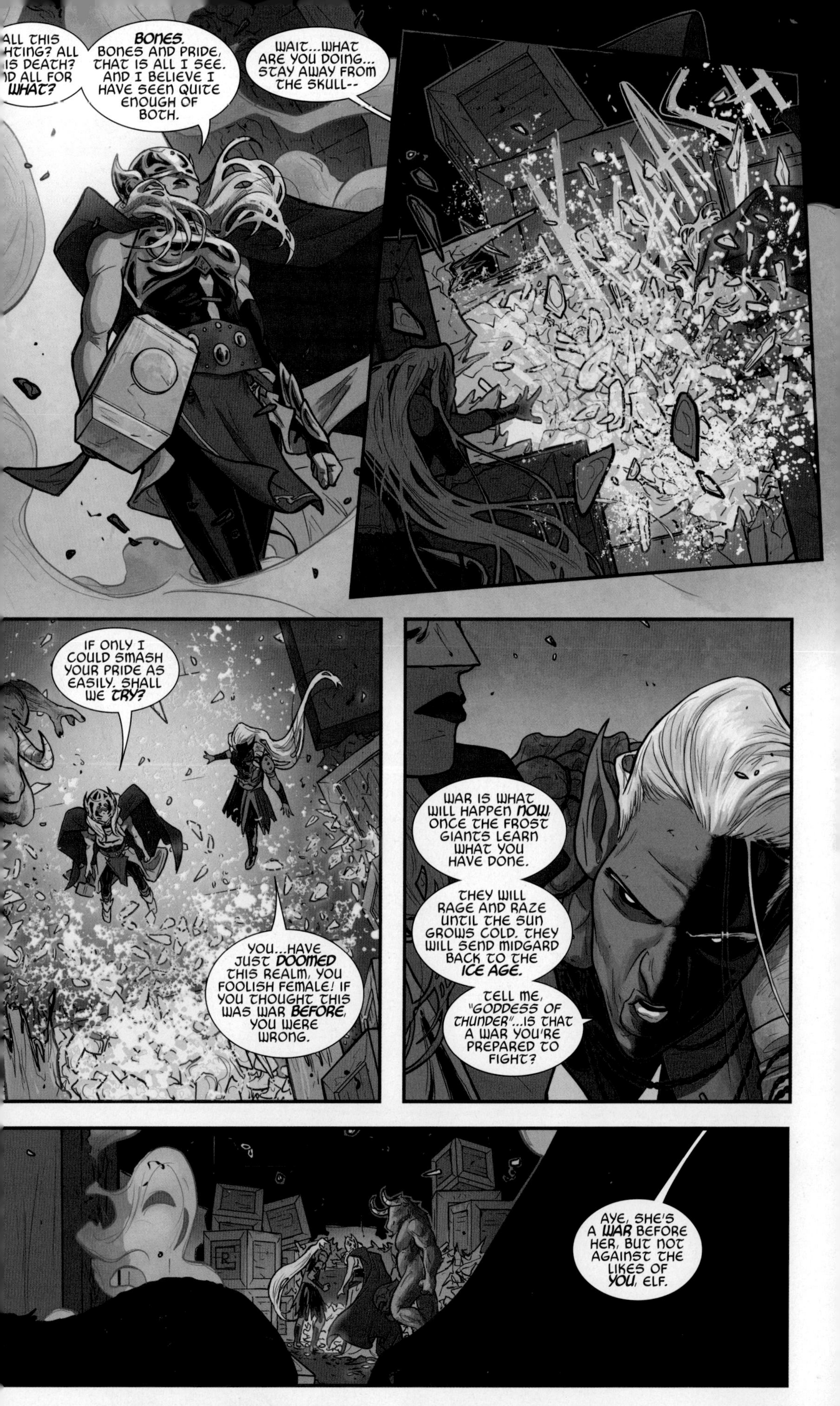
ALL THIS HTING? ALL IS DEATH? D ALL FOR WHAT?
BONES. BONES AND PRIDE. THAT IS ALL I SEE. AND I BELIEVE I HAVE SEEN QUITE ENOUGH OF BOTH.
WAIT...WHAT ARE YOU DOING... STAY AWAY FROM THE SKULL--
IF ONLY I COULD SMASH YOUR PRIDE AS EASILY. SHALL WE TRY?
YOU...HAVE JUST DOOMED THIS REALM, YOU FOOLISH FEMALE! IF YOU THOUGHT THIS WAS WAR BEFORE, YOU WERE WRONG.
WAR IS WHAT WILL HAPPEN NOW, ONCE THE FROST GIANTS LEARN WHAT YOU HAVE DONE.
THEY WILL RAGE AND RAZE UNTIL THE SUN GROWS COLD. THEY WILL SEND MIDGARD BACK TO THE ICE AGE.
TELL ME, "GODDESS OF THUNDER"...IS THAT A WAR YOU'RE PREPARED TO FIGHT?
AYE, SHE'S A WAR BEFORE HER, BUT NOT AGAINST THE LIKES OF YOU, ELF.

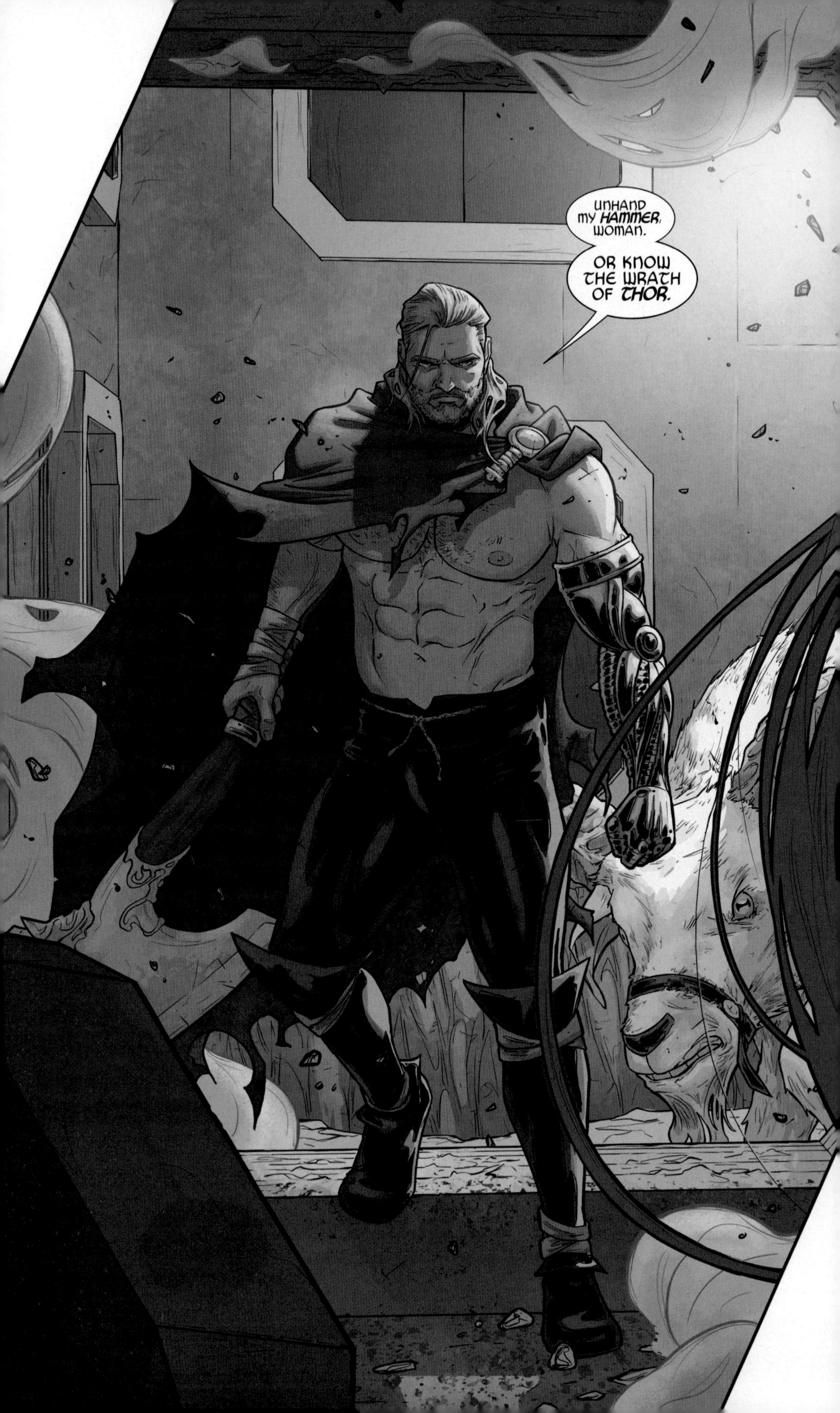
UNHAND MY *HAMMER*, WOMAN.
OR KNOW THE WRATH OF *THOR*.

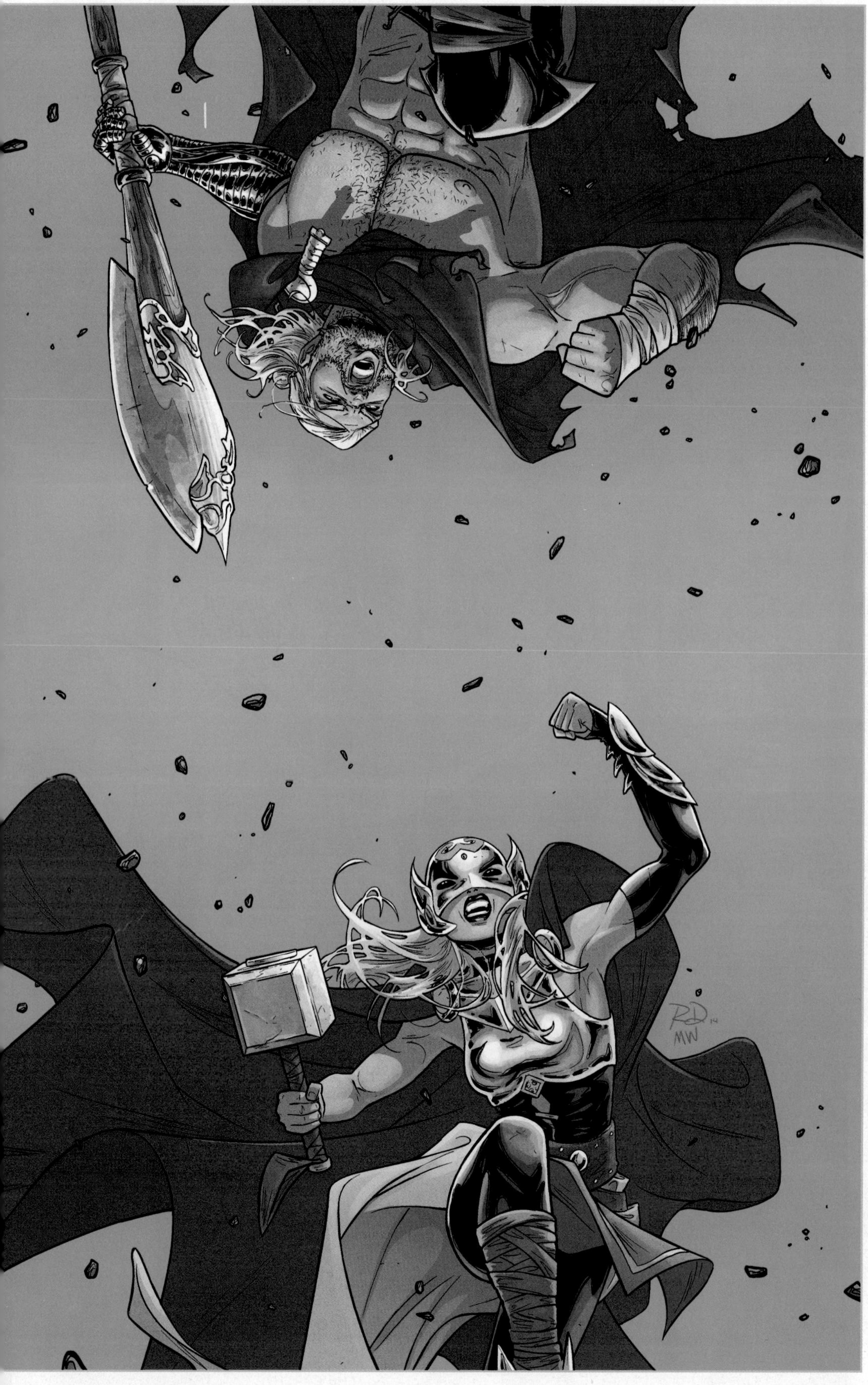

— 4 —

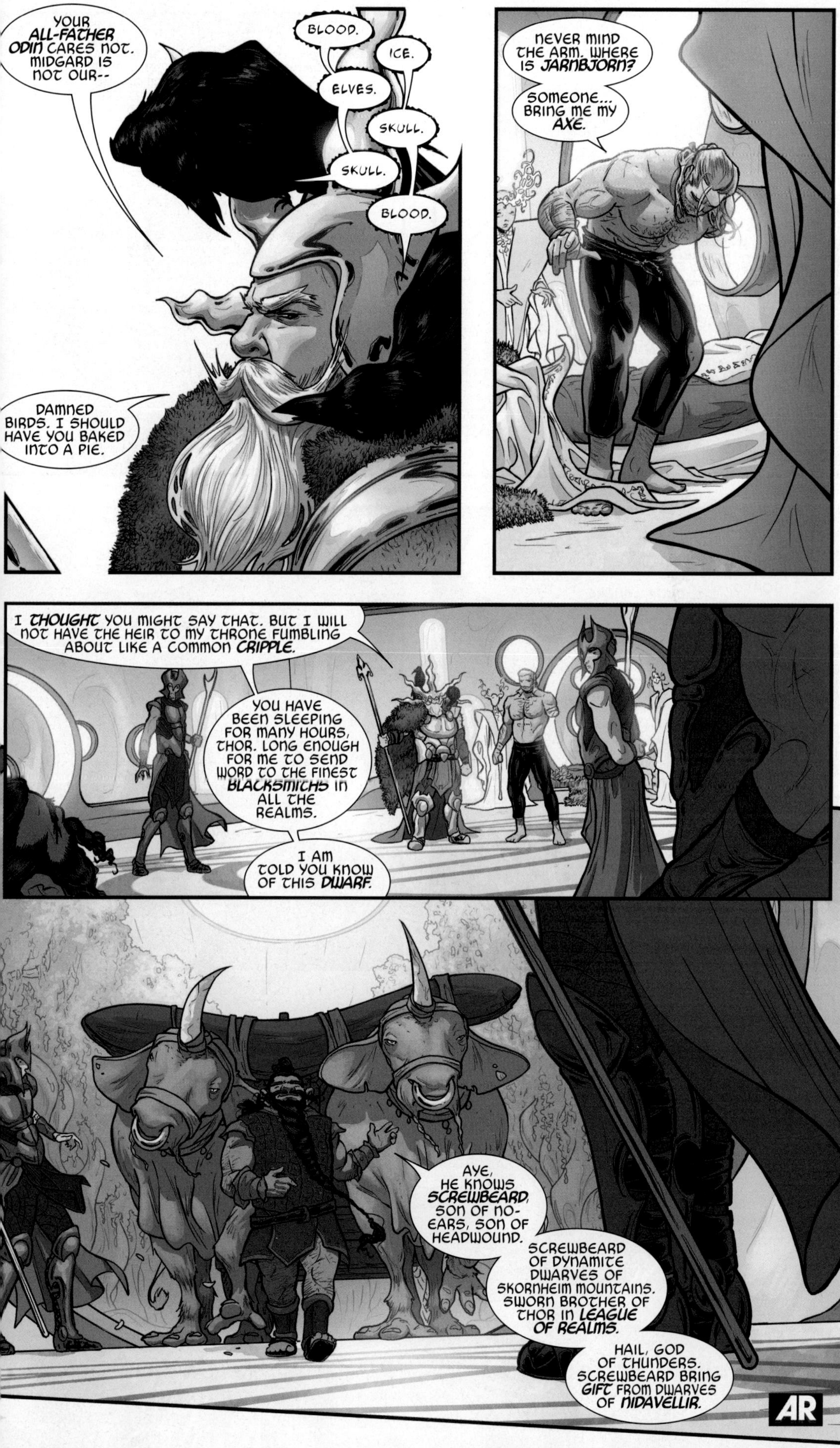

YOUR ALL-FATHER ODIN CARES NOT. MIDGARD IS NOT OUR--
BLOOD.
ICE.
ELVES.
SKULL.
SKULL.
BLOOD.
DAMNED BIRDS. I SHOULD HAVE YOU BAKED INTO A PIE.
NEVER MIND THE ARM. WHERE IS JARNBJORN?
SOMEONE... BRING ME MY AXE.
I THOUGHT YOU MIGHT SAY THAT. BUT I WILL NOT HAVE THE HEIR TO MY THRONE FUMBLING ABOUT LIKE A COMMON CRIPPLE.
YOU HAVE BEEN SLEEPING FOR MANY HOURS, THOR. LONG ENOUGH FOR ME TO SEND WORD TO THE FINEST BLACKSMITHS IN ALL THE REALMS.
I AM TOLD YOU KNOW OF THIS DWARF.
AYE, HE KNOWS SCREWBEARD, SON OF NO-EARS, SON OF HEADWOUND.
SCREWBEARD OF DYNAMITE DWARVES OF SKORNHEIM MOUNTAINS. SWORN BROTHER OF THOR IN LEAGUE OF REALMS.
HAIL, GOD OF THUNDERS. SCREWBEARD BRING GIFT FROM DWARVES OF NIDAVELLIR.
AR

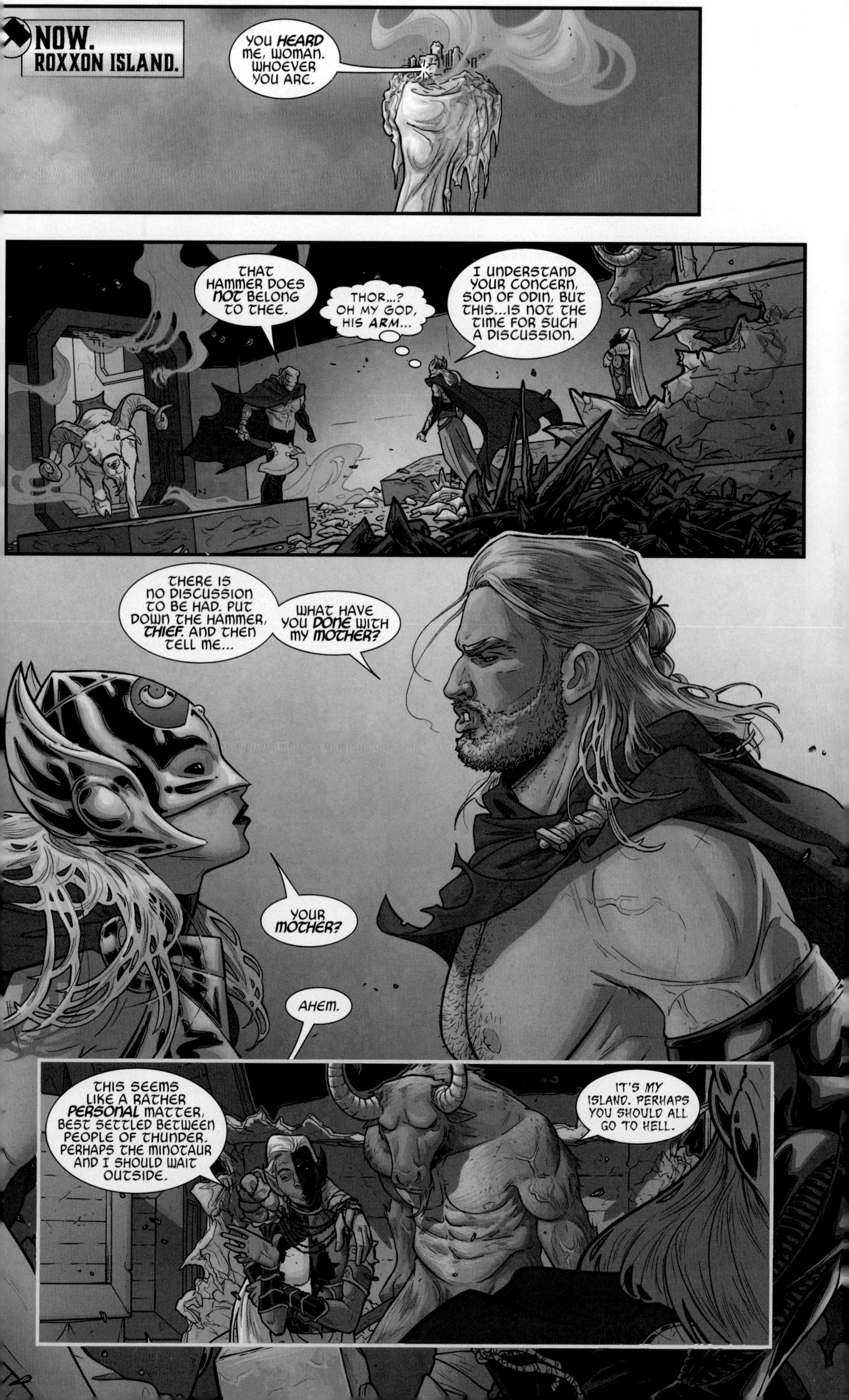
NOW. ROXXON ISLAND.
YOU HEARD ME, WOMAN. WHOEVER YOU ARE.
THAT HAMMER DOES NOT BELONG TO THEE.
THOR...? OH MY GOD, HIS ARM...
I UNDERSTAND YOUR CONCERN, SON OF ODIN, BUT THIS...IS NOT THE TIME FOR SUCH A DISCUSSION.
THERE IS NO DISCUSSION TO BE HAD. PUT DOWN THE HAMMER, THIEF. AND THEN TELL ME...
WHAT HAVE YOU DONE WITH MY MOTHER?
YOUR MOTHER?
AHEM.
THIS SEEMS LIKE A RATHER PERSONAL MATTER, BEST SETTLED BETWEEN PEOPLE OF THUNDER. PERHAPS THE MINOTAUR AND I SHOULD WAIT OUTSIDE.
IT'S MY ISLAND. PERHAPS YOU SHOULD ALL GO TO HELL.

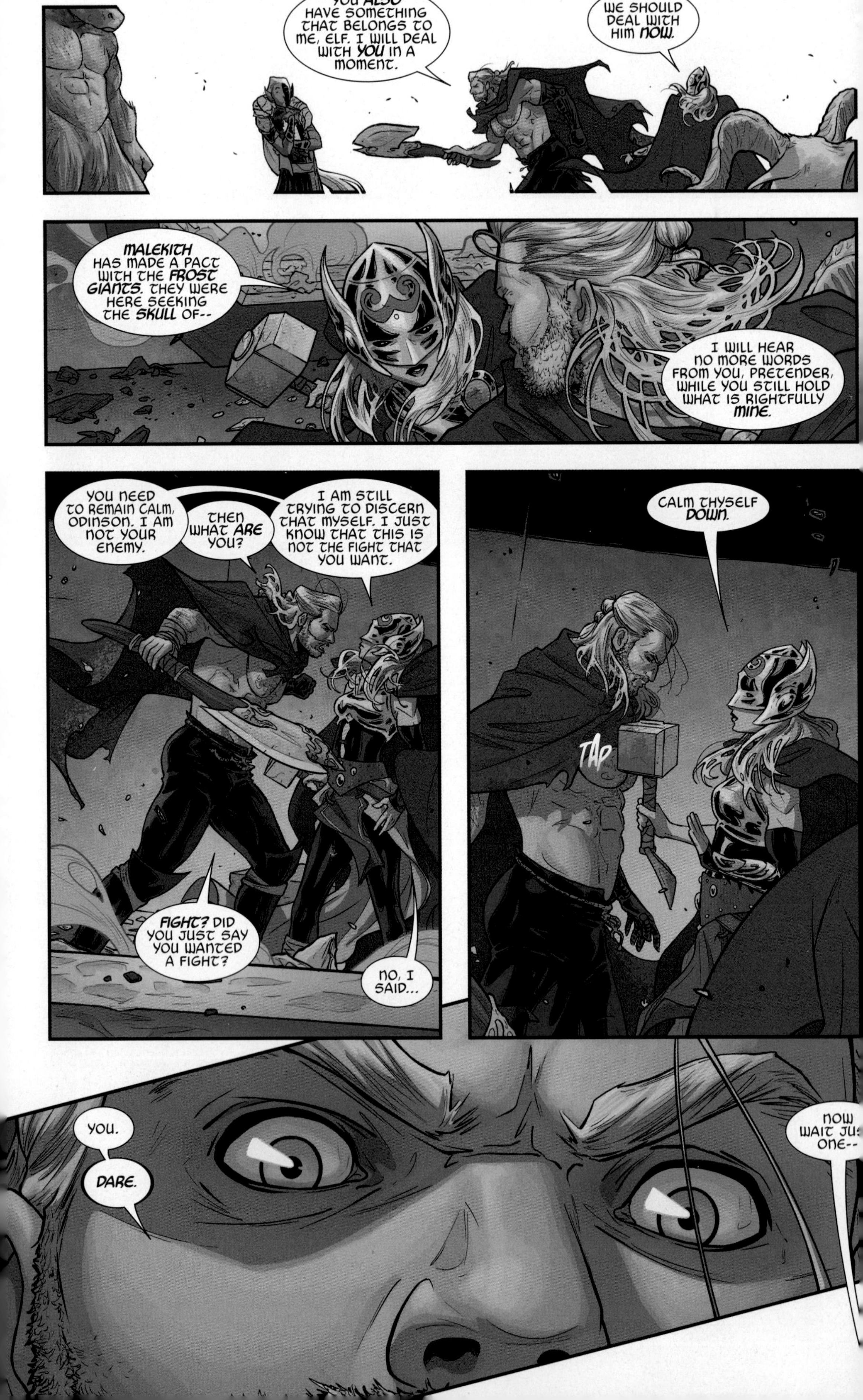
YOU ALSO HAVE SOMETHING THAT BELONGS TO ME, ELF. I WILL DEAL WITH YOU IN A MOMENT.
WE SHOULD DEAL WITH HIM NOW.
MALEKITH HAS MADE A PACT WITH THE FROST GIANTS. THEY WERE HERE SEEKING THE SKULL OF--
I WILL HEAR NO MORE WORDS FROM YOU, PRETENDER, WHILE YOU STILL HOLD WHAT IS RIGHTFULLY MINE.
YOU NEED TO REMAIN CALM, ODINSON. I AM NOT YOUR ENEMY.
THEN WHAT ARE YOU?
I AM STILL TRYING TO DISCERN THAT MYSELF. I JUST KNOW THAT THIS IS NOT THE FIGHT THAT YOU WANT.
FIGHT? DID YOU JUST SAY YOU WANTED A FIGHT?
NO, I SAID...
CALM THYSELF DOWN.
TAP
YOU.
DARE.
NOW WAIT JUS ONE--

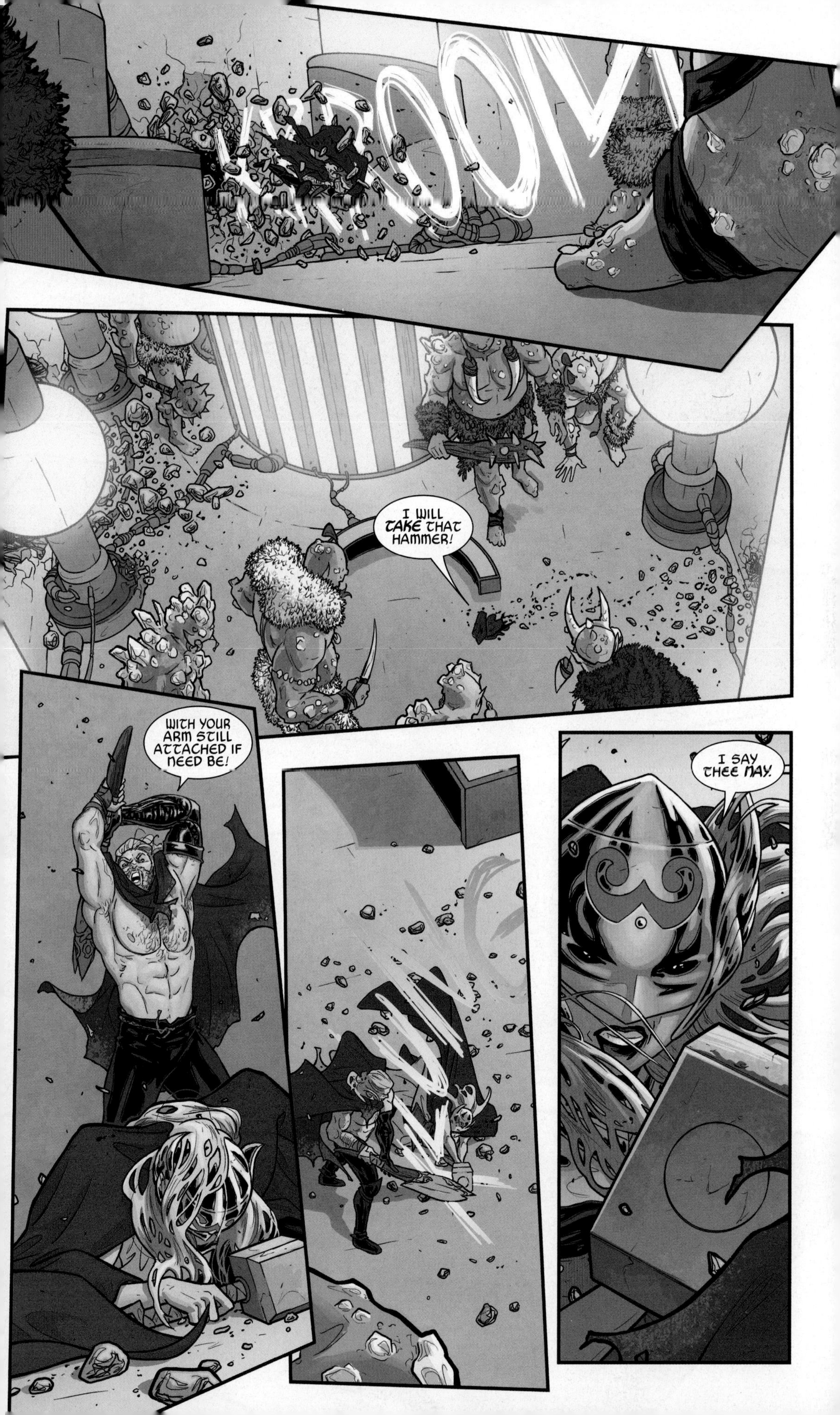
KRA-BOOOM
I WILL TAKE THAT HAMMER!
WITH YOUR ARM STILL ATTACHED IF NEED BE!
I SAY THEE NAY.

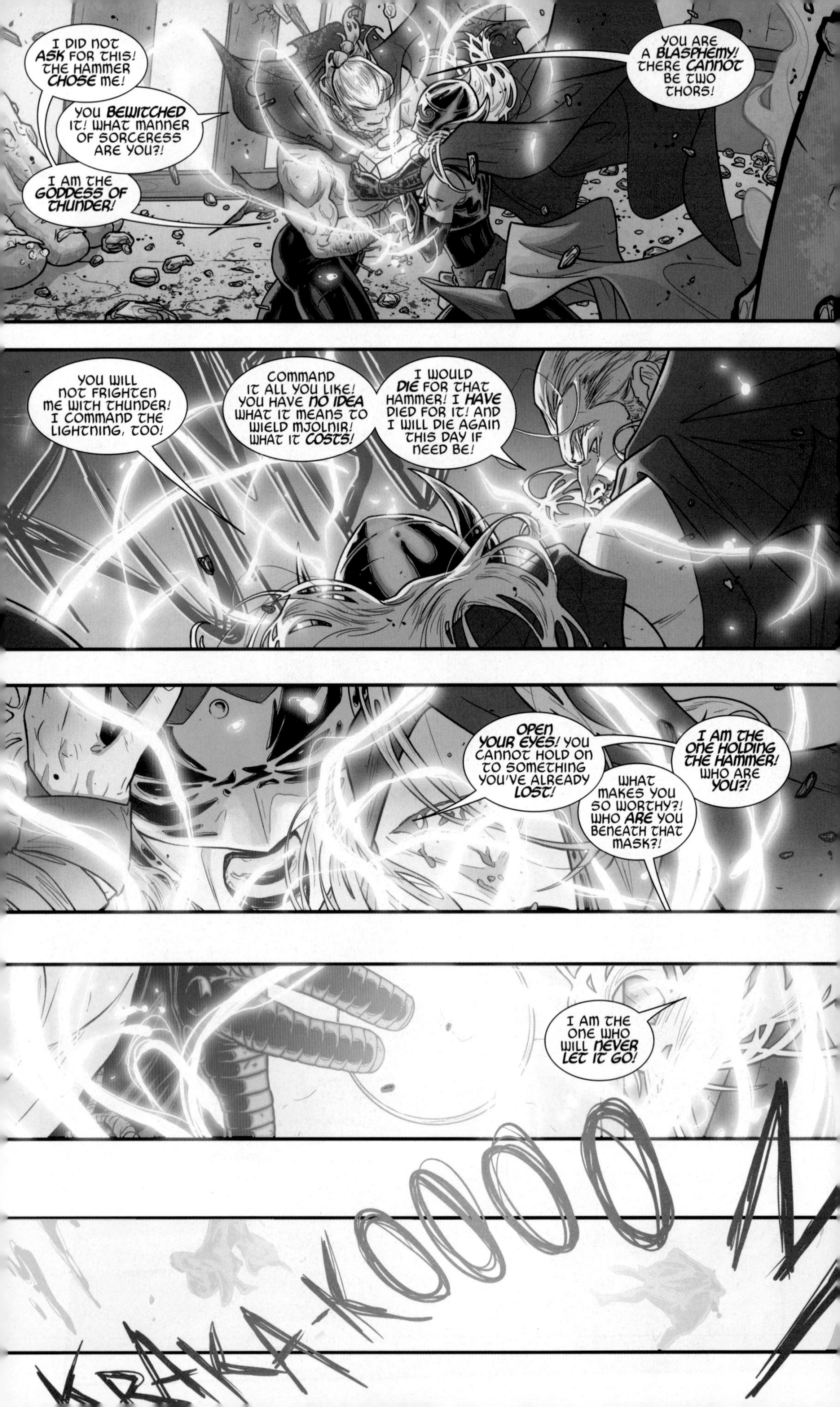

I DID NOT ASK FOR THIS! THE HAMMER CHOSE ME!
YOU ARE A BLASPHEMY! THERE CANNOT BE TWO THORS!
YOU BEWITCHED IT! WHAT MANNER OF SORCERESS ARE YOU?!
I AM THE GODDESS OF THUNDER!
YOU WILL NOT FRIGHTEN ME WITH THUNDER! I COMMAND THE LIGHTNING, TOO!
COMMAND IT ALL YOU LIKE! YOU HAVE NO IDEA WHAT IT MEANS TO WIELD MJOLNIR! WHAT IT COSTS!
I WOULD DIE FOR THAT HAMMER! I HAVE DIED FOR IT! AND I WILL DIE AGAIN THIS DAY IF NEED BE!
OPEN YOUR EYES! YOU CANNOT HOLD ON TO SOMETHING YOU'VE ALREADY LOST!
I AM THE ONE HOLDING THE HAMMER! WHO ARE YOU?!
WHAT MAKES YOU SO WORTHY?! WHO ARE YOU BENEATH THAT MASK?!
I AM THE ONE WHO WILL NEVER LET IT GO!
KRAKA-KOOOOOM

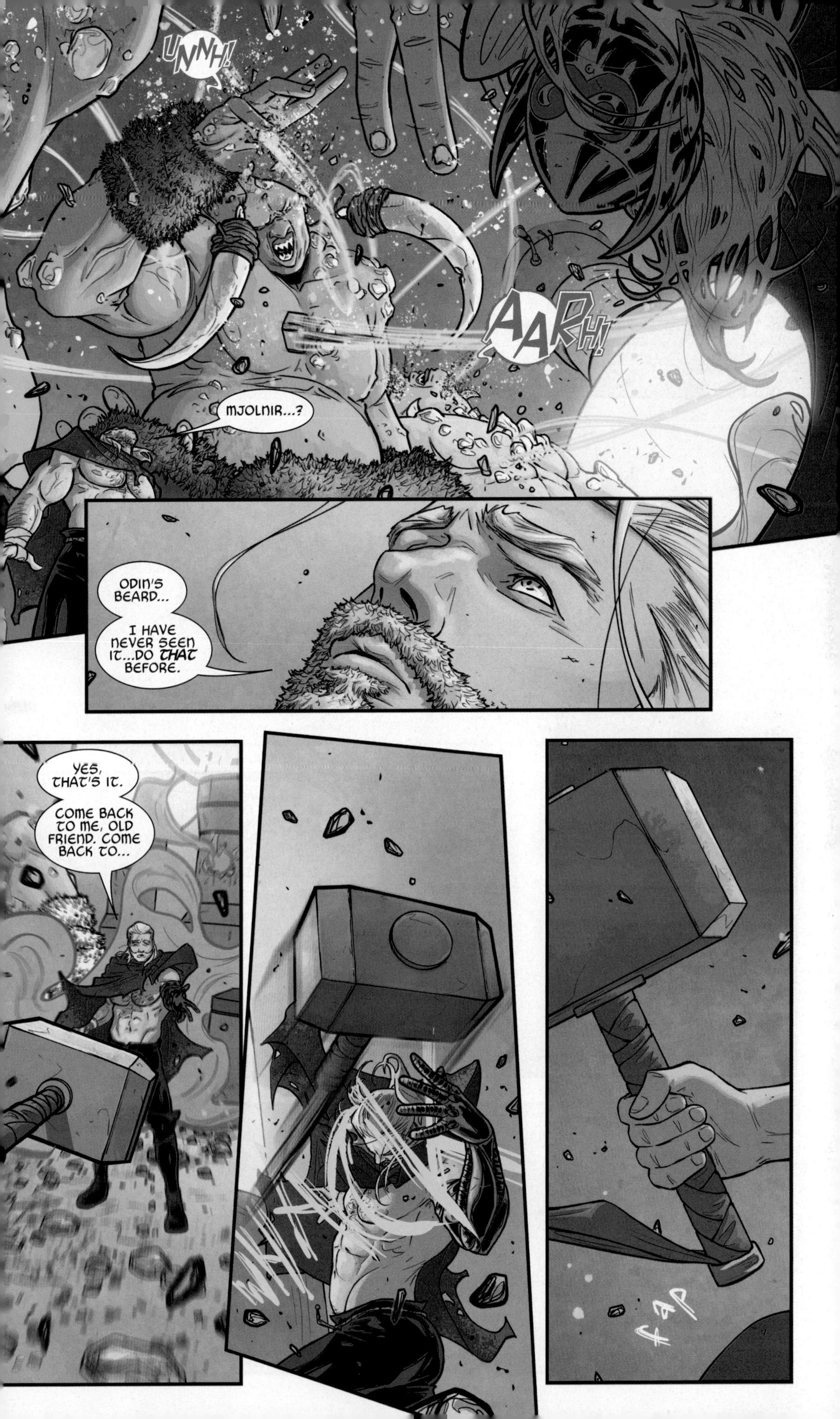

UNNH!
AARGH!
MJOLNIR...?
ODIN'S BEARD...
I HAVE NEVER SEEN IT...DO *THAT* BEFORE.
YES, THAT'S IT.
COME BACK TO ME, OLD FRIEND. COME BACK TO...

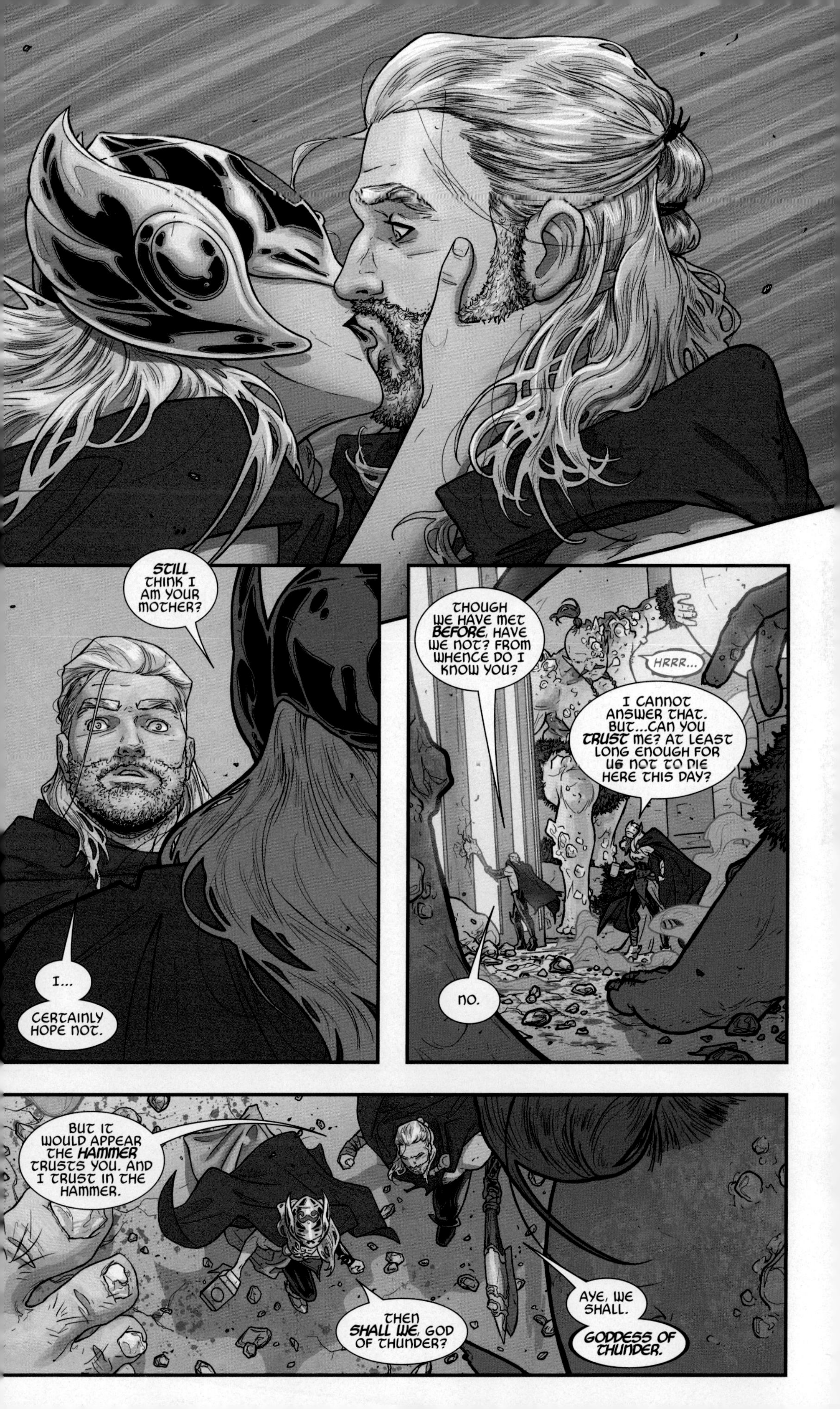
STILL THINK I AM YOUR MOTHER?
I...
CERTAINLY HOPE NOT.
THOUGH WE HAVE MET BEFORE, HAVE WE NOT? FROM WHENCE DO I KNOW YOU?
HRRR...
I CANNOT ANSWER THAT. BUT...CAN YOU TRUST ME? AT LEAST LONG ENOUGH FOR US NOT TO DIE HERE THIS DAY?
NO.
BUT IT WOULD APPEAR THE HAMMER TRUSTS YOU. AND I TRUST IN THE HAMMER.
THEN SHALL WE, GOD OF THUNDER?
AYE, WE SHALL.
GODDESS OF THUNDER.

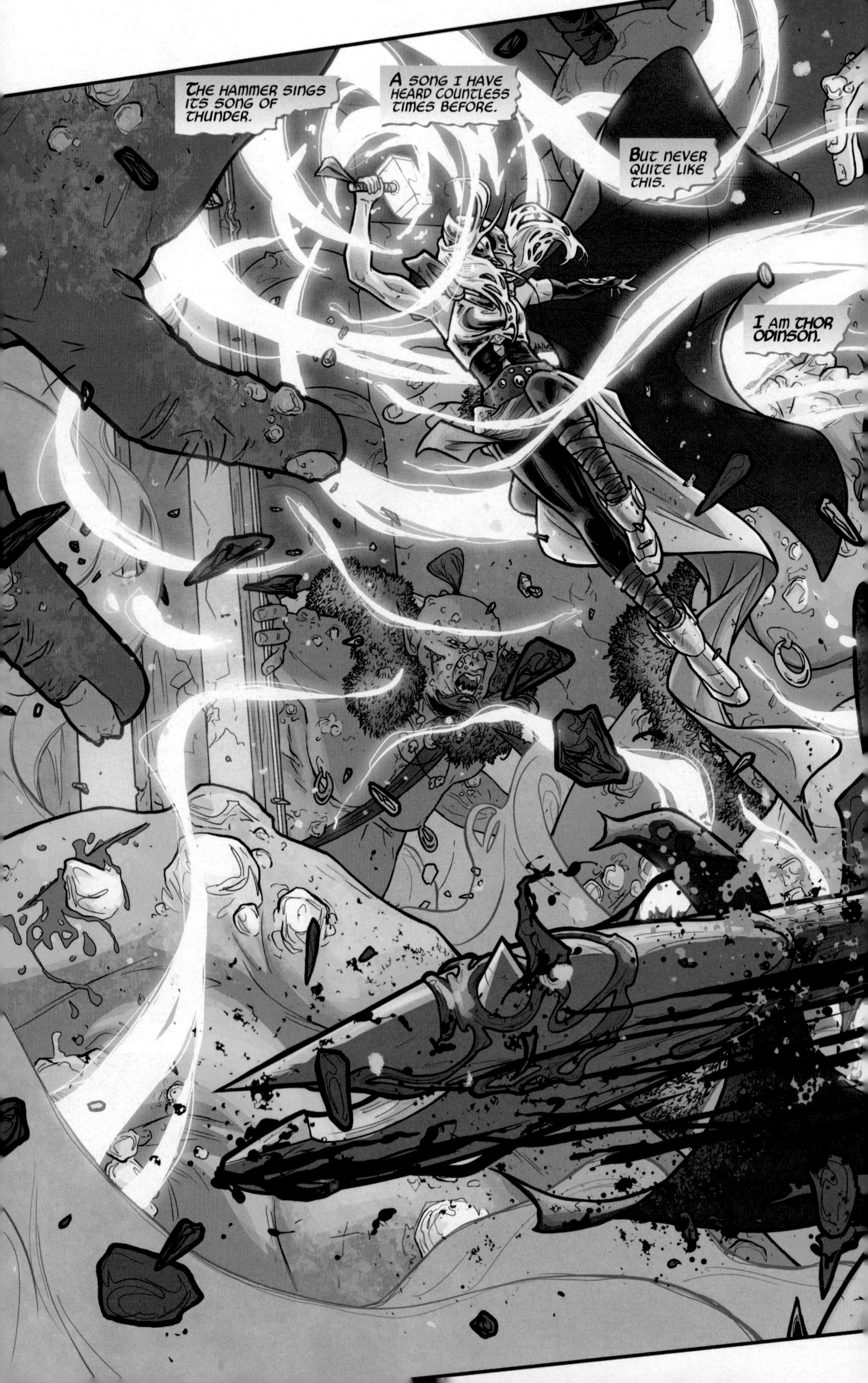
THE HAMMER SINGS ITS SONG OF THUNDER.
A SONG I HAVE HEARD COUNTLESS TIMES BEFORE.
BUT NEVER QUITE LIKE THIS.
I AM THOR ODINSON.

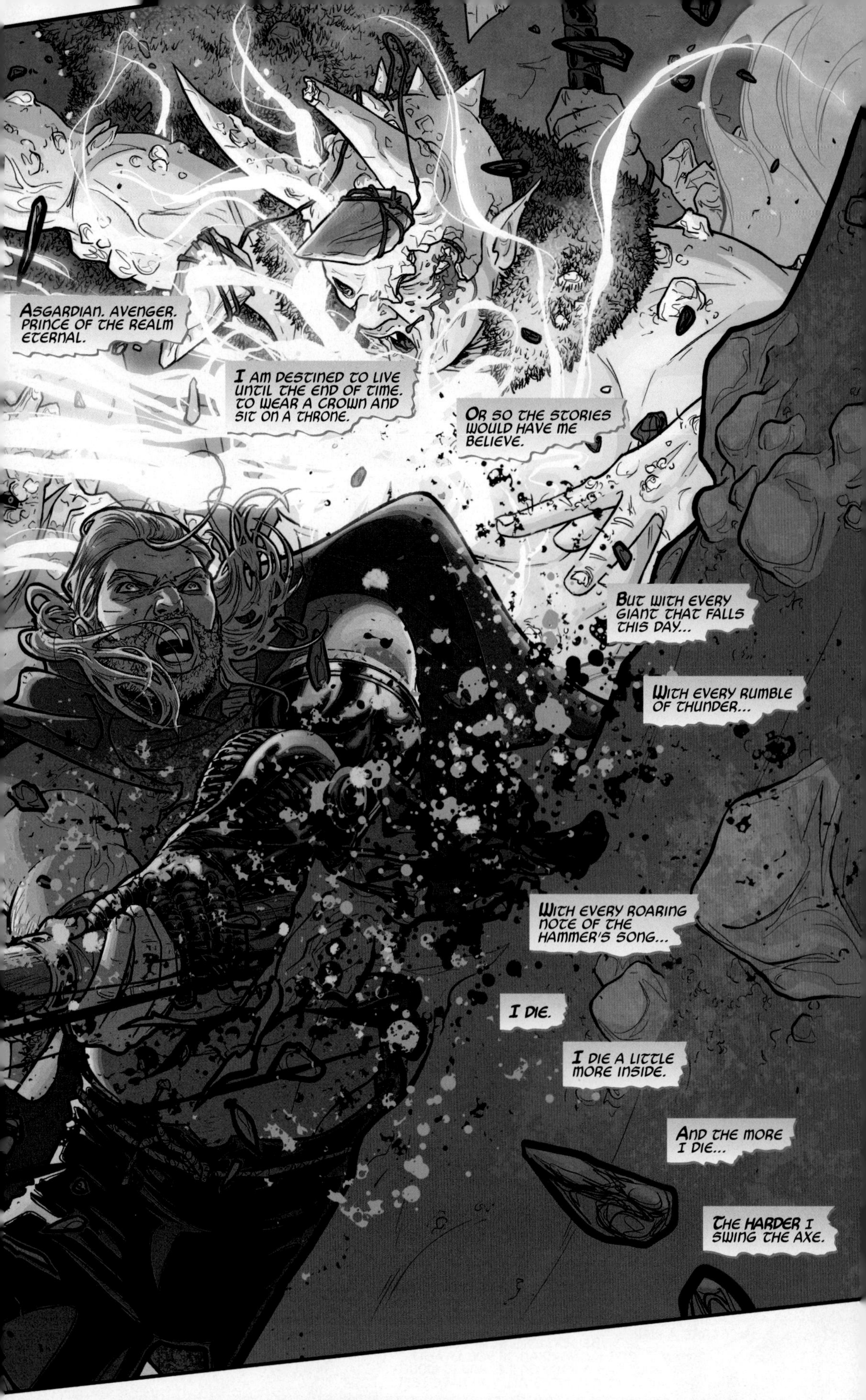
ASGARDIAN. AVENGER. PRINCE OF THE REALM ETERNAL.
I AM DESTINED TO LIVE UNTIL THE END OF TIME. TO WEAR A CROWN AND SIT ON A THRONE.
OR SO THE STORIES WOULD HAVE ME BELIEVE.
BUT WITH EVERY GIANT THAT FALLS THIS DAY...
WITH EVERY RUMBLE OF THUNDER...
WITH EVERY ROARING NOTE OF THE HAMMER'S SONG...
I DIE.
I DIE A LITTLE MORE INSIDE.
AND THE MORE I DIE...
THE HARDER I SWING THE AXE.

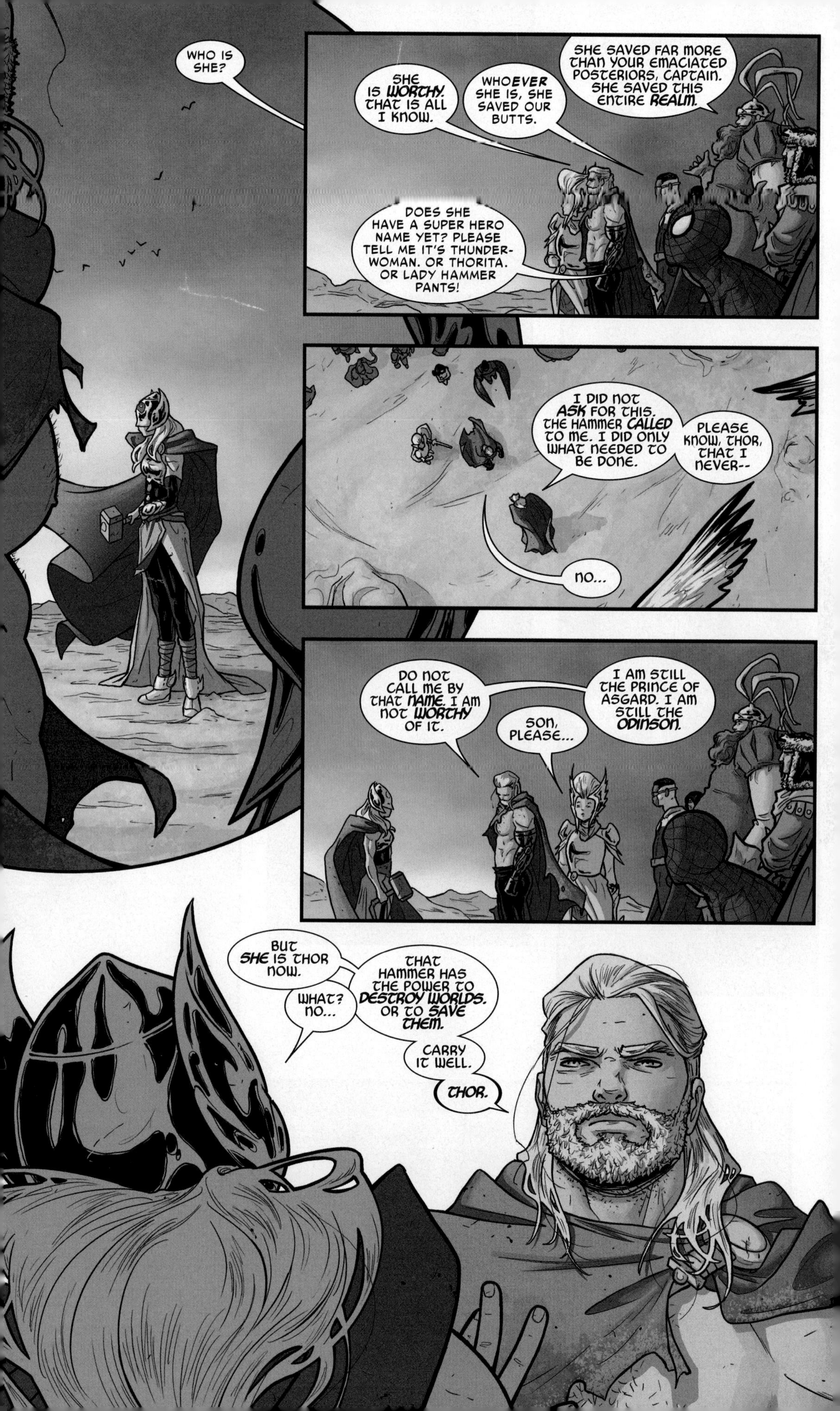

WHO IS SHE?
SHE IS WORTHY. THAT IS ALL I KNOW.
WHOEVER SHE IS, SHE SAVED OUR BUTTS.
SHE SAVED FAR MORE THAN YOUR EMACIATED POSTERIORS, CAPTAIN. SHE SAVED THIS ENTIRE REALM.
DOES SHE HAVE A SUPER HERO NAME YET? PLEASE TELL ME IT'S THUNDER-WOMAN. OR THORITA. OR LADY HAMMER PANTS!
I DID NOT ASK FOR THIS. THE HAMMER CALLED TO ME. I DID ONLY WHAT NEEDED TO BE DONE.
PLEASE KNOW, THOR, THAT I NEVER--
NO...
DO NOT CALL ME BY THAT NAME. I AM NOT WORTHY OF IT.
I AM STILL THE PRINCE OF ASGARD. I AM STILL THE ODINSON.
SON, PLEASE...
BUT SHE IS THOR NOW.
WHAT? NO...
THAT HAMMER HAS THE POWER TO DESTROY WORLDS. OR TO SAVE THEM.
CARRY IT WELL.
THOR.

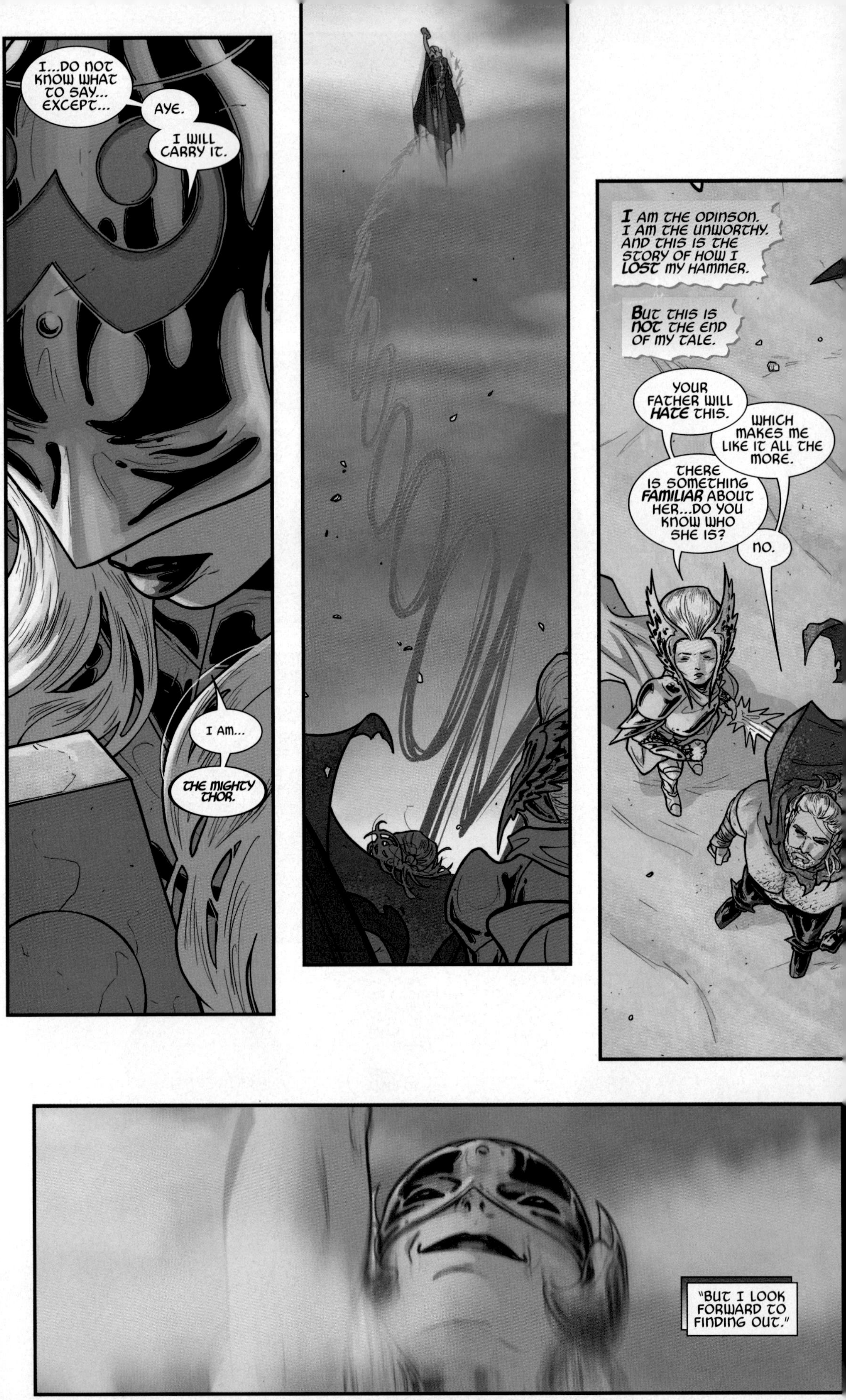
I...DO NOT KNOW WHAT TO SAY... EXCEPT...
AYE.
I WILL CARRY IT.
I AM...
THE MIGHTY THOR.
I AM THE ODINSON. I AM THE UNWORTHY. AND THIS IS THE STORY OF HOW I LOST MY HAMMER.
BUT THIS IS NOT THE END OF MY TALE.
YOUR FATHER WILL HATE THIS.
WHICH MAKES ME LIKE IT ALL THE MORE.
THERE IS SOMETHING FAMILIAR ABOUT HER...DO YOU KNOW WHO SHE IS?
NO.
"BUT I LOOK FORWARD TO FINDING OUT."

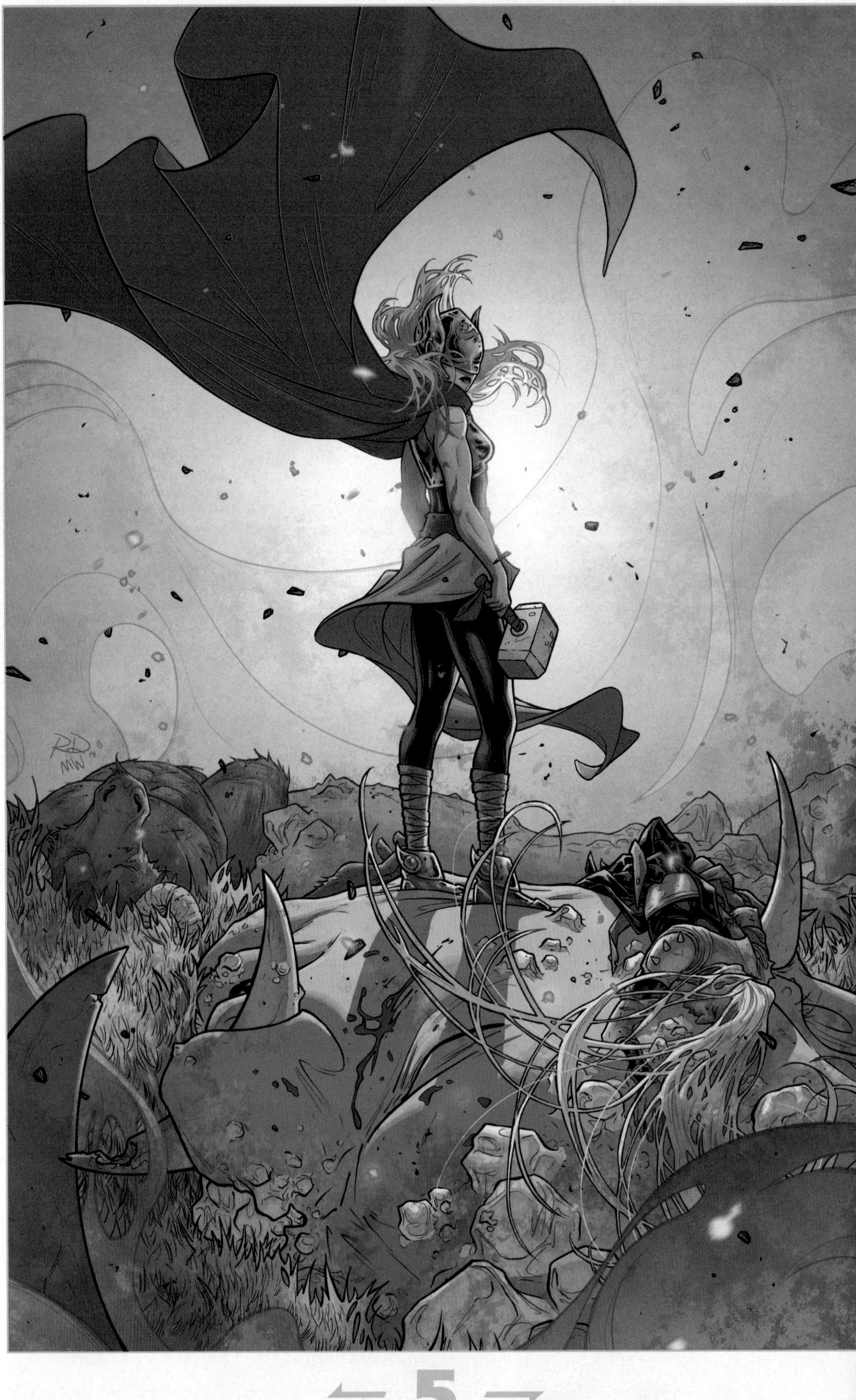

5

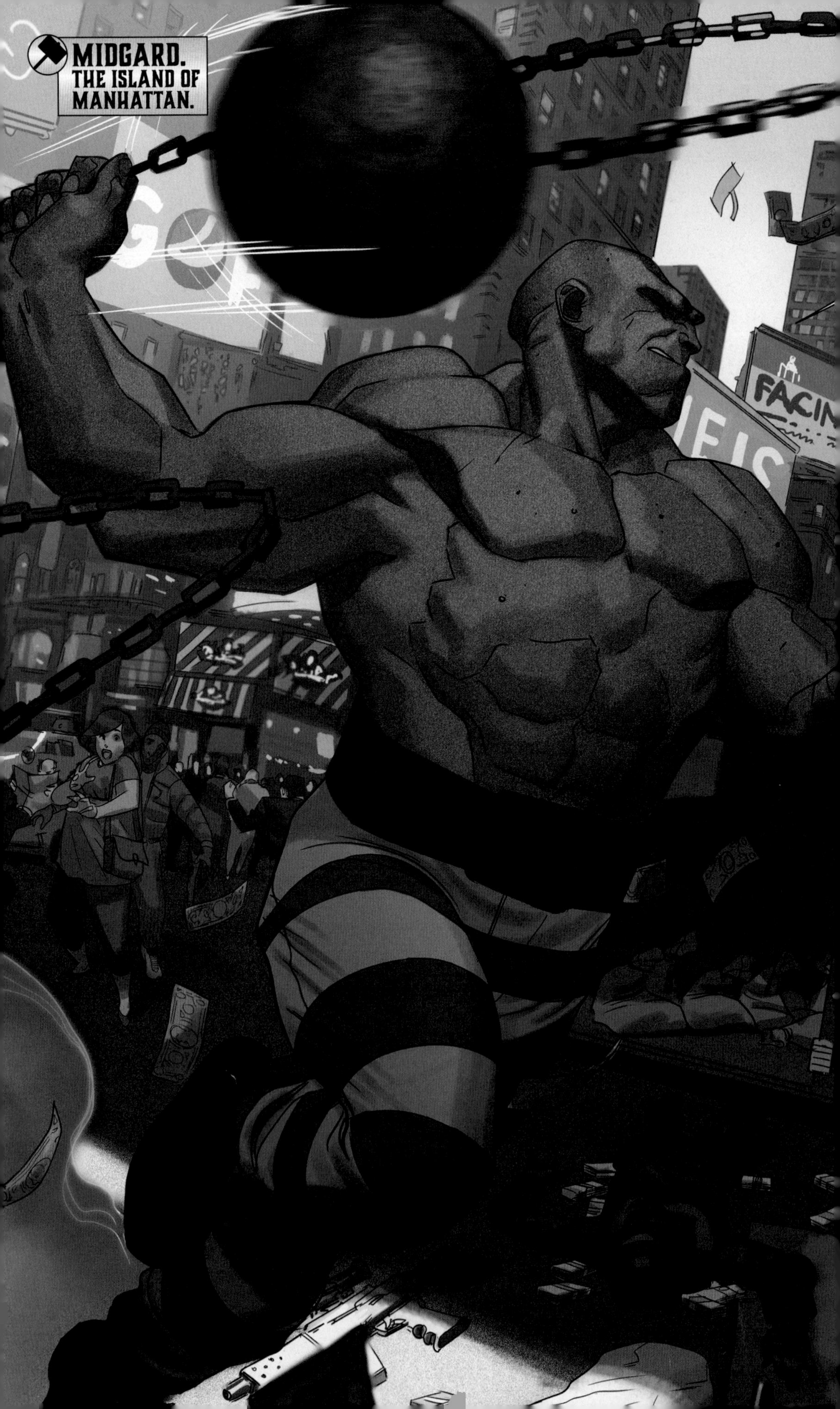
MIDGARD. THE ISLAND OF MANHATTAN.

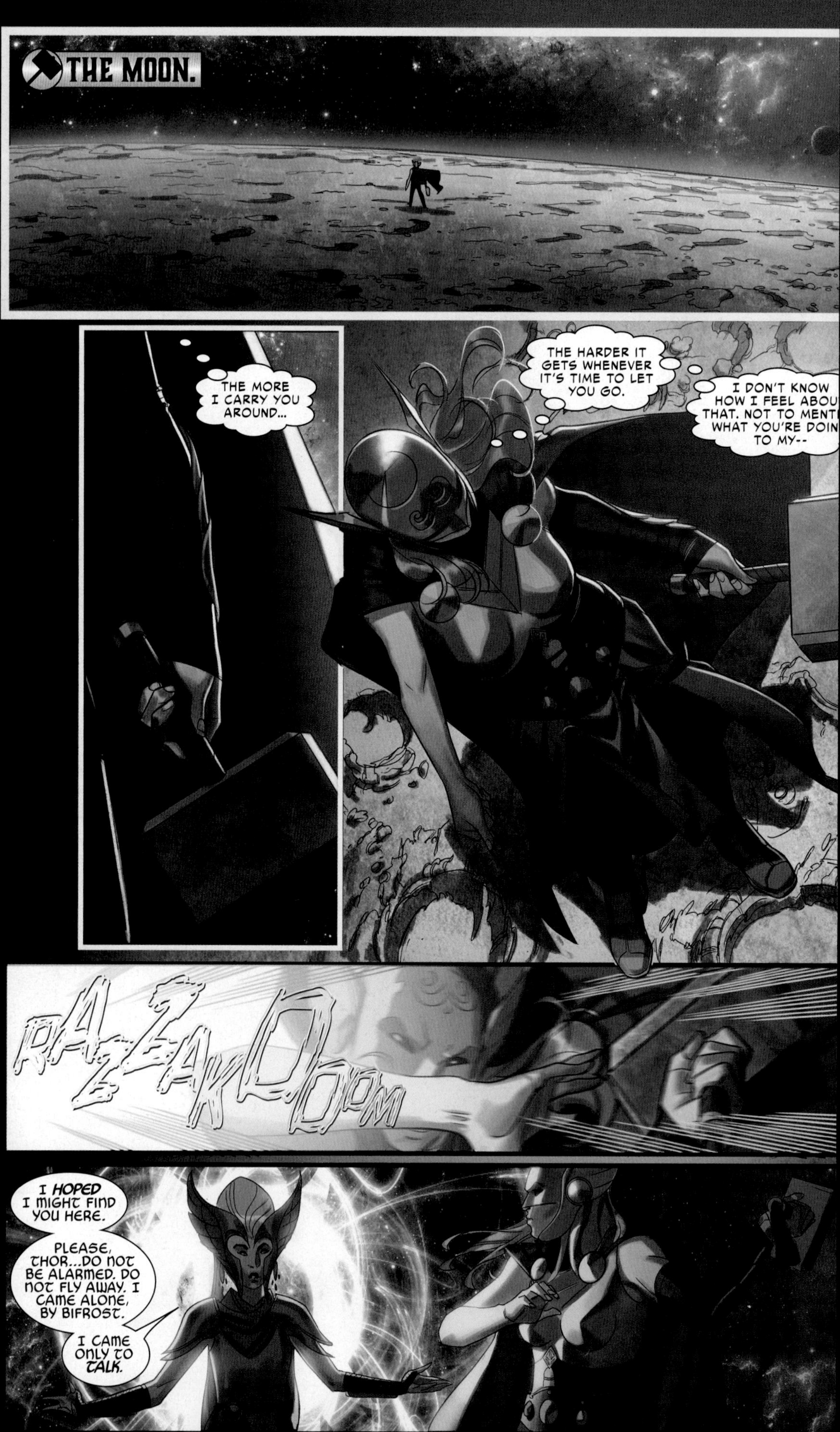
THE MOON.
THE MORE I CARRY YOU AROUND...
THE HARDER IT GETS WHENEVER IT'S TIME TO LET YOU GO.
I DON'T KNOW HOW I FEEL ABOU THAT. NOT TO MENT WHAT YOU'RE DOIN TO MY--
RAZZAKOOOM
I HOPED I MIGHT FIND YOU HERE.
PLEASE, THOR...DO NOT BE ALARMED. DO NOT FLY AWAY. I CAME ALONE, BY BIFROST.
I CAME ONLY TO TALK.

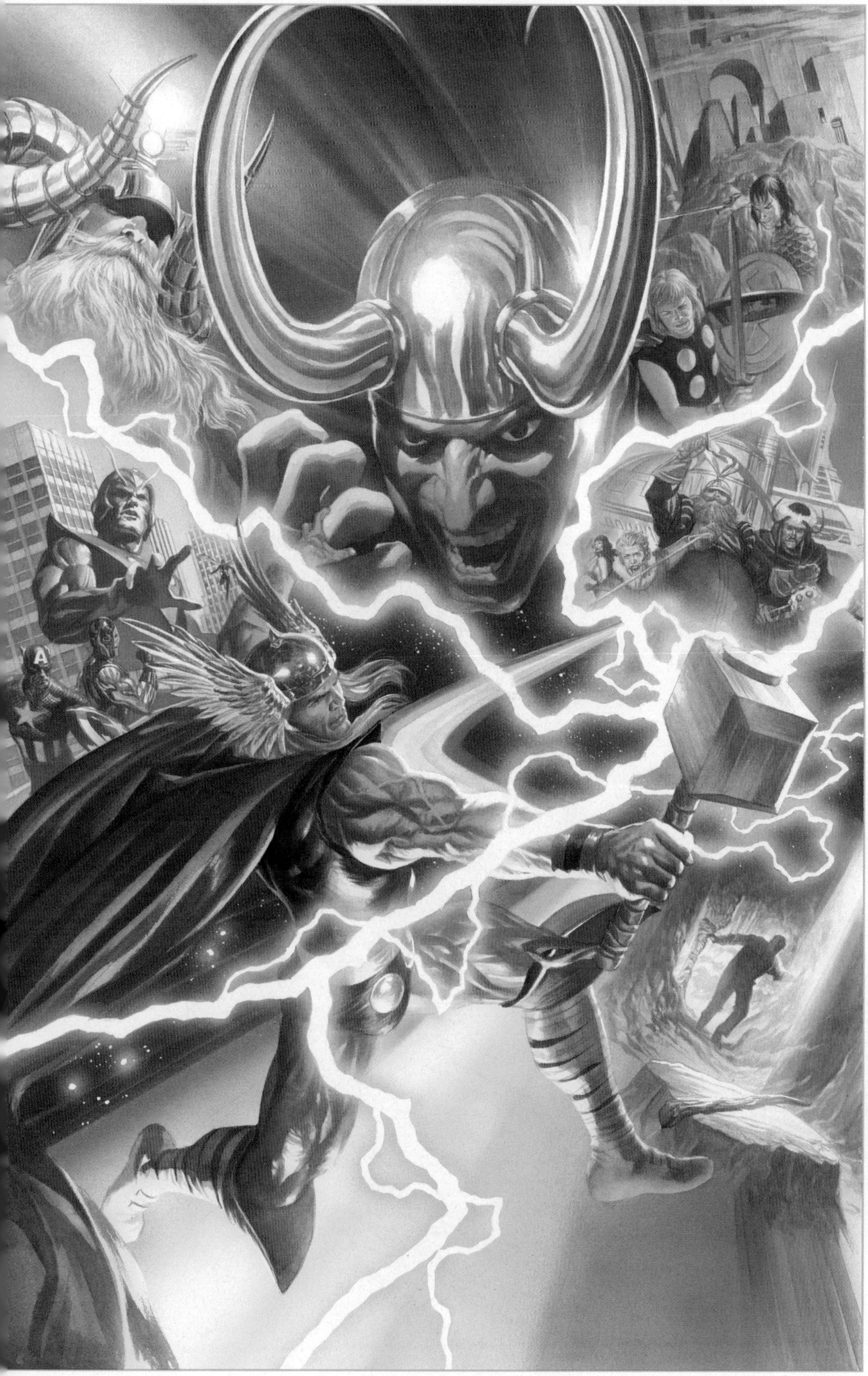

THOR # 1 75TH ANNIVERSARY VARIANT
BY **ALEX ROSS**

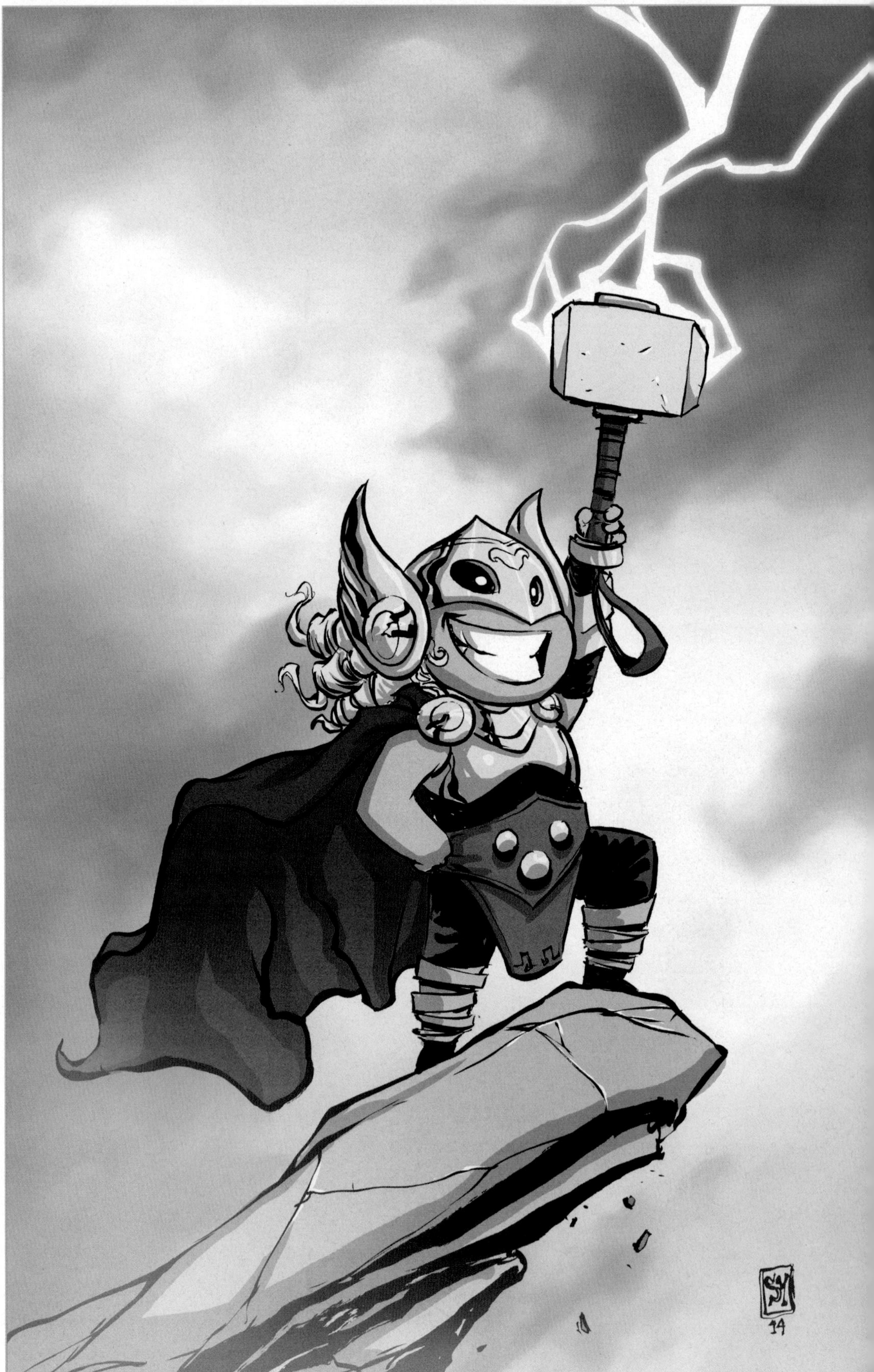

THOR # 1 VARIANT
BY **SKOTTIE YOUNG**

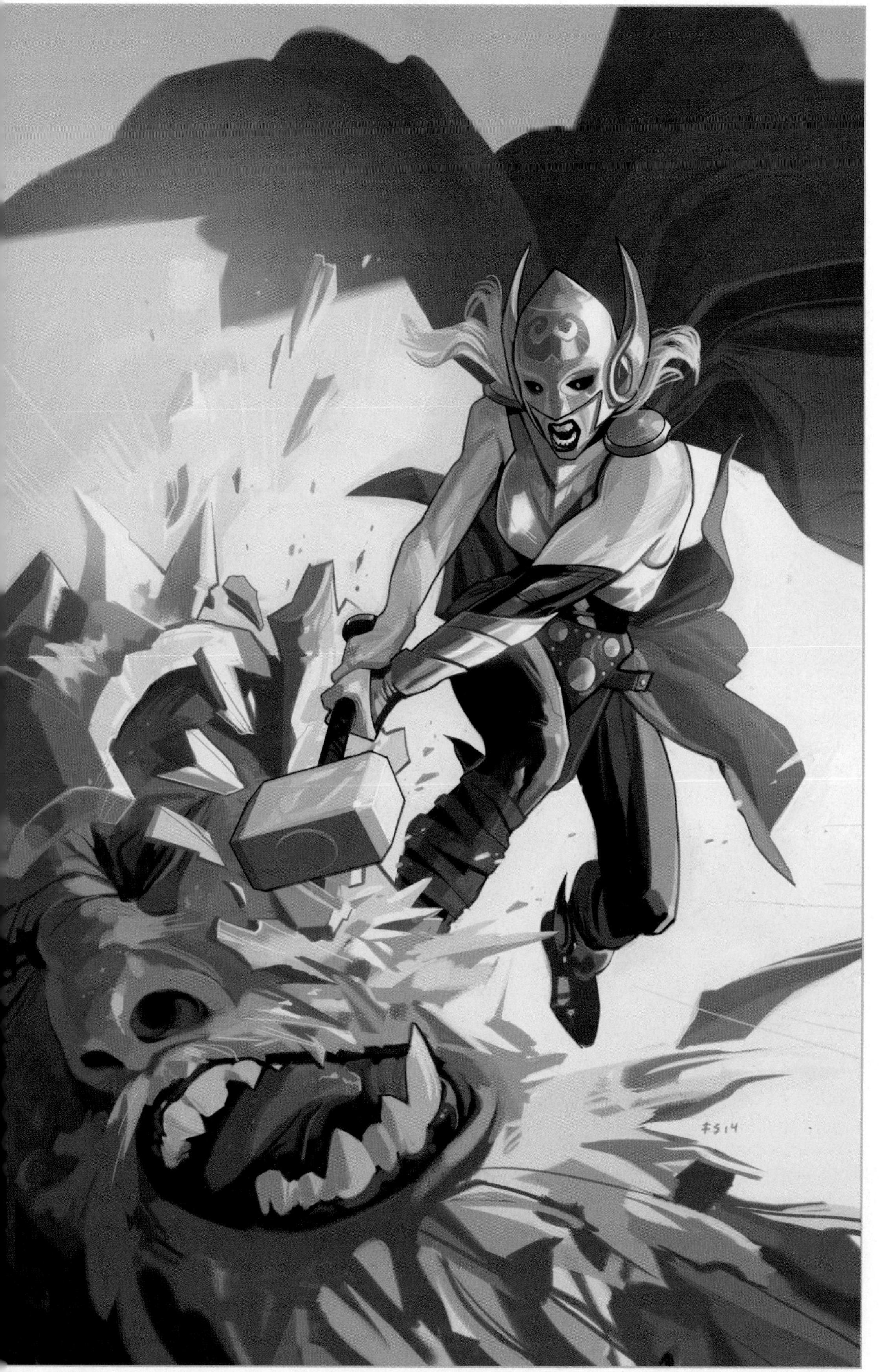

THOR # 1 VARIANT
BY **FIONA STAPLES**

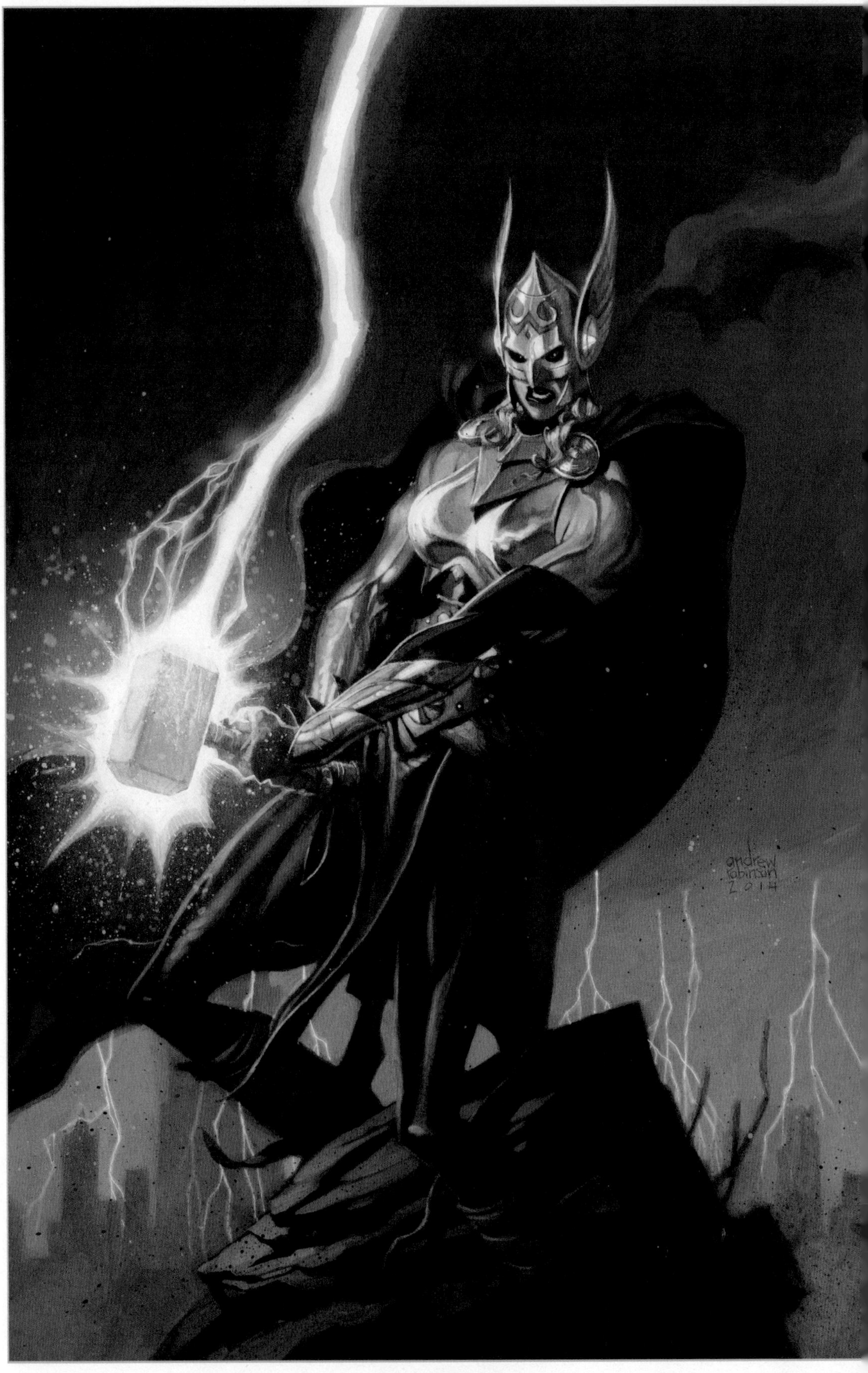
andrew robinson 2014

THOR # 1 VARIANT
BY **ANDREW ROBINSON**

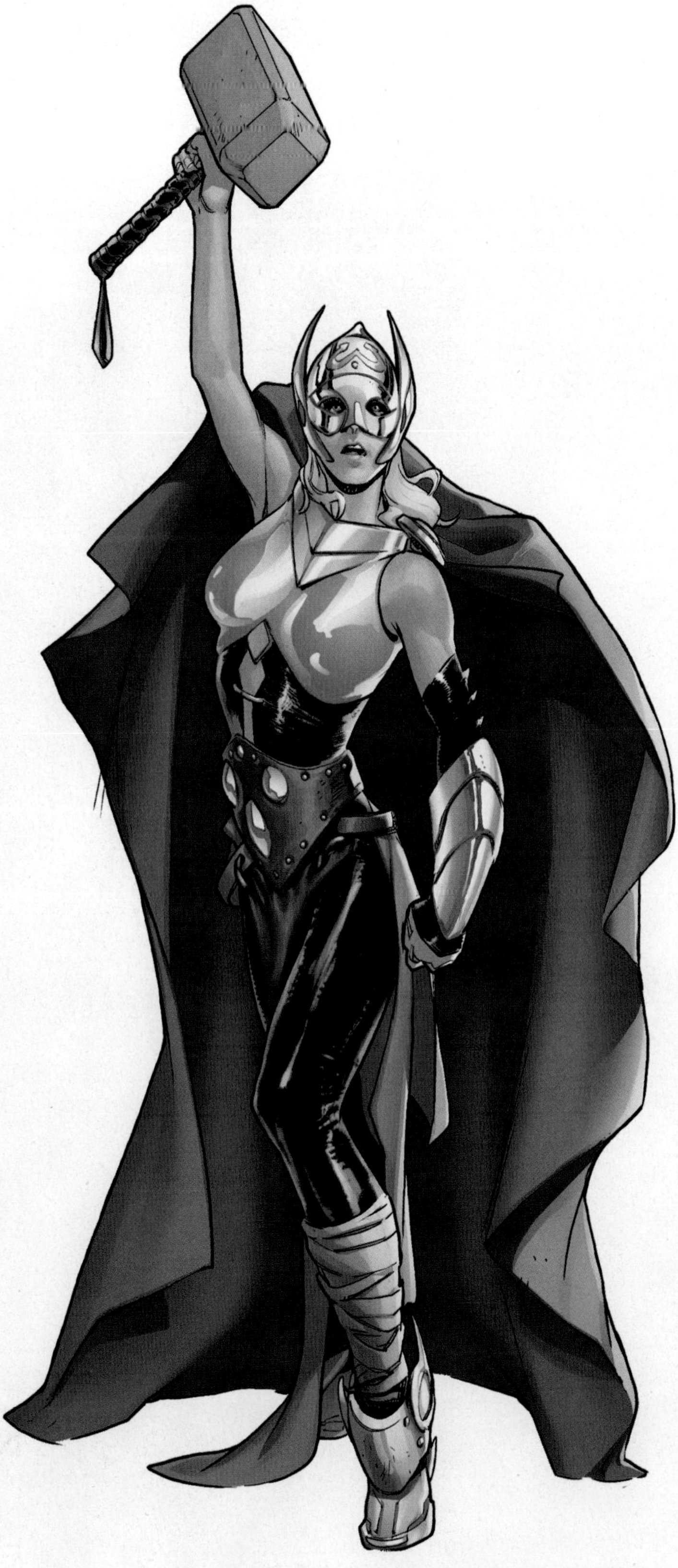

THOR # 1 VARIANT
BY **SARA PICHELLI & LAURA MARTIN**

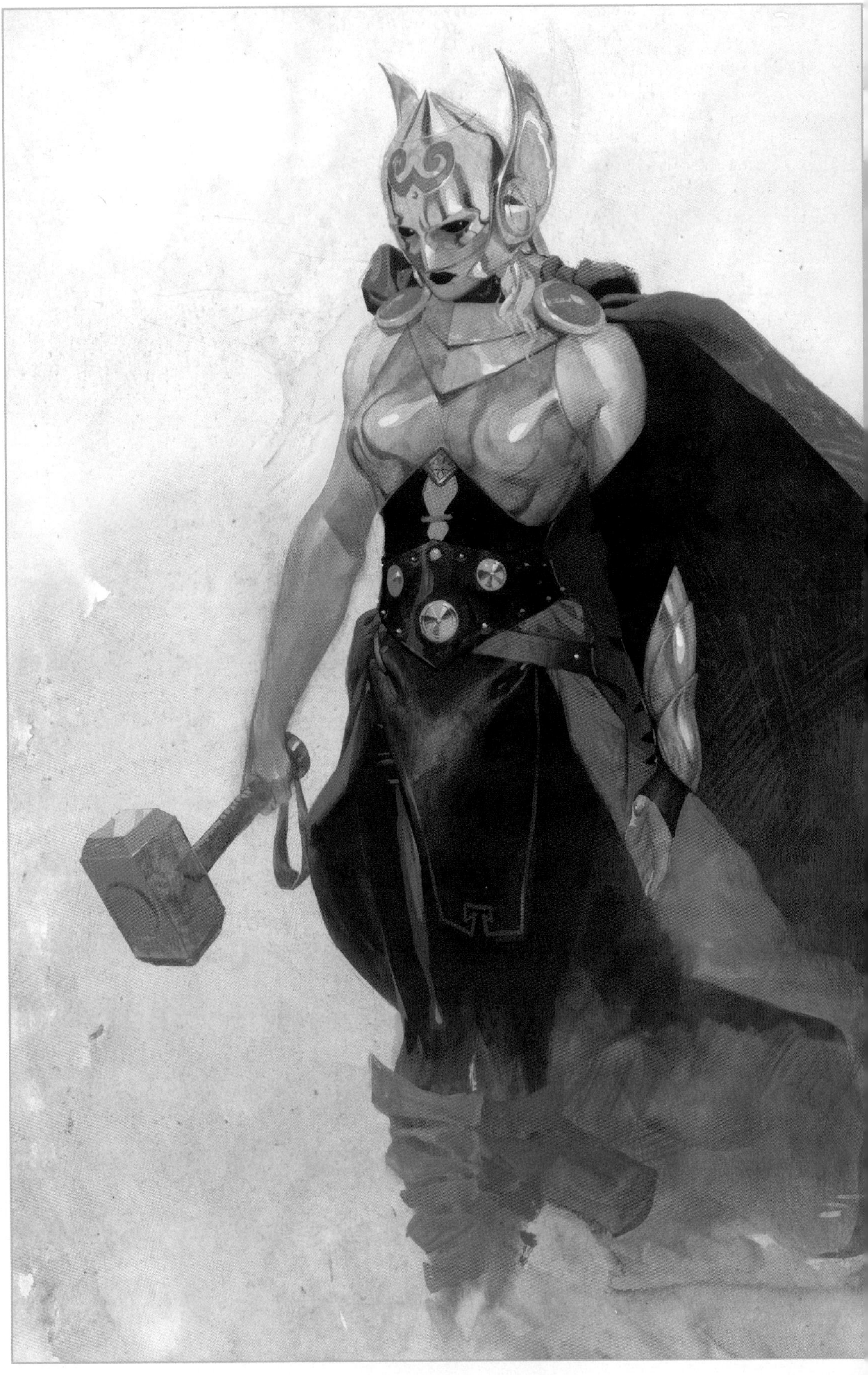

THOR # 1 DESIGN VARIANT
BY **ESAD RIBIC**

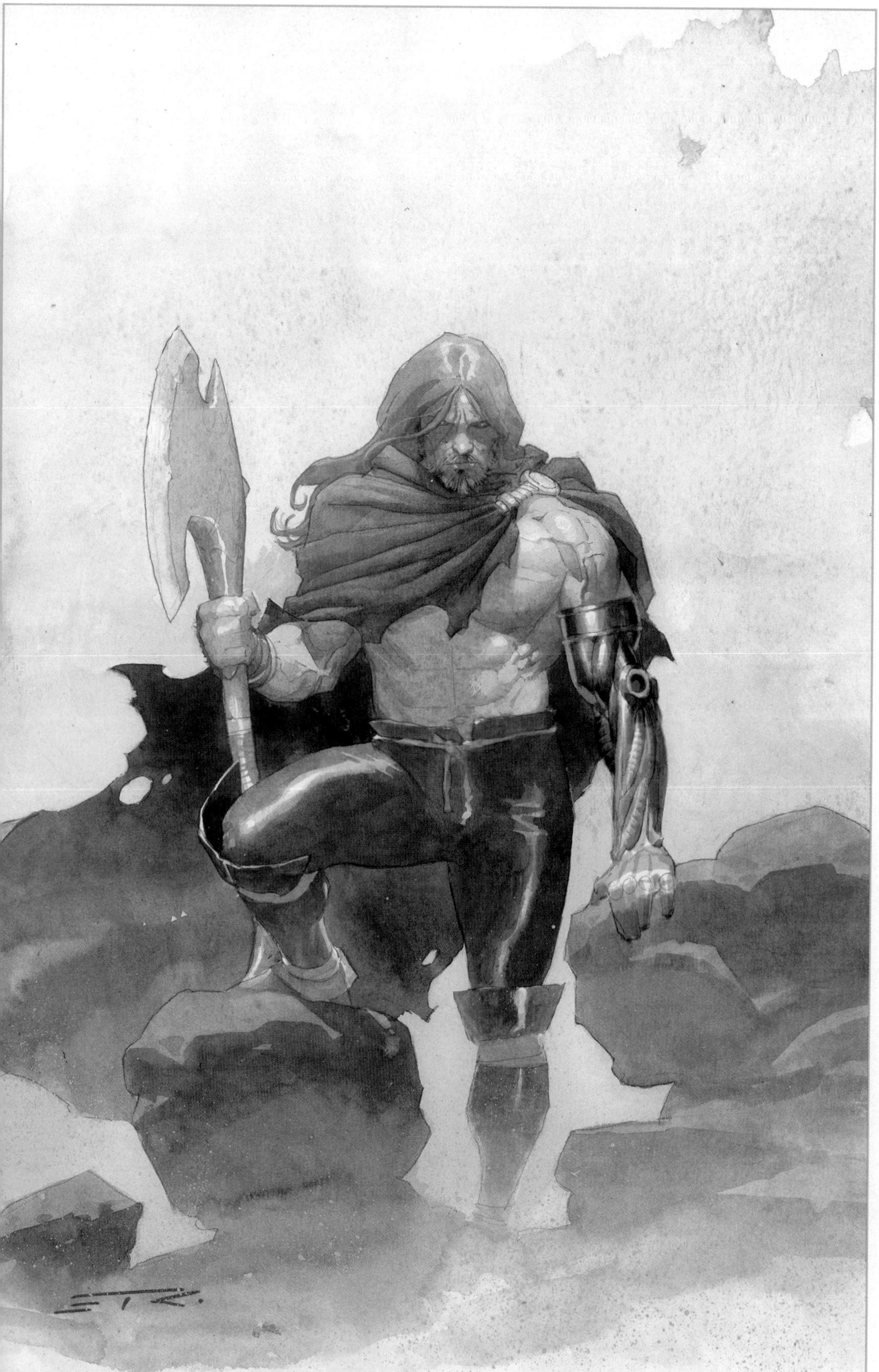

THOR # 2 VARIANT
BY **ESAD RIBIC**

THOR # 2 VARIANT
BY **CHRIS SAMNEE & MATTHEW WILSON**

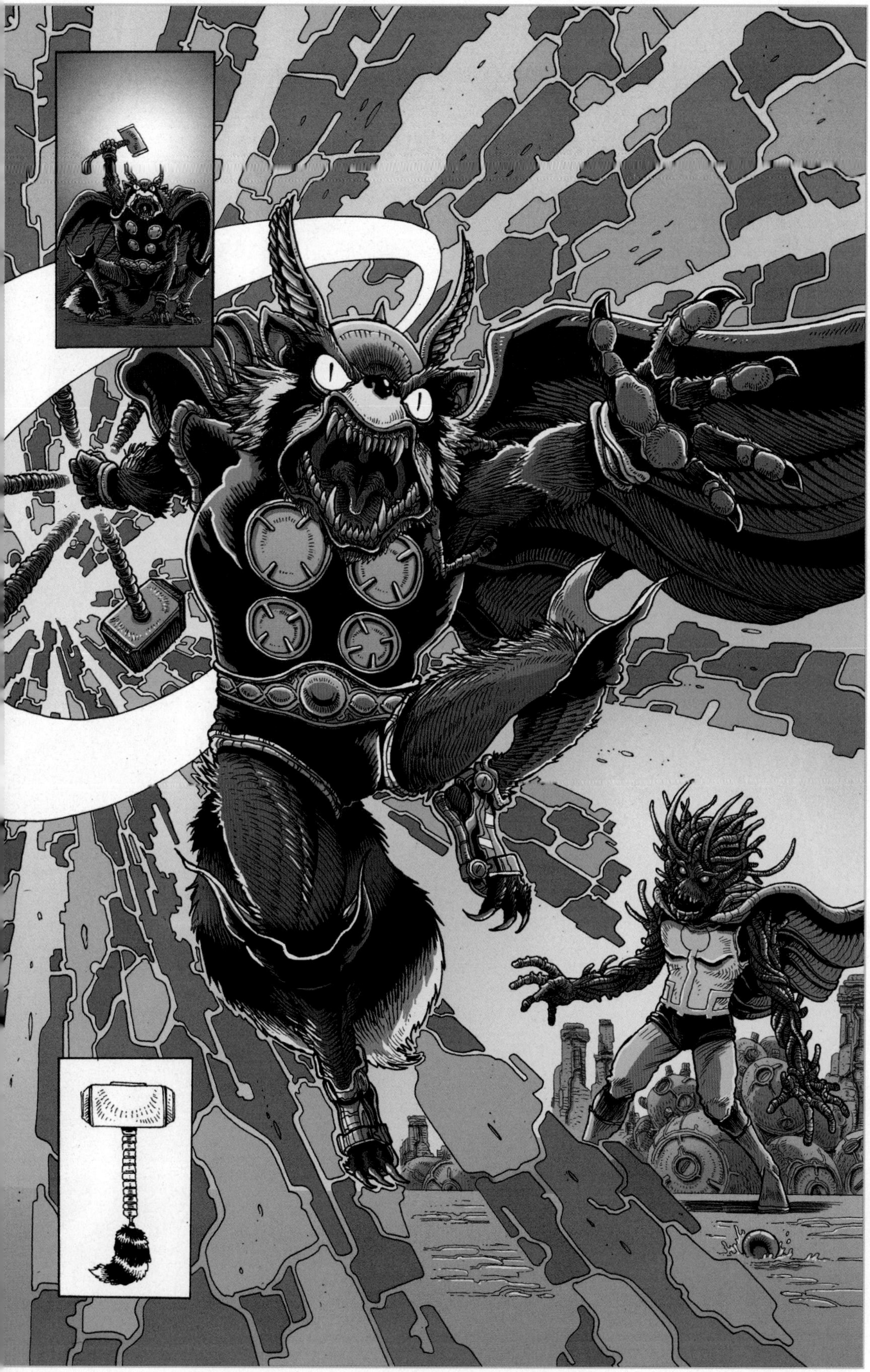

THOR # 2 ROCKET & GROOT VARIANT
BY **JAMES STOKOE**

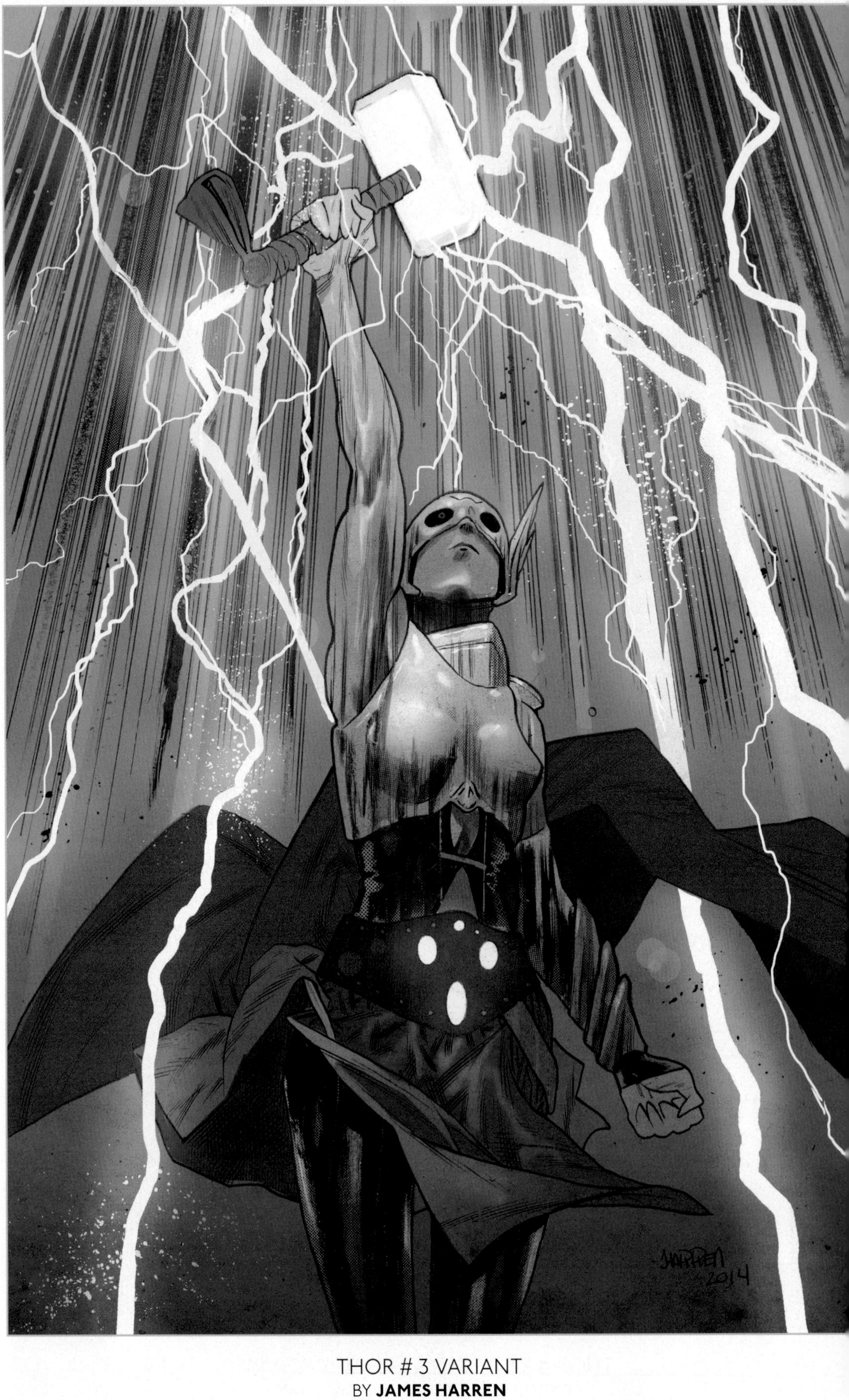

THOR # 3 VARIANT
BY **JAMES HARREN**

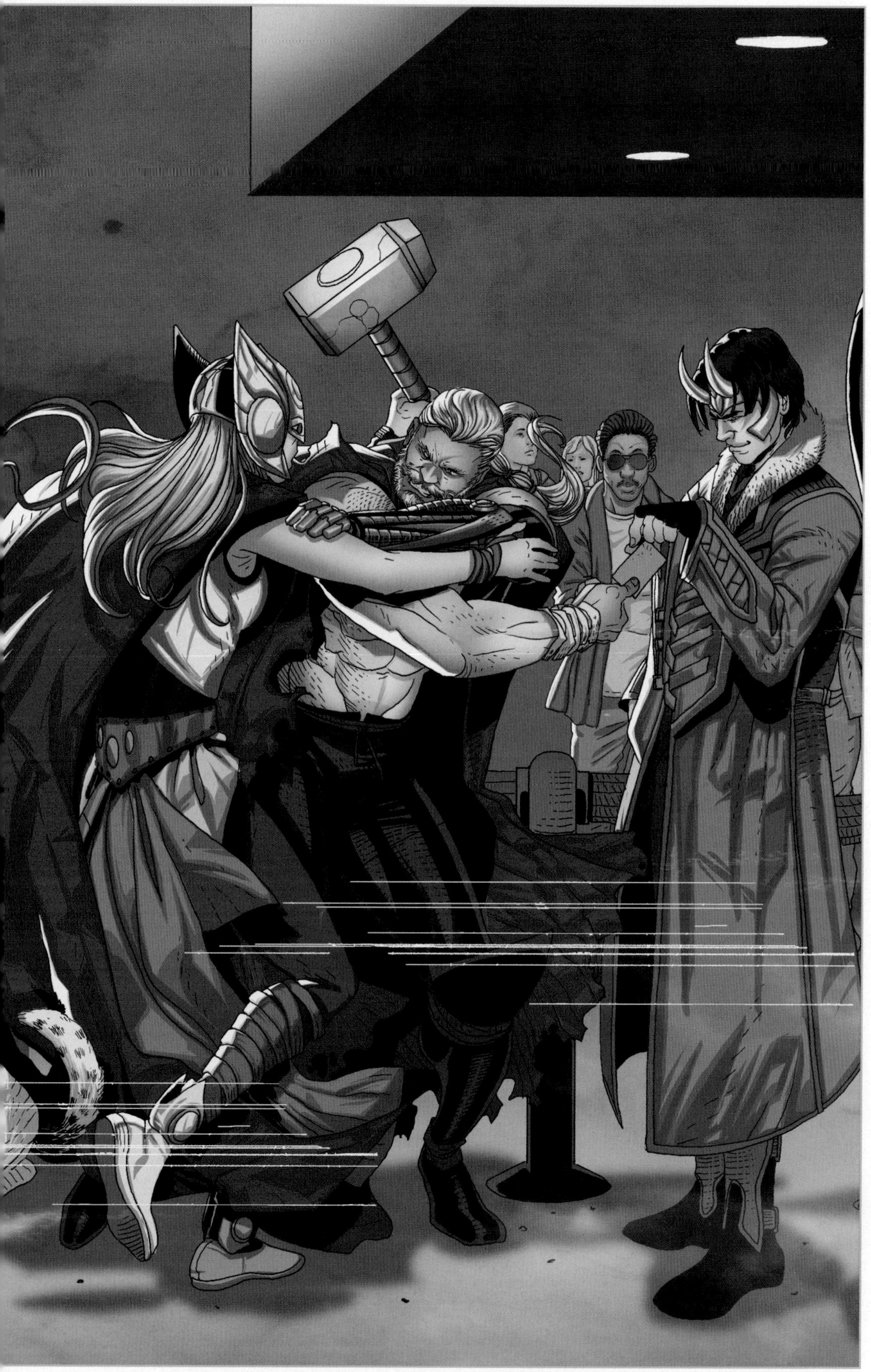

THOR # 4 WELCOME HOME VARIANT
BY **SALVADOR LARROCA & ISRAEL SILVA**

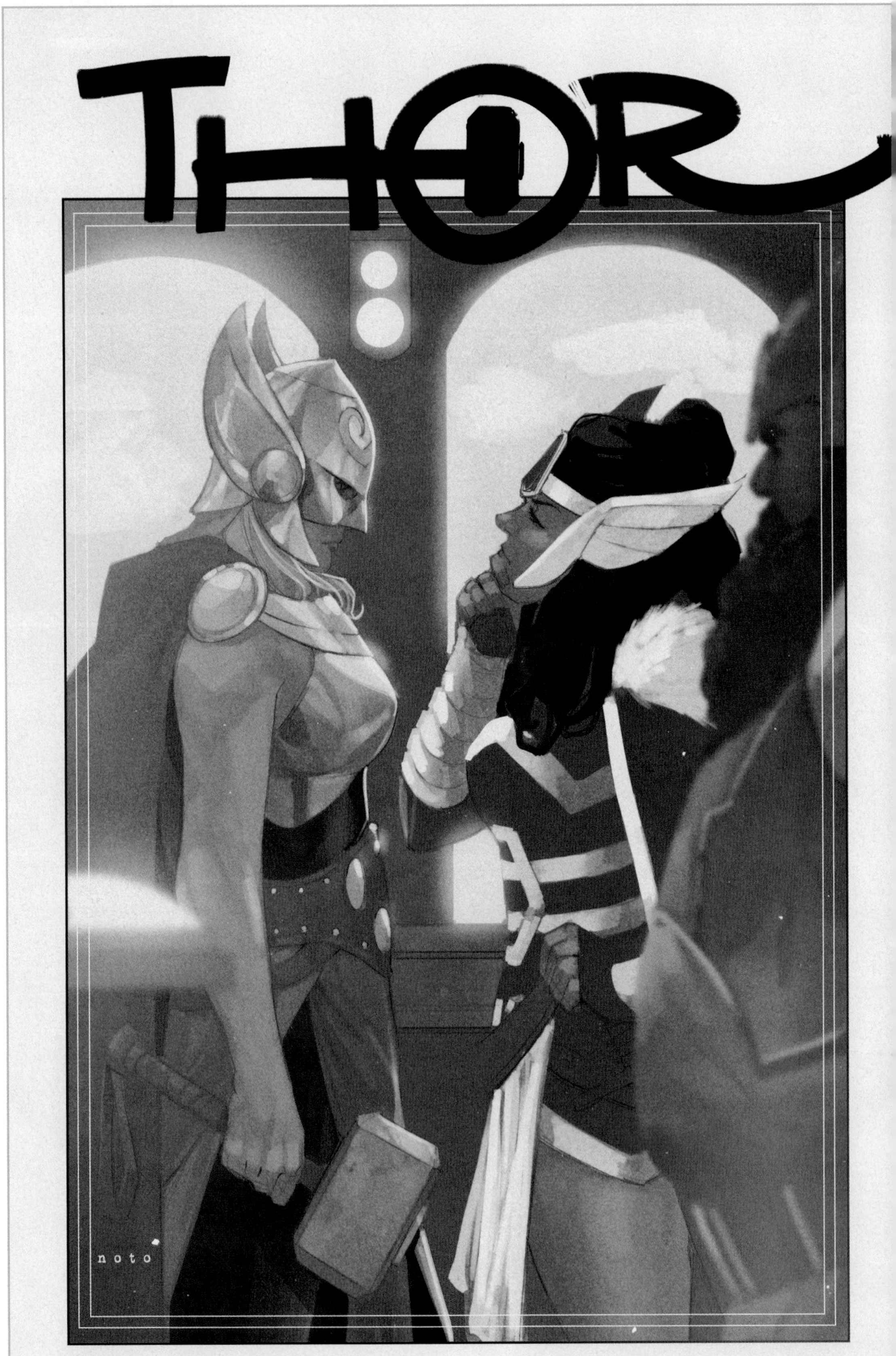
THOR
noto

THOR # 5 VARIANT
BY **PHIL NOTO**

CHARACTER DESIGNS
BY RUSSEL DAUTERMAN

THOR

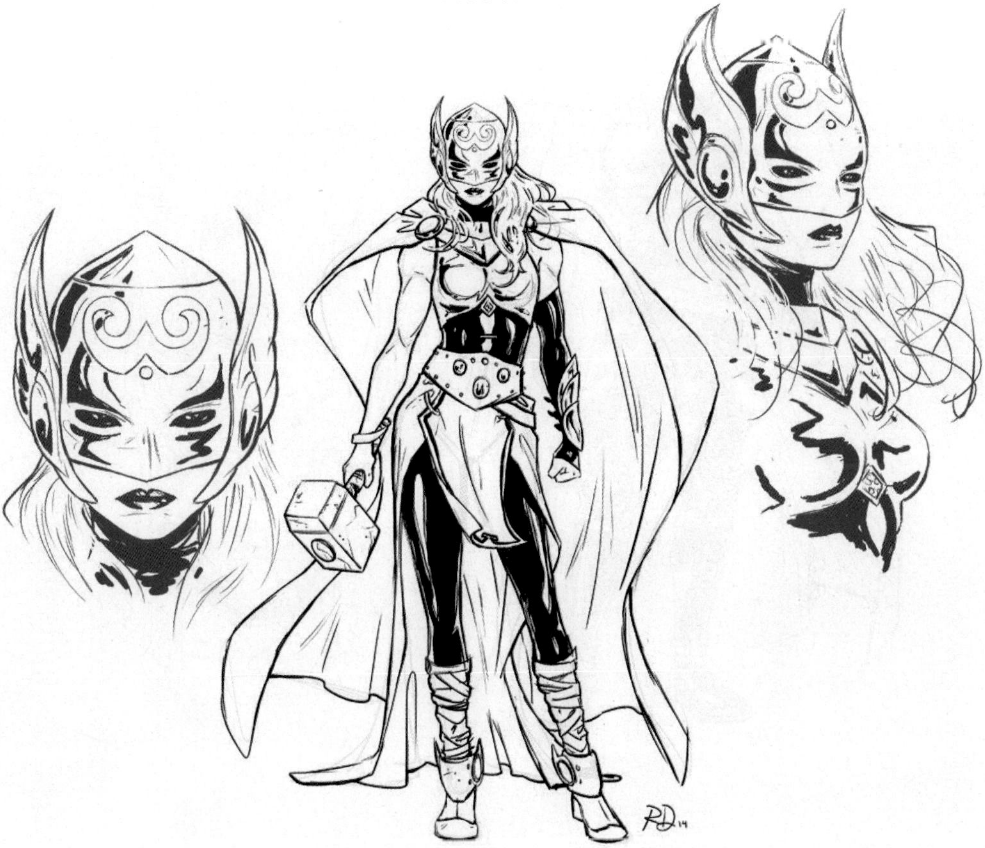

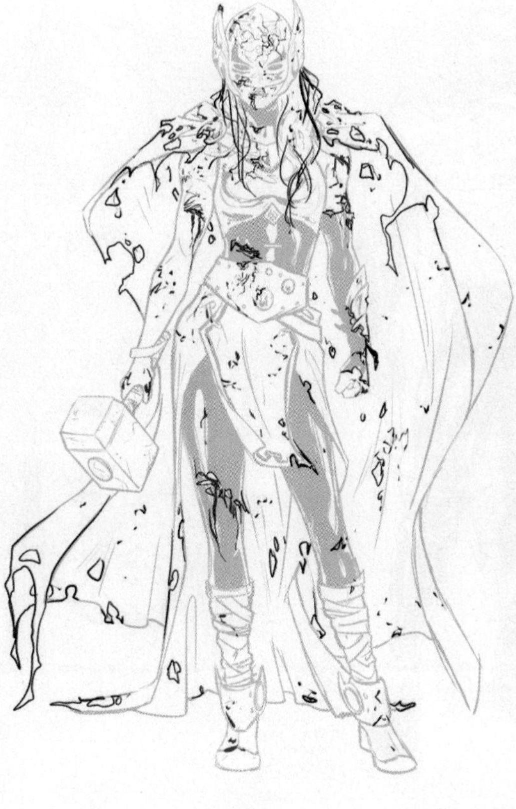

BATTLE DAMAGE

ODINSON

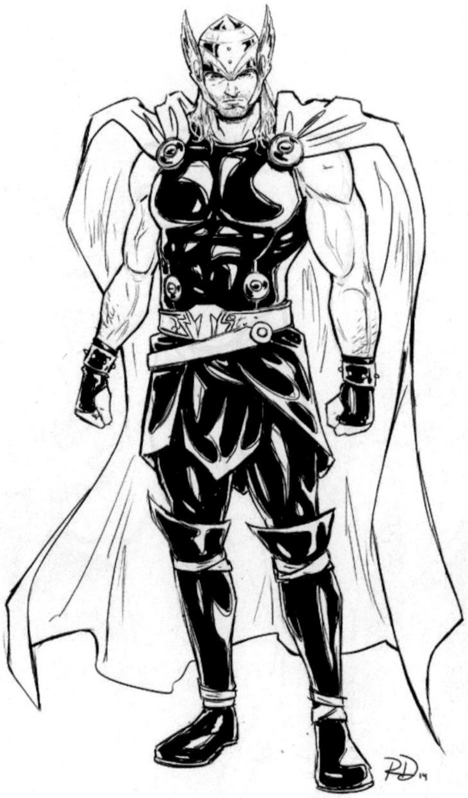

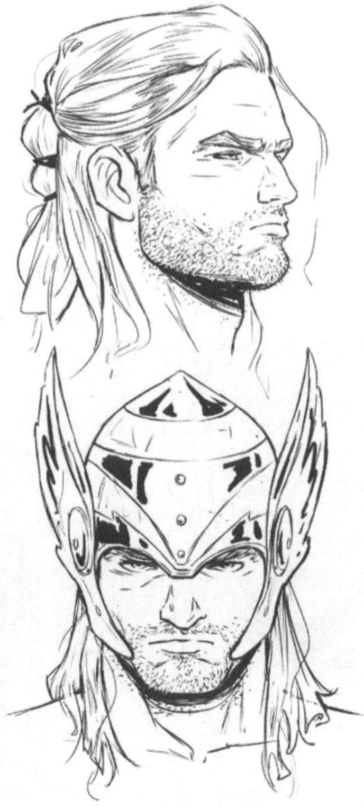

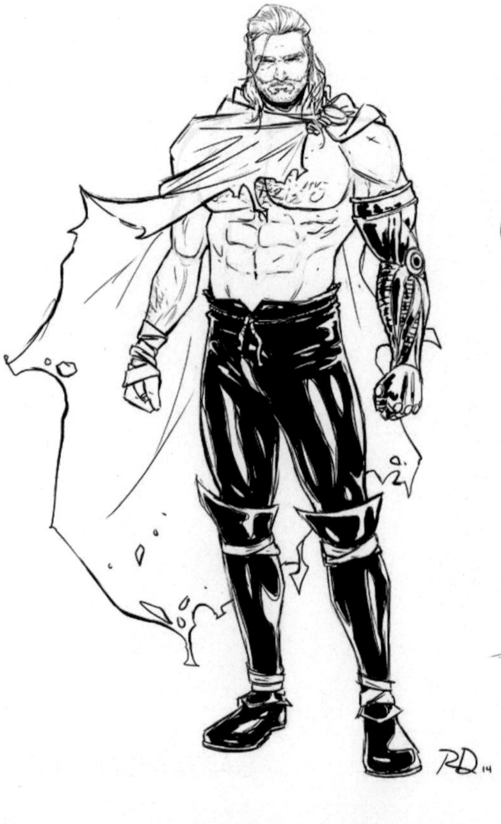

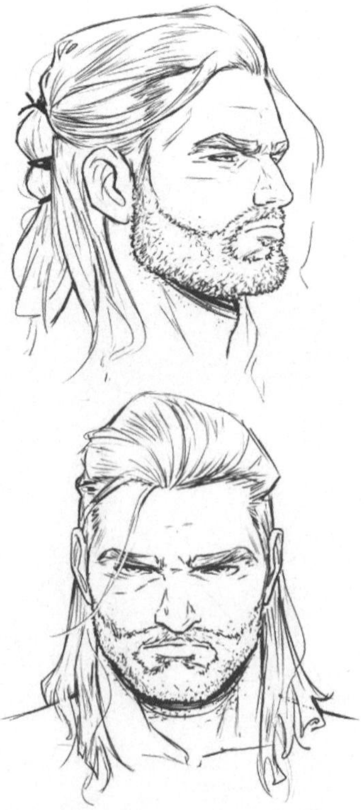

ODIN & FREYJA

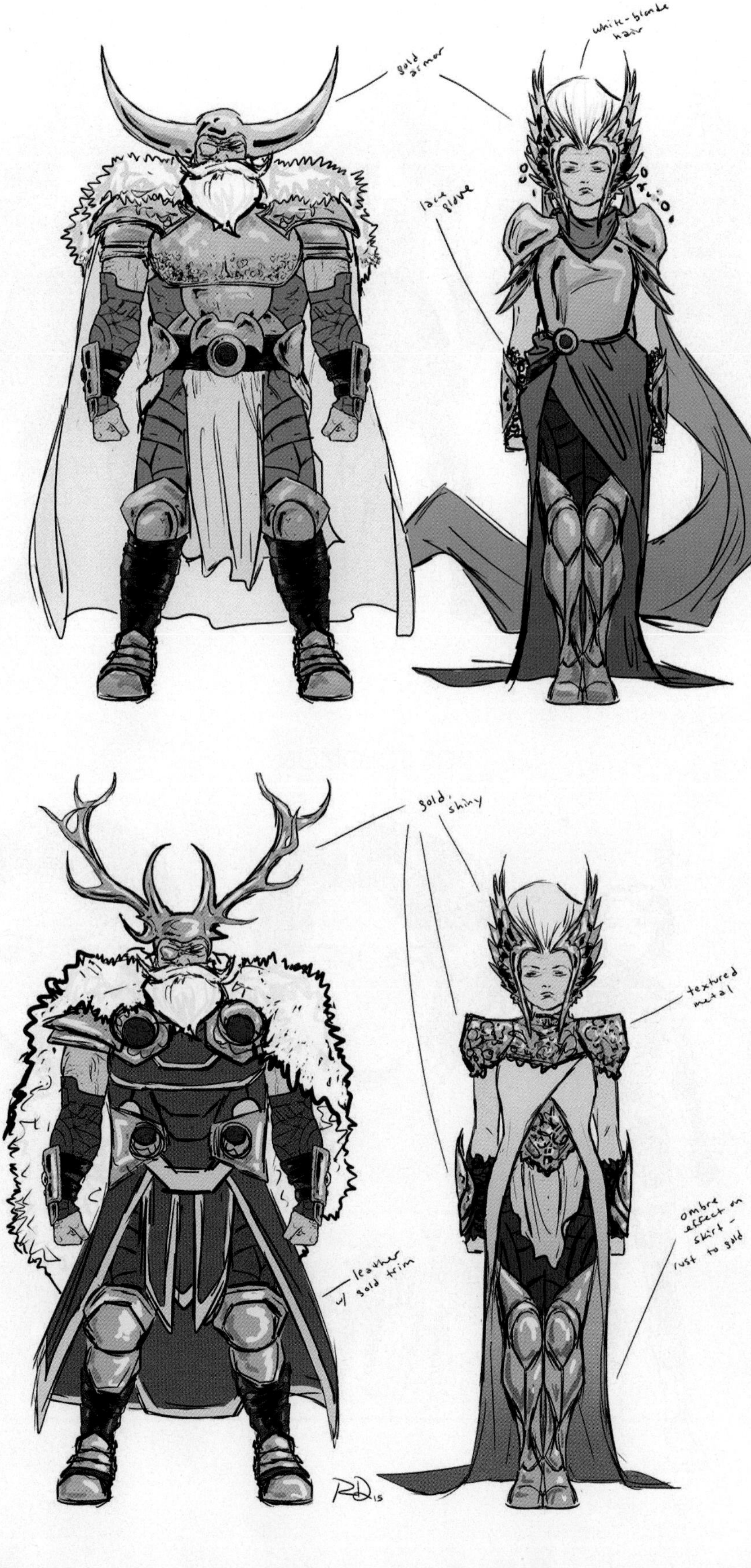
gold armor
white-blonde hair
lace glove
gold, shiny
textured metal
leather w/ gold trim
ombre effect on skirt - rust to gold

MALEKITH

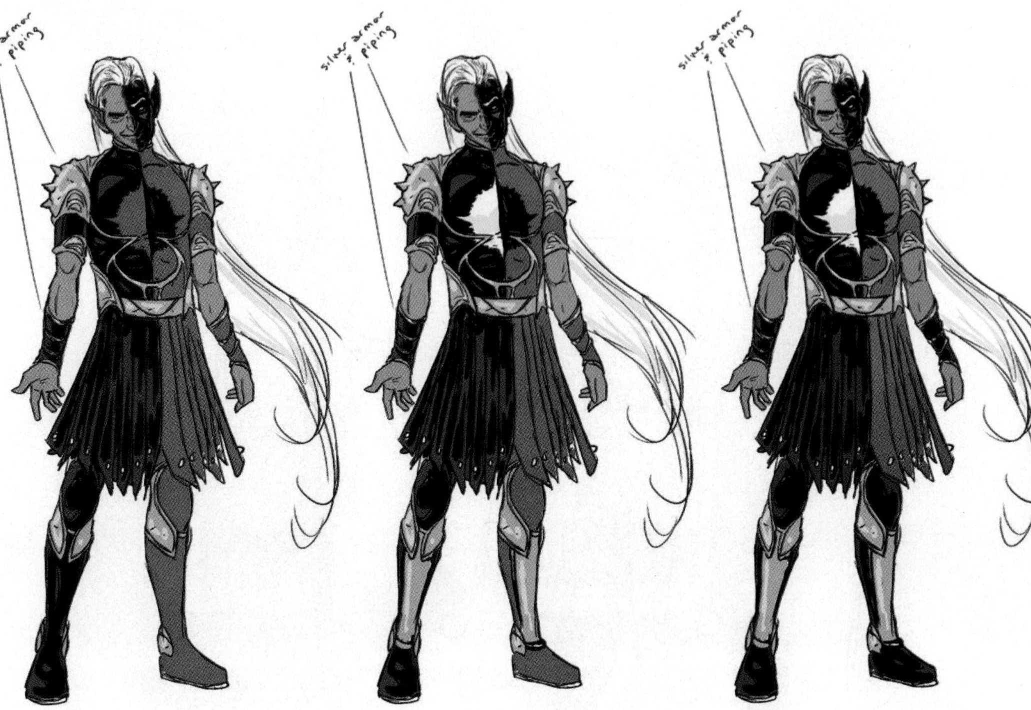

silver armor & piping
silver armor & piping
silver armor & piping

ROZ SOLOMON

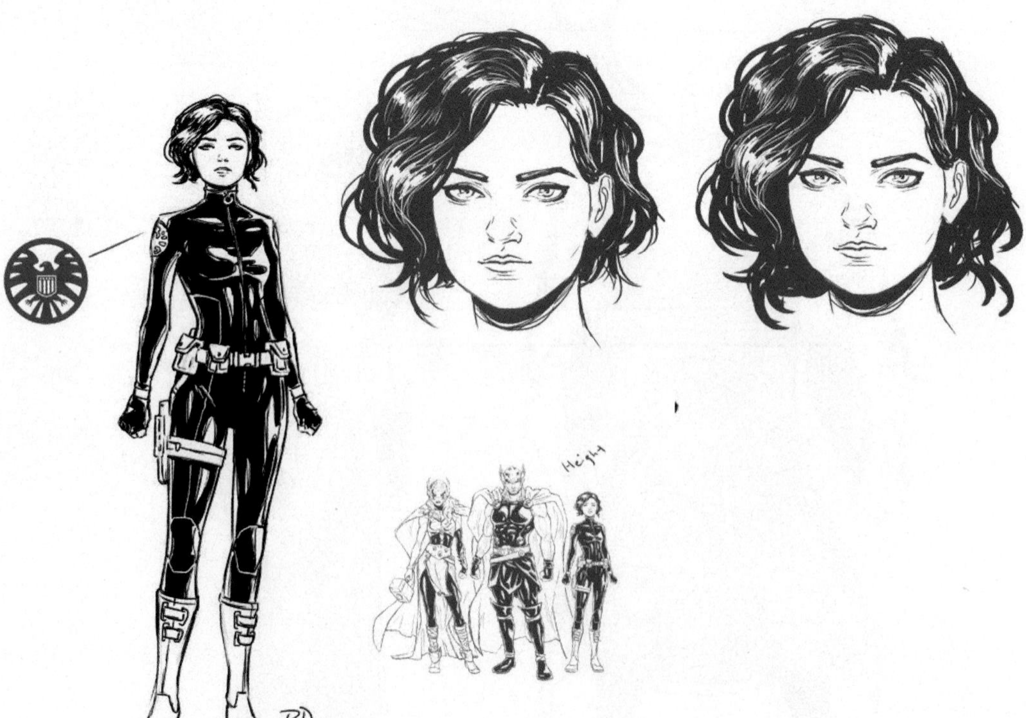

Height

#1 PAGE 21, LAYOUTS AND INKS

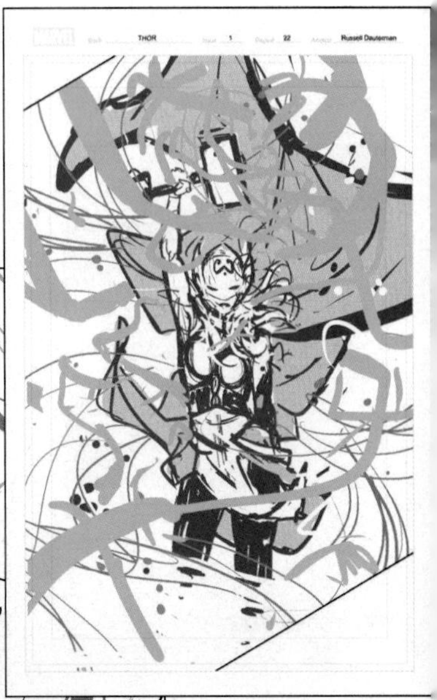
THOR
1
22
Russell Dauterman

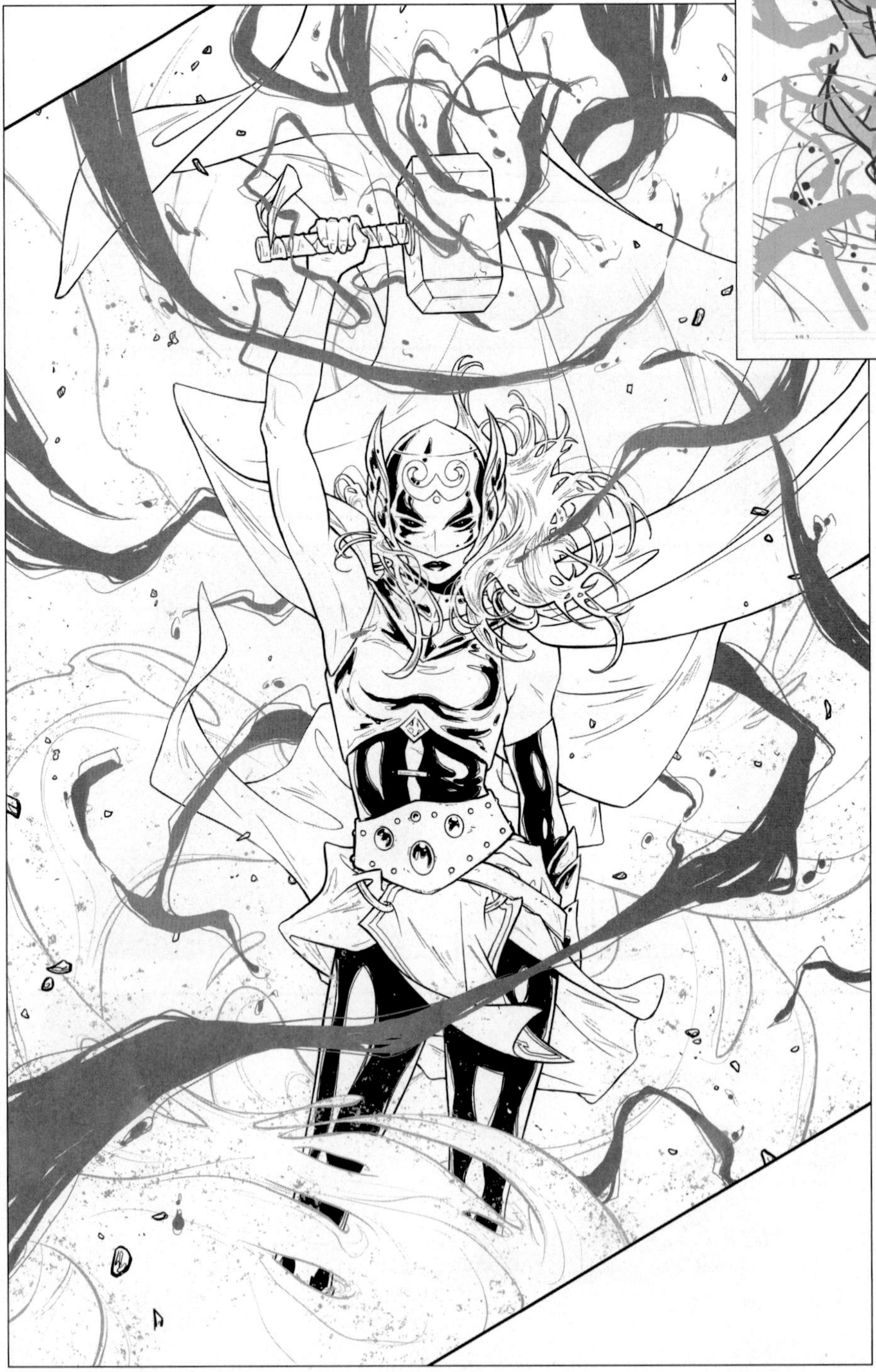

#1 PAGE 22, LAYOUTS AND INKS

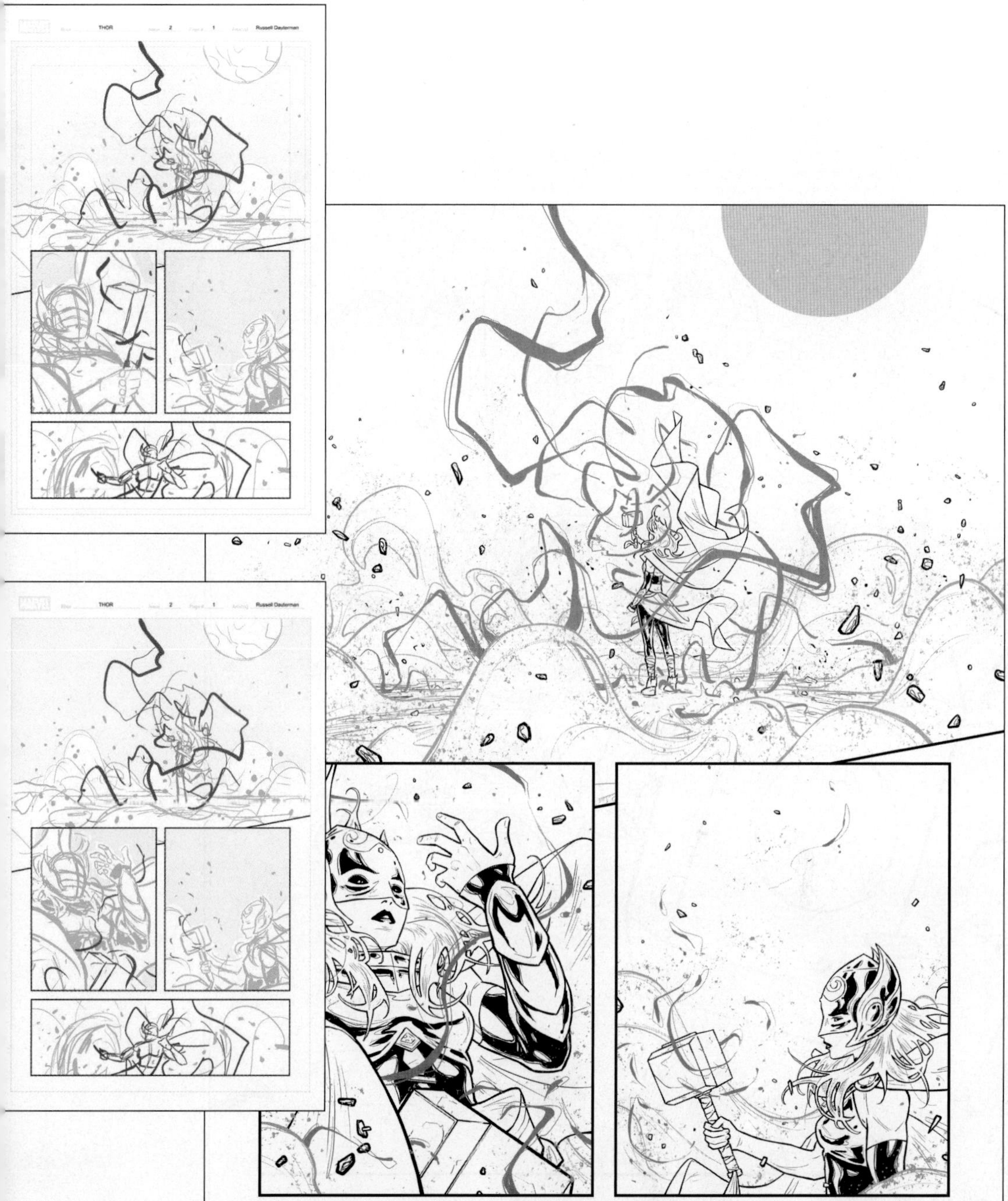
THOR
Russell Dauterman

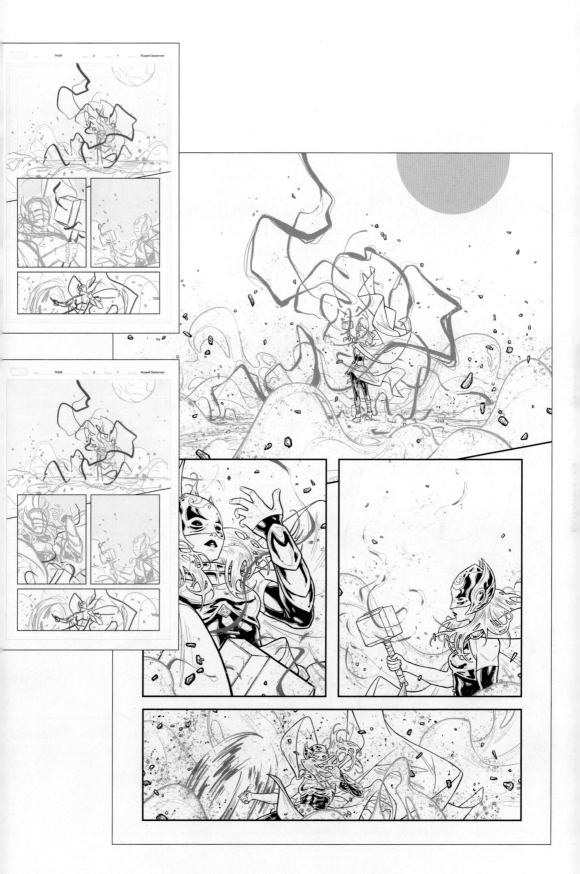

#2 PAGE 1, LAYOUTS AND INKS

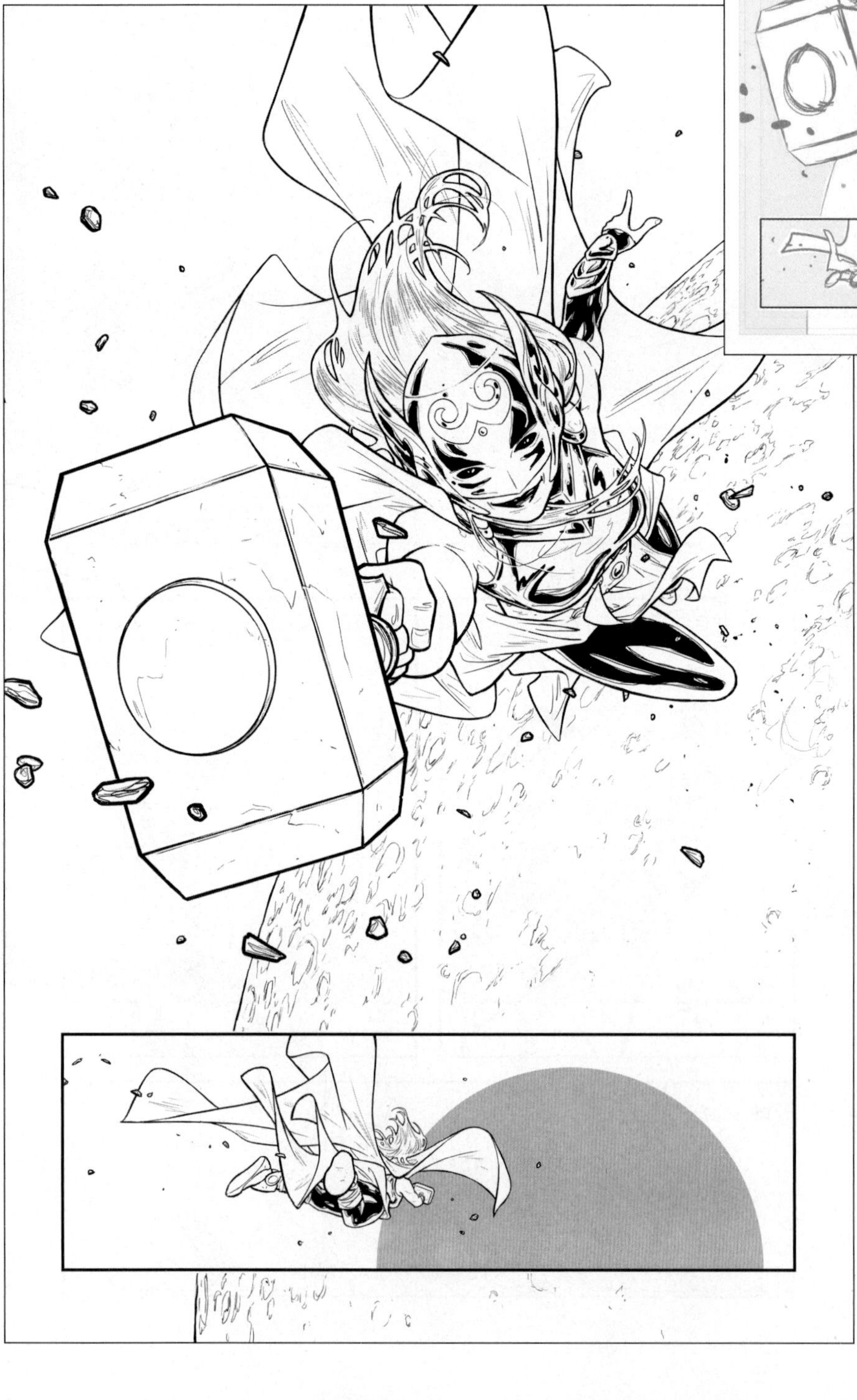

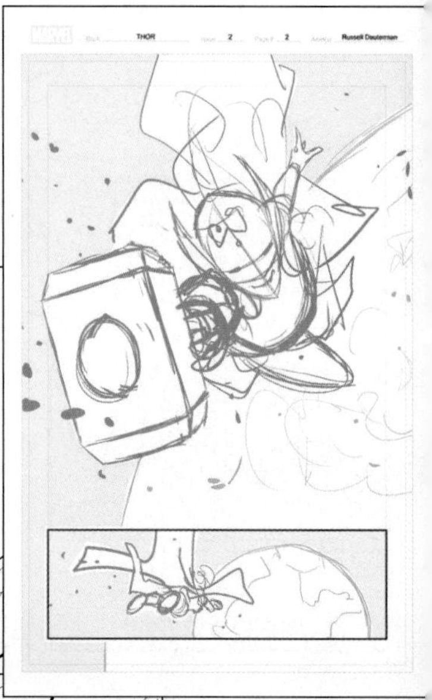
THOR
2
2
Russell Dauterman

#2 PAGE 2, LAYOUTS AND INKS

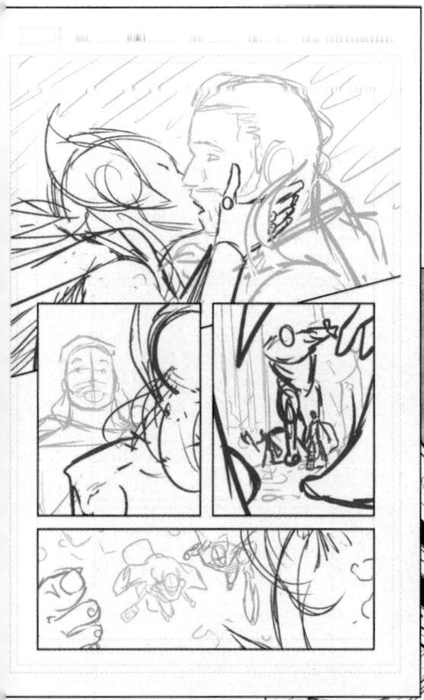

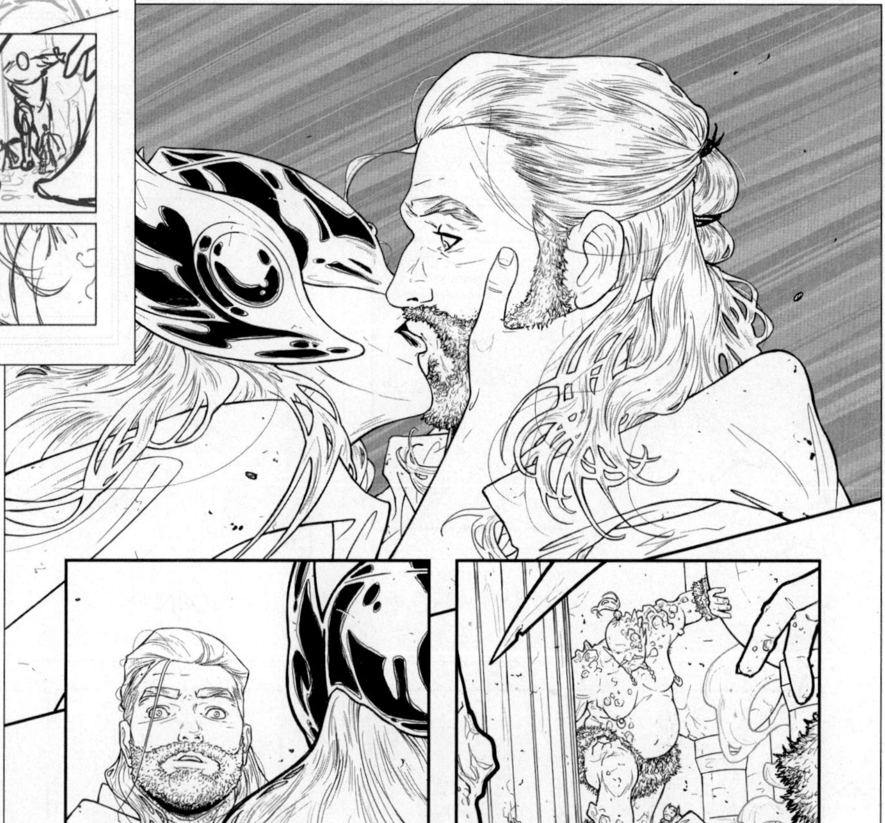

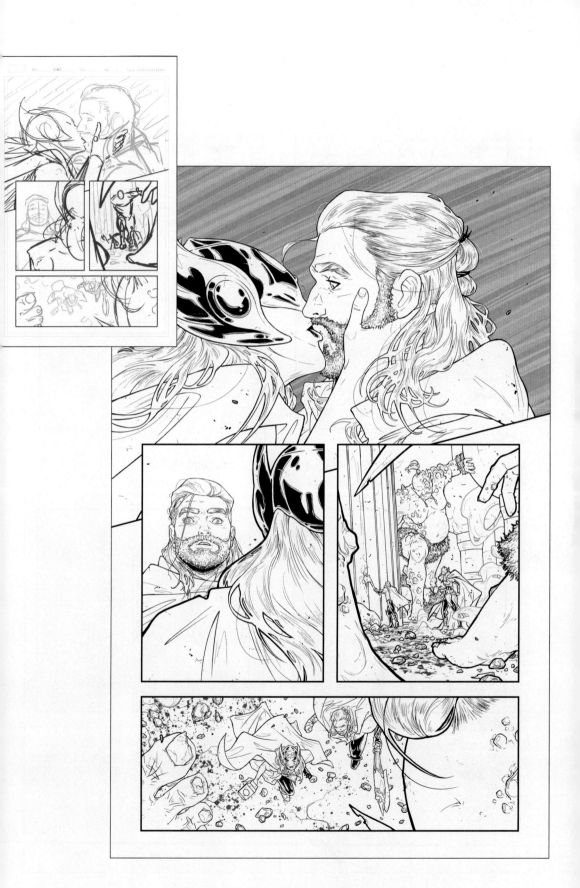

#4 PAGE 12, LAYOUTS AND INKS

ART PROCESS
BY JORGE MOLINA

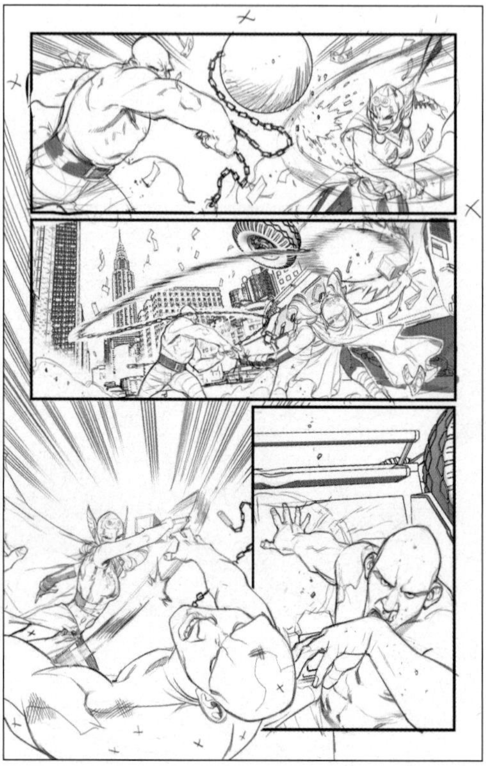

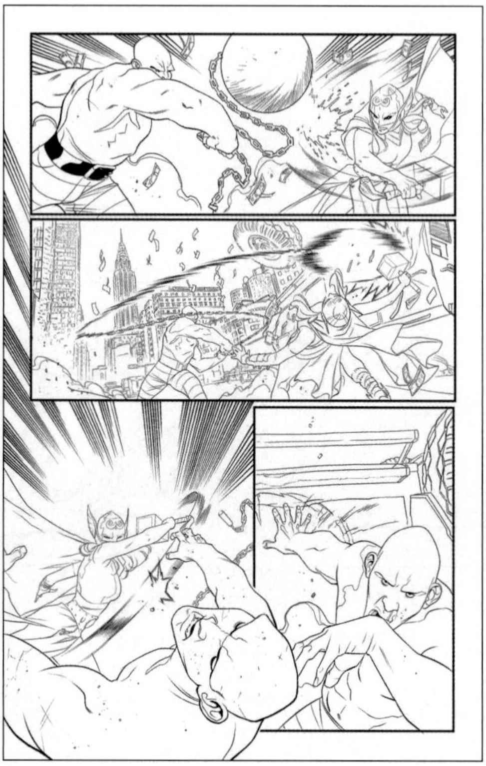

#5 PAGE 4, PENCILS AND INKS

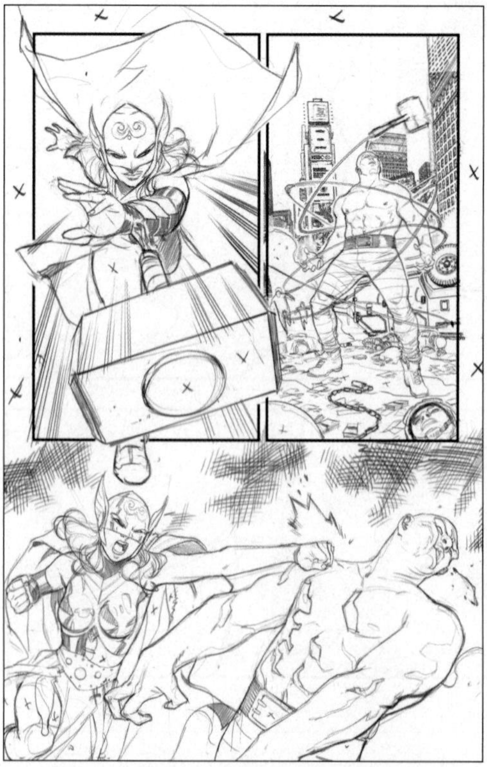

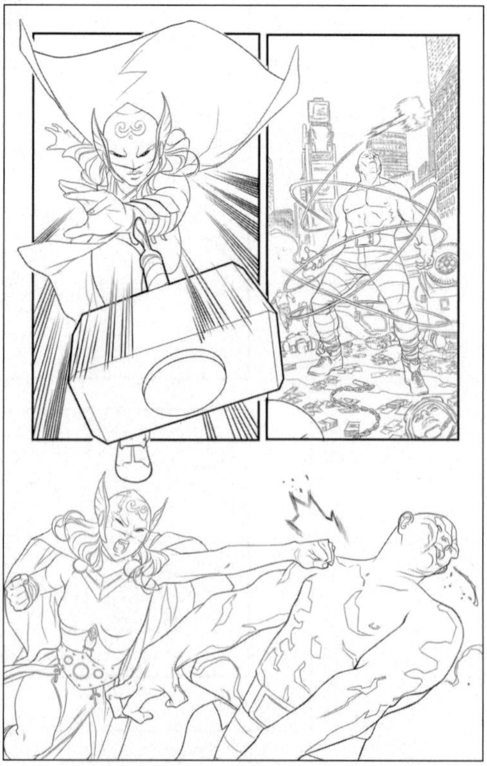

#5 PAGE 5, PENCILS AND INKS

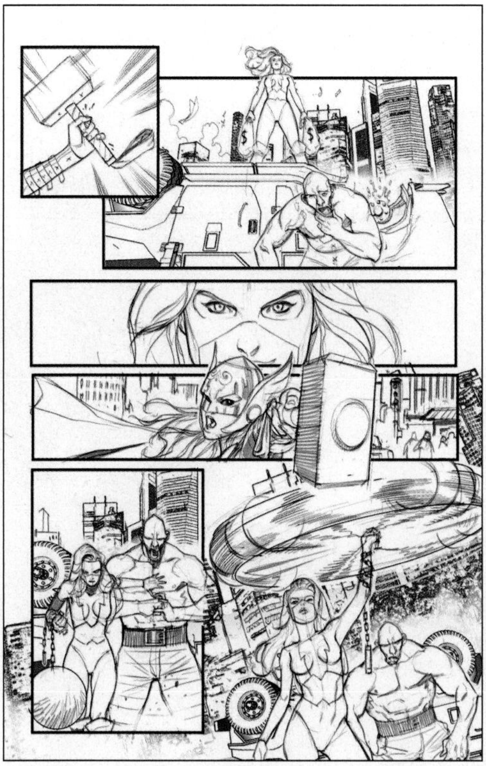

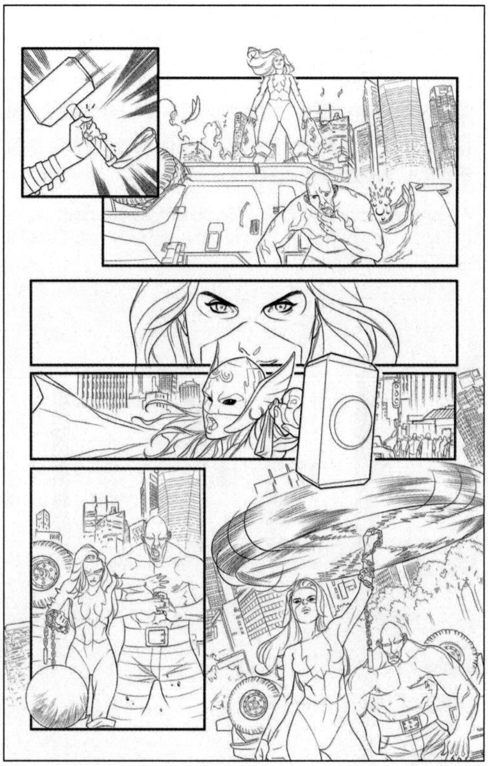

#5 PAGE 6, PENCILS AND INKS

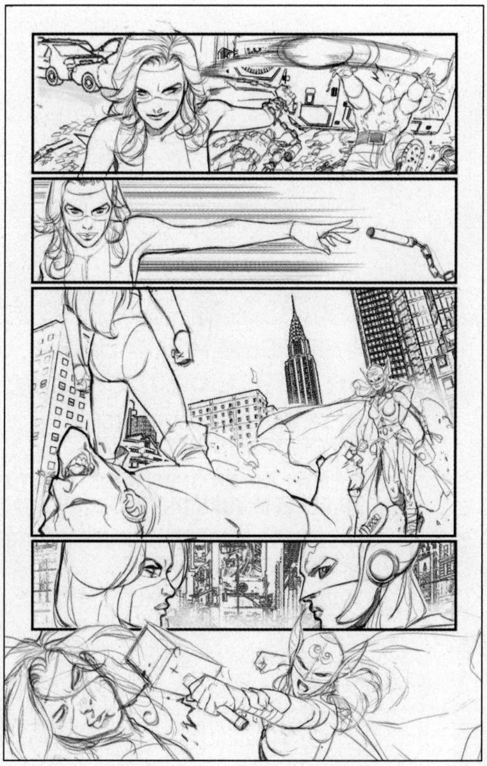

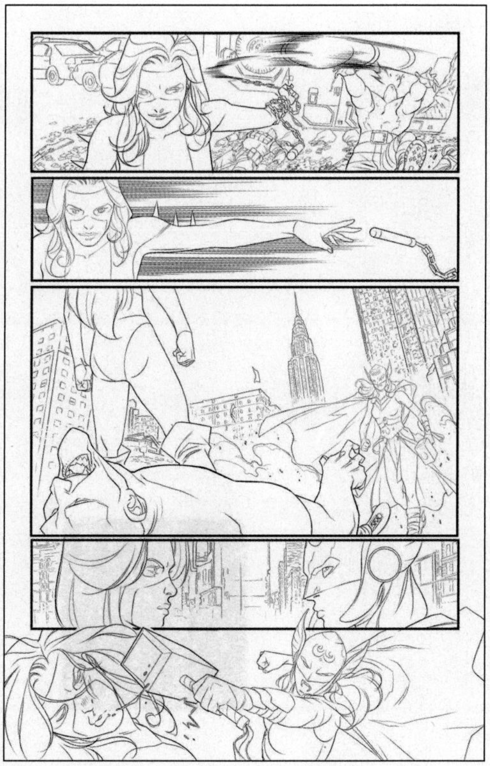

#5 PAGE 7, PENCILS AND INKS

MARVEL AR AUGMENTED REALITY

MARVEL AUGMENTED REALITY (AR) ENHANCES AND CHANGES THE WAY YOU EXPERIENCE COMICS!

TO ACCESS THE FREE MARVEL AR CONTENT IN THIS BOOK*:

1. Locate the AR logo within the comic.
2. Go to Marvel.com/AR in your web browser.
3. Search by series title to find the corresponding AR.
4. Enjoy Marvel AR!

*All AR content that appears in this book has been archived and will be available only at Marvel.com/AR – no longer in the Marvel AR App. Content subject to change and availability.

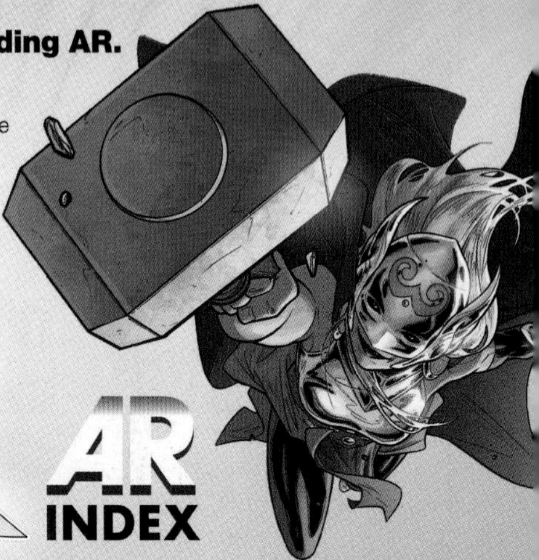

THOR AR INDEX

TMAYXLRWXXUN

TO REDEEM YOUR CODE FOR A FREE DIGITAL COPY:

1. GO TO MARVEL.COM/REDEEM. OFFER EXPIRES ON 5/13/17.
2. FOLLOW THE ON-SCREEN INSTRUCTIONS TO REDEEM YOUR DIGITAL COPY.
3. LAUNCH THE MARVEL COMICS APP TO READ YOUR COMIC NOW!
4. YOUR DIGITAL COPY WILL BE FOUND UNDER THE *MY COMICS* TAB.
5. READ & ENJOY!

YOUR FREE DIGITAL COPY WILL BE AVAILABLE

MARVEL COMICS APP FOR APPLE® iOS DEVICES

MARVEL COMICS APP FOR ANDROID™ DEVICE